CINE-SCAPES

Cine-scapes explores the relationship between urban space, architecture and the moving image. While an impressive amount of research has been done with regards to the way in which architecture is portrayed in film, this book offers a new perspective...

What happens if we begin to see the city as a place for an embodied visual consumption; a visual apparatus or, perhaps, a system that is based on movement, light and the body, and which we can explore in kinematic, kinetic and kinaesthetic ways?

Using film as a lens through which we look at urban spaces and places, Richard Koeck reveals the filmic and cinematic phenomena and spatial qualities that are present in postmodern landscapes, and which are perhaps otherwise disregarded or merely passively consumed.

Drawing on the author's extensive knowledge derived from architectural and film practice, *Cine-scapes*:

- offers insight into architecture and urban debates through the eyes of a practitioner working in the fields of film and architectural design;
- emphasises how filmic/cinematic tendencies take place or find their way into urban practices;
- can be used as a text for educators, students and practitioners in architecture and urban design to communicate and discuss design issues with regard to contemporary architecture and cities.

Cine-scapes ignites new ways of seeing, thinking and debating the nature of architecture and urban spaces.

Richard Koeck is a Senior Lecturer in Architecture and Director of the Centre for Architecture and the Visual Arts (CAVA) at the University of Liverpool, UK. He is Founding Director of CineTecture Ltd, a Liverpool-based production and post-production company.

For Maxine

CINE-SCAPES

Cinematic Spaces in Architecture and Cities

Richard Koeck

Routledge
Taylor & Francis Group

NEW YORK AND LONDON

First published 2013
by Routledge
2 Park Square, Milton Park, Abingdon, Oxon OX14 4RN

Simultaneously published in the USA and Canada
by Routledge
711 Third Avenue, New York, NY 10017

Routledge is an imprint of the Taylor & Francis Group, an informa business

© 2013 Richard Koeck

British Library Cataloguing in Publication Data
A catalogue record for this book is available from the British Library

Library of Congress Cataloging in Publication Data
A catalog record for this book has been requested from The Library of
Congress

ISBN: 978-0-415-60078-1 (hbk)
ISBN: 978-0-415-60079-8 (pbk)

Typeset in Aldine and Swiss
by Book Now Ltd, London

Printed and bound in Great Britain by
TJ International Ltd, Padstow, Cornwall

Contents

Figures

Preface and Acknowledgements

In recent years, the relationships between film, architecture and cities has become a thriving theme that has informed many academic and professional debates. A considerable amount of critical thought has addressed how architectural debates and practices have influenced the representation of a space, architecture and urban environments in film. *Cine-scapes* aims to expand the argument of the reciprocity between architecture and film in what might be considered the opposite direction. It examines the ways that properties and methods traditionally situated in the sphere of film have influenced spatial practices in contemporary architecture and urban design. In doing so, this book is not intended to be read as a dogmatic approach to how people ought to view the spaces that surround them or they inhabit, but instead hopes to inspire the reader to think about cities and architectural spaces in ways they might not have thought before. It aims to emphasise that architectural and urban sites can have filmic, or even scenographic, dimensions that might not be obvious in our everyday passive perception of cities.

The interdisciplinary angle from which this book is written means that my arguments are underpinned by literature from a range of disciplines relating to film and architecture, such as philosophy, sociology, and geography; yet, I would not go so far as to say that the book is profoundly multi-disciplinary. Instead, the considerations and opinions expressed take into account personal observations that relate to living and working in three different countries in the last fifteen years, as well as practical experience in the two fields that are addressed here – filmmaking and architectural design. *Cine-scapes* is a book that aims to show that the study of film and architecture – two cultural phenomena that take a predominant role in people's lives – is not solely the province of specialists. Ultimately, this book is written for students, scholars and professionals from varying fields who have an ontological interest film and architecture in the broadest sense, as well as the narrative, embodied, scopic regimes found in contemporary cities. In doing so, this text seeks to explore existing perspectives, as well as offering new ones with regard to the way we perceive and engage with architectural and urban spaces.

This book owes its inspiration to the work of some wonderful friends and colleagues, particularly Francois Penz, Maureen Thomas, Andong Lu, Helmut Weihsmann, Dietrich Neumann and Luis Urbano, from whose diverse backgrounds and critical input I have profited immensely for many years. Time management has been one of the greatest challenges when working on this book and I therefore wish to thank two department heads, Robert Kronenburg and Andre Brown, at the University of Liverpool, my home institution, for their support in recent years. I am indebted to Gary Warnaby, with whom I wrote a joint paper on urban advertisement and place marketing, and which added tremendously to this book. I am grateful to many of my Masters and PhD students in our architectural school who I had the pleasure of teaching over the years, and who have allowed me to develop and test some of the concepts and ideas explored in this book.

I express my particular gratitude to the organisations, professional photographers and individuals – including Alex Billington, Rachel Berardinelli, Jürgen Götzke, Keith Hamilton, Charlie May, Babik Paviz, Werner Paul, James Perry, Kate Stevens and Alan Tansey – who have given permission for their images to be used, and in some instances even went on location scouting missions for me. I wish to particularly thank our PhD students Jane Clayton, Anna Gogh and Antoinette McKane for kindly assisting me at various stages of producing my manuscript, as well as Francesca Ford and Laura Williamson from Routledge who have supported my journey from the commissioning to the production of this book. Most importantly, I wish to thank my wife Monika, with whom I have not only worked throughout my professional career, but also whose artistic sense and professional expertise in dance, architecture and filmmaking has remained my greatest inspiration over the last twenty years. This book is dedicated to my daughter Maxine, whose arrival added yet another dimension to the production of this book.

Introduction

CONTEXT

Cinema and Landscapes

Describing it in the broadest terms, *Cine-scapes* is a text that explores the affinity between urban space, architecture and the moving image. For a book that is dedicated to establishing these links, it is perhaps unusual to start by highlighting what sets the two spatial spheres apart. Nevertheless, I think it is essential to recognise the margins between both spheres before embarking on a journey that will invite the reader to see both spaces with different eyes. The spaces of architecture and cities in films are fundamentally different from those in real life. When watching a film or movie, we might say that we temporally inhabit the spaces seen on the screen, yet these do not have, of course, the same material, social and economic function as the spaces created by true architecture and cities. Spaces portrayed as moving images normally have a narrative function, while buildings and cities primarily give us shelter and provide us with living space. It is critical to bear in mind that spaces and places seen in movies never truly mirror spatial reality, but are mediated and altered by the medium itself; a *filmic illusion* at best, regardless of whether we watch an actuality, newsreel, documentary, fiction or a movie belonging to any other genre. Even early film history's most innocent portrayals of cities never portray a space in its entirety. In 1897, for instance, when Alexandre Promio filmed urban scenarios in cities such as Liverpool, Dublin and Belfast for the Lumière company, his city portrayals were constructed by deliberate decisions on when, where, what and how he filmed a particular space at the time.[1] Although a city scene might be filmed from the seemingly unmediated point of view of a passive observer, his city visions were actually composed for a particular purpose, namely to attract a paying audience to the

Figure I.1   Liverpool. Still from Lumière clip N°701. Lime Street. Scene taken by A. Promio, 1897. © Association frères Lumière.

screening. To achieve this objective, Promio employed particular tactics to film the cities he visited. In reiterating the distinction between film spaces and actual spaces, I would like nonetheless to argue that it is worth bearing in mind that the moving image, just like architecture, is a medium that skilfully and proficiently engages with spatial and temporal matters. By illustrating a few urban cinematic practices and tactics, I invite the reader to challenge established perceptions and to view the city through the lens of a camera, or through the eyes a filmmaker. With this in mind, I hope to inspire the reader to a rethinking of the spaces we inhabit, and henceforth our future of being in the city.

Going to the movies has a totally different meaning today than it had in the formative years of cinema, or even only twenty or thirty years ago. While in the early years, moving images were shown as part of a fairground attraction, and later a theatrical visit, in the majority of cases today we encounter moving images outside such distinct spatial events or acts. Not only did television and video transform our living spaces to home theatres, changing the moving image event from a collective to a more individual practice, but also the consumption of moving images evolved from a space-specific to a space-independent act. Also, the digital revolution has meant that moving images today are an indispensable means of information, communication and advertisement, as well as narrative film. Although we are living at a time when small cinemas are gradually disappearing from city centres, inner cities show, paradoxically, more and more signs of filmic or cinematic influences. Living in the twenty-first century means that we are now surrounded by digital moving images 'anytime and everywhere',[2] and with a frequency and intimacy that is unprecedented in human history. While in the past we would consume films and moving images primarily in the cinema, and later in our homes, the digital age means that they have now conquered almost every spatial corner of our urban life. Marshall McLuhan once noted that 'Mechanization was never so vividly fragmented or sequential as in the birth of the movies' and that the movie 'by sheer speeding up the mechanical, carried us from the world of sequence and connections into the world of creative configuration and structure' (McLuhan 2006 [1964]: 110). One wonders if this notion of configuration and structure is limited to a reading of pictures, or if the medium of film has contributed to new ways in which the city presents itself or is perceived and, ultimately, has an impact on our being in space. Screens being mounted in urban spaces, installed in buildings and held in our hands invite us to passively consume moving images in university food halls, hotel lobbies, medical surgeries, public toilets and on the street. Even during those times when we ourselves are on the move, such as on buses, trains and aeroplanes, movies are an inescapable by-product of modern lifestyle. Following on from this basic observation, I hope to demonstrate that film and cinema, either as mental or physical constructs, can provide a meaningful context and frame of reference for spatial phenomena found in contemporary architecture and urban spaces. My interest lies more in the visual analysis, design and image-based marketing strategies of architecture and urban spaces, as well as in the occurrence of public activities that relate to film and cinema, rather than in a concrete study of the underlying urban socio-economic forces leading to such phenomena. However, this is done not without consideration and admiration for the work of Henri Lefebvre, Manuel Castells, David Harvey, Edward Soja, Saskia Sassen, Steven Miles and others working in this rich field.

A considerable amount of critical thought has been dedicated to the exploration of the *architectural significance* of film. Evidence for the richness of this debate can be found in the number of conferences and symposia dedicated to this topic, and the publication of critical texts in the last two decades, including Albrecht (2000 [1986]), Weihsmann (1988), Neumann (1999), Clarke (1997), Thomas and Penz (1997), Konstantarakos (2000), Lamster (2000), Vogt (2001), Sanders (2001), Shiel and Fitzmaurice (2001), Barber (2002), Dimendberg (2004), Marcus and Neumann (2007), Brunsdon (2007), Mennel (2008), Webber and Wilson (2008), Koeck and Roberts (2010). This body of work shows the range and depth of research that has been done with regard to the study of architecture portrayed in film, in terms of its spatial, cultural, gender, psychoanalytical and other qualities. There is little doubt among scholars that film can 'reflect' a modern or postmodern urban condition in many ways and, indeed, it has done so very successfully throughout the history of film which spans well over a century. However, while this is an important milestone to which I will return in my argument later in this book, it does not lie in the centre of my investigations. Conversely, the *filmic significance* and *properties* of architecture and urban environments – in other words using film as a lens through which we look at architecture and cities – is a field of research that by comparison is still relatively unexplored. This is an issue that has been raised for more than a decade (cf. Aitken and Zonn 1994; Clarke 1997), and it seems there is a growing interest in considering film, film history and film theory as a means of making sense of the *places* in which we live (cf. Pallasmaa 2001; Vidler 2002; AlSayyad 2006; Koeck 2008).

The title of this book is made from the combination of the words 'cine' and 'scapes', which is admittedly problematic as it adds yet more artificial and inflationary terminology to an already burdened literature of 'landscape'. It would be fair to say that the term has been chosen with a degree of resentment; however, it seems to denote the two spatial realms that lie at the centre of my deliberations in this book – *cinema* and *landscapes* – or to be precise, filmic and cinematic phenomena related to urban landscapes. The title of the book is not meant to describe a singular situational fact, but instead to point to a widening ontological discourse on visual media and architectural spaces that includes some of the things considered in this book, but it by no means covers the complete spectrum. Living in times of accelerated technological innovation, it is often forgotten that we have just left behind the *analogue age* of manually splicing and gluing film stock, or drawing architectural plans and sections. Instead, as we have only recently been thrown into the *digital age* of unlimited image manipulation (meant in a filmic, as well as city-branding sense), I would prefer to see the phenomenon of *Cine-scapes* as an 'incomplete project', along the lines of Jürgen Habermas' famous dictum made in 1980.[3] Of course, in saying this, the book does not seek to compare itself with the importance of Habermas' work, but rather the way architectural, cultural and intellectual thought models related to modernity resurface throughout this book.

Filmic and Cinematic

This book is written from the interdisciplinary and practice-based perspective of film and architecture and, therefore, is intended as a critical text addressing the question of how our understanding of movies and film language can inform contemporary debates in architecture and urban design.

Figure I.2 Nanning, China. The experience of taking a Tuk Tuk taxi in China. Being moved through and by urban space.

This means my arguments are underpinned by literature from a number of disciplines related to film and architecture, such as philosophy, sociology and geography, although I would not go so far as to say that the book is profoundly multi-disciplinary. I hope to show that if we use film as a lens through which we look at urban spaces and places, a cinematic gaze can reveal *filmic* and/or *cinematic* phenomena and qualities that are present in postmodern landscapes, and which perhaps are otherwise disregarded or merely passively consumed. By *filmic*, I mean that architecture and urban landscapes can have the qualities and characteristics of spaces and places that can be compared to those we have seen in films or other forms of motion pictures. In fact, it is not only these filmic reflections that influence our perception of cities that we seem to know so well. I believe we engage with spaces and places in our daily life in ways that are essentially *cinematic*. The term *cinematic*, in this context, is meant to convey its etymological origins found in the word *cinema*. The Greek term κινεῖν or *kinema*, meaning 'to move' or 'movement', also appears in the word stem of *kinematic*, *kinetic* and *kinaesthetic*. The term *cinema* signifies an architectural space in which we become part of a visual system that allows us to perceive a sensation of *movement* and in which we are *moved*. My argument is indebted to Giuliana Bruno, who describes cinema and movies as a form of 'geopsychic exploration' (Bruno 2002: 15), a cartographic process serving the probing of spaces. This definition begins to challenge the boundaries of a defined architectural space – that of the cinema – and opens itself up to seeing movement-based spatial recognition and consumption as a process that shares common ground with a much larger territory, such as a city.

The relation of cinema to an interdisciplinary dialogue around movement and perception goes back to the beginning of cinema. By nature, cinema as a mode of production and consumption transgresses disciplinary boundaries. Auguste Choisy, in *Histoire de l'architecture* (Choisy 1899), published four years after the Lumière brothers' first film demonstration in Paris, considered visual strategies that would overcome the single perspective view of a building, and came to the conclusion that axonometric drawings enable a mode of visual perception that enunciated 'virtual movement' and, as such, offers a quasi-cinematic function as observed by Yve-Alain Bois (1989: 114–15). In doing so, Choisy laid the foundation for the concept of a cinematic perception of architecture, which is one aspect that this book will explore further. A similar interdisciplinary argument comes from Sergei Eisenstein, who looked at the phenomena of sequentiality and montage in paintings. By introducing the notion of *cinématisme* for such visual articulations (a term to which I will return below), he explicitly linked the art of painting with cinema (Bois 1989: 112–3). Therefore, it seems legitimate to link the visual phenomena associated with film and cinema to architecture and urban spaces. Thus this text will ask the question as to what would happen if we begin to imagine the city as a place for embodied visual consumption: a visual apparatus or, perhaps, a system that is based on *movement*, *light* and the *body*, and which we can explore in *kinematic*, *kinetic* and *kinaesthetic* ways. In this way, *Cine-scapes* aims to expand the argument of the reciprocity between architecture and film in what, for many, is considered an opposite direction. It will examine the ways that properties and methods normally situated in the sphere of film have influenced spatial practices in contemporary architecture and urban design. I would like to propose the provocative idea that the creative act of shaping architecture and cities relies not soley anymore with architects and planners of 'abstract spaces' (Lefebvre 1991 [1974]: 229–91), but with a population that is film literate and has the ability to interpret and appropriate spaces and places. We live in an age in which film has become the frame of reference for our urban existence, and our activities and thoughts are intertwined with screen-based realities. I argue that we have reached a point today in which *film* and *architecture* are not only related disciplines that have mutually informed each other, but are, indeed, inseparable. Architectural and urban sites can have filmic, or even scenographic, dimensions, which might not be obvious in our everyday passive perception of cities. In doing so, this book will shed light on urban cinematic practices as well as the thought models related to these, such as (with respect to advertising) sign-like architecture or our sequential movement through space, and which may get obscured by the way we increasingly take for granted the spectacles of everyday life.

ARCHITECTURE, CITIES AND FILM

We will recognize cinema as the synthesis of all the arts ,
underlying them. It will be our immaterial Temple, Parthenor

(c

Modern Reciprocities

Ben Highmore gives a definition of modernity that is simple, yet captures
what lies at the heart of it: 'Modernity, as I understand it, is the experience of
being caught up in, and at times overtaken by, dramatic changes' (Highmore
2005: 12). This simple definition applies to both spheres of mass culture,
namely cinema and cities. While film brought dramatic changes to the way in
which images of real or imagined landscapes, events or people were captured
and shared with the public, not least through cinema itself and the changed
physical fabric of the city, cities of the western world simultaneously under-
went enormous transformations.[4] It is during these formative years that film
and cities built an affinity and dependency that can be still felt today.

Key scholars in both fields have recognised that the beginnings of the relationship between film and cities is also linked to concepts and practices that
have their roots in the early years of an emerging urban modernity. James
Donald (1999), Dietrich Neumann (1999), Barbara Mennel (2008) and others recognise that it is this modernity that links the theories and practices of
urbanism with that of cinema. Donald (1999: 63–92) recalls that early cinema,
in the words of Phil Hubbard,

> ... should be understood as an urban phenomenon not merely because cinemas were
> located *in* the city, but because they were *of* the city, using new narrative devices, visual
> technologies and editing techniques to communicate the *pace* of modern urban life.
>
> (Hubbard 2006: 135).

AlSayyad comments that 'Berlin's modernity was the product of a new experience of space, time and motion', and demonstrates that the concept of the
modern city and street life was the sharing of the same characteristics as those
found in cinema, thus providing a 'collective understanding of place'
(AlSayyad 2006: 34). Indeed, this book, which primarily aims to identify ways
of understanding contemporary urban conditions, will rely considerably
upon the writings of, and concepts developed by, pioneers in film and modern
architecture, such as Hans Richter, Sergei Eisenstein, A. and L. Lumière,
Robert Mallet-Stevens and Le Corbusier.

Of the celebrated 'coincidences' that the birth of cinema shared with other
emerging modernist projects, such as psychoanalysis, nationalism, consumerism and imperialism (Shohat and Stam 1994: 100), cinema's emergence as a

urban set of practices has ensured that the city and the moving ve, from the very outset, remained as intertwined constituents of the rn urban imaginary. At the turn of the twentieth century, the fascination nd spectacle of the moving image experienced by early cinema audiences drew its strength and affective potency from the technological, perceptual and spatial transformations that were shaping rapid processes of urbanisation in large parts of the industrialised world.

When the pioneers of film captured moving images of cities, during a time when cinematic apparatus recorded only images without sound, filmmaking was a light and mobile practice that was often carried out in the bustling streets and landscapes of the metropolis. This scopic affinity between medium and place can perhaps be explained by the fact that the emerging modern city seemed to naturally complement the ability of the cinematic apparatus to capture the city's defining characteristics: its architectural forms, movements, illuminations and, of course, its people. Film – arguably better than any other medium – seems to be able to engage with the city's physical disposition, its simultaneity, temporality and ephemerality in ways that had hitherto only been imagined.

This symbiotic relationship between two emerging phenomena of modernity – the city and film – manifested itself not only in terms of capturing the spaces in 'transition' (Webber and Wilson 2008), but also in the form of screenings to an urban audience. Internationally, such early projections of urban life were made possible by entrepreneurs and pioneers such as the Skladnowski brothers in Germany, the Lumière Company in France, the Mitchell & Kenyon company in England and Thomas Edison in the United States. The pioneering endeavours of these early luminaries gradually turned film from being a 'scientific curiosity' and fairground attraction into a 'seventh art' (as noted by Ricciotto Canudo) that would eventually transform the appearance, geography and socio-spatial organisation of cities (in the form of, for example, nickelodeons, leisure parks and film theatres) (Canudo 1988a [1911]: 67, 1988b [1923]: 291; see also Albrecht 2000 [1986]: 27–34). Thanks to the seminal texts of a series of scholars,[5] we continue to gain a detailed understanding of how early film activities, such as production, distribution and exhibition, have operated within, and shaped, modern cities.

Although the first three decades of the twentieth century are often regarded as the Golden Age of the visionary architect and planner, even the designs of the avant-garde of architectural modernity, such as Adolf Loos, Ludwig Hilberseimer, Bruno Taut, Le Corbusier and Walter Gropius, proved to be simply unbuildable in a politically-charged and economically devastating climate. During the same period, the film industry, on the other hand, often employed directors and designers who were architecturally trained and were able to create imagined architectures and urban environments that not only benefited from the lack of constraints which modernist urban designers were otherwise confronted with, but were also remarkable in terms of the increasing tectonic quality that characterised the work of this new breed of film professionals.

The fact that, in the 1920s, a number of prominent architects, particularly in Germany and France, contributed to professional film productions, suggests a longstanding 'applied' reciprocity between the disciplines of architecture and film. Prominent examples include the architects Hans Poelzig, who built the set for Carl Boese's and Paul Wegener's expressionist film classic, *Der Golem, wie er in die Welt kam* (1920); Robert Mallet-Stevens who worked on the set design for Marcel L'Herbier's film, *L'Inhumaine* (1924), and whose architecture featured in Man Ray's surrealist film, *Les Mystères du Château de Dé* (1928/29); Le Corbusier who collaborated with Pierre Chenal on the documentary film, *L'Architecture d'aujourd'hui* (1929); and László Moholy-Nagy who contributed a special effects sequence to Alexander Korda's futuristic feature film *Things to Come* (1936).[6]

While, at first glance, these notable examples appear to demonstrate an intense engagement between architects and film production in the early twentieth century, it is worth remembering that the group mentioned above forms an exception to the rule. The majority of their forward-looking contemporaries were more sceptical towards narrative film and did not consider it to be an expedient medium for their practice. Many considered that narrative film as a genre was too derivative of stage arts and thus could not be considered an art in its own right. Therefore, it is debateable whether any of the filmic products mentioned above actually informed the architectural practices of those architects involved. However, they may have informed the architectural practices of other architects, especially if one accepts the idea that, for example, Mallet-Stevens and Le Corbusier's portrayal of ultramodern architecture in film promoted a short-lived, but triumphant phase of architectural modernism in Europe.

These and other links between the two industries have caught the attention of a new generation of interdisciplinary scholars who, profiting from and inspired by the high-quality set design of this modern period, set out to find a new method of reading films; one that moves away from seeing film solely as a genre-dependent *text*, but also as a rich *map* of socio-cultural, political, economic and, of course, architectural discourses. This is supported by a number of encyclopaedic publications dedicated to the specificity of urban location portrayed in film in a global context, such as *Die Stadt im Kino* (Vogt 2001), *Celluloid Skyline* (Sanders 2001), *La Ville au Cinéma* (Jousse and Paquot 2005), *City + Cinema* (Griffiths and Chudoba 2007) and *Cinematic Rotterdam* (Paalman 2011).

As in the case of these latter publications, with increasing frequency, architectural schools are producing scholars specialising in the analysis of *projected architecture* and *places* found, most prominently, in feature films, but also in documentaries, city symphonies and computer games (Thomas and Penz 1997), which they regard as a rich source for the contextualisation of what Helmut Weihsmann poetically refers to as the *Architektur des filmischen Raums* (Weihsmann 1995: 25): the architecture of filmic space. Yet it is not just the formal merits of architectural objects found in film that warrant scholarly investigation. Projected cities can share with real cities a sense of place in an almost infinite *matrix* of space and time, as in the Wachowski brothers' 1999 film of the same name; one that goes well beyond the Weimar years, or, in the words of Dietrich Neumann, 'from *Metropolis* to *Blade Runner*' (Neumann 1999).

Proto-cinematic Reading of Cities

While it is well established that architectural skills, thoughts and forms have infiltrated filmic productions, it is less clear how filmic and cinematic principles have impacted discussions of architecture and urban design. Are there any filmic properties found in architecture and cities today and, if so, what are they? Interestingly, these and other enquiries bear, once again, a relationship to the aforementioned history of film and architecture. Mallet-Stevens, one of the pioneers of French architectural modernism, claimed that although film has a distinct influence on modern architecture, this modern architecture also shares filmic properties, since both essentially consist of 'images in movement' (Mallet-Stevens 1925: 96).[7] Along similar lines, in 1928, Sigfried Giedion insisted that only film (rather than photography) could intelligibly capture the essence of Le Corbusier's work (Giedion 1995 [1928]: 176). It could be argued that, by commenting on the problem of visual representation, Giedion draws attention to the multi-perspectival character (movement) and hence *cinematic* element that is embedded in the design (space) of certain examples modern architecture.

A further intellectual breakthrough can be seen when filmmakers rediscovered the city as location for shooting, such as Italian Neorealist cinema and the French New Wave. For instance, during the latter period of French filmmaking in the late 1950s and 1960s, celebrated figures such as Godard, Truffaut, Rohmer, Chabrol and Rivette, drew attention to a type of filmmaking practice that, after a long period of studio productions, took the camera on to the streets of Paris and other cities. Perhaps it is no coincidence that this transition from studio to street was directly preceded by a series of architectural writings that considered both the fragmented/disjointed and linear/sequential nature of the city, considering urban space as an almost proto-cinematic entity. For example,

Gordon Cullen's *The Concise Townscape* (Cullen 2005 [1961]) developed the concept of 'serial vision'. Similar to those methods employed by storyboard artists, he undertook a shot-by-shot analysis while travelling at constant pace through a series of urban spaces. Likewise, Christopher Alexander's work, *A Pattern Language: Towns, Buildings, Construction* (Alexander 1977), scientifically dissects architectural design into a grammar of discrete units or *patterns*. Depending on the particular situation, and by making use of his rules and regulations, these patterns can be reassembled (edited) and applied to any scheme, so that the result, once again, produces a harmonious environment. Colin Rowe argues in his book *Collage City* written in association with Fred Koetter that, since the seventeenth century, cities (being a 'didactic instrument') consist of 'ambiguous and composite buildings' (Rowe and Koetter 1984 [1978]: 121, 168). As such, they are disintegrated and fragmented, and call for an enlightened, pluralistic design strategy in which historical references reside, collage-like, alongside and within contemporary architectural articulations.

The 1960s also saw the foundation of Archigram (1961–74) at the Architectural Association in London, whose dynamic urban environments, such as *Living City* (1963–64), *Walking City* (1964) and *Instant City* (1968), were expressions of a pro-consumerist and technocratic vision of the future. Many of the ideas developed by the members of the team – Warren Chalk, Peter Cook, Dennis Crompton, David Greene, Ron Herron and Michael Webb – could not be communicated through conventional architectural drawings. Early on, therefore, the group relied heavily on various formats, including imagery, graphics and text, that often showed influences of comic books, collage and pop art. This shows a commitment to a language of fragmentation in which images and architecture formed a new composite of a utopian future. Archigram became one of the influences on the Italian firm Superstudio, led by Adolfo Natalini and Cristiano Toraldo di Francia. Founded in 1966 in Florence, Italy, the group propagandised a rapid expansion of architecture and a total urbanisation spanning – and unifying – the entire world. This was explored in three research strands, namely the *architecture of the monument*, the *architecture of the image* and *technomorphic architecture*. As with Archigram before them, the group relied on printed media (in this case the magazine *Casabella*) to distribute their utopian ideas, for which they developed fictional stories, storyboard illustrations and photomontages. Also formed in the 1960s, and collaborating with Superstudio, the group *Archizoom Associati* was the second influential and radical architectural collective from Florence. While today Superstudio is probably best remembered for their project *Continuous Monumenti*, which was first shown as a series of enigmatic photo-collages produced in 1969,[8] Archizoom is best known for its radical, modernist vision of a mass-produced *No-Stop City* (1969). Both of these avant-garde fantasies have never been realised, and exist only as imagined places in the form of printed images, montages, models, installations and films (see Budzknski 2011: 1), yet their work has arguably inspired that of Zaha Hadid, Rem Koolhaas, Bernard Tschumi and other progressive architects.

The aforementioned term 'practice' does not, of course, limit itself to a unilateral form of knowledge transfer, but includes the production of architecture and urban space as well as its consumption. The public on the streets of a typical city in the western hemisphere are, in most cases, surrounded by the products of architects and planners. However, most people who use these spaces are not trained in a planning discipline, but instead have grown up in a culture that, since the early years of childhood, exposes them to an active and passive consumption (or reading) of moving images. It is not, therefore, too farfetched to hypothesise that the concepts surrounding film production, such as the way a film is edited, could inform our consumption of architecture in an urban context. Central to this investigation is the realisation that film and architecture share a number of properties, of which 'narration' is arguably one of the most important agents in the transfer of spatially-embedded information. As many filmmakers will confirm, no matter how well it is put together, any film narrative will fail without a decent plot.[9] The same could perhaps be applied to cities. Cities that have no coherent spatio-narrative structure tend to be places that leave little lasting impression on our memory. The plot, which an experienced film or video editor normally assembles on the timeline of a multitude of small visual fragments (shots), seems to be missing in many contemporary cities today.

Contemporary urban landscapes have been problematised as sites that are often filled with commercialised tourist spaces or generic consumer architecture that fundamentally lack a relationship to their surrounding geography. Edward Relph's concept of the 'placelessness' of urban landscapes (Relph 1976, 1987) describes the phenomenon that our increase of mass communication and mobility produced spaces that are short of distinctiveness, become increasingly alike and ubiquitous, and lack a sense of place. This is echoed in Marc Augé's notion of 'non-places' – fleeting and fragmented spaces, such as hotels, airports and motorways – that have been brought about by a new supermodernity that cannot be defined as relational or historical, and is not concerned with identity (Augé 1995: 77–78; see also Dovey: 2002 [1999]). In this book, then, I do not attempt to further categorise the 'spaces for consumption' (Miles 2010) and define them as *cinescapes*, but argue that contemporary urban spaces have a common quality that links them to principles first recognised in the context of the emerging modern city and cinema. In so doing, I concur with two important arguments. First, that of Peter Wollen, when he says that even the supermodern spaces of Augé are not too dissimilar from the modern urban sensations described by Walter Benjamin, since they are both experienced as 'dynamic spaces rather than static, to which our relationship is kinetic rather than contemplative'. Our movement through urban space creates an interactive relationship with such spaces (Wollen 2002: 201). Second, I agree with James Donald, whose superb book *Imagining the Modern City* (Donald 1999) highlights, for me, that the city cannot only be judged as a product of society and its structure, but that it produces a 'way of seeing'.[10] In probing the relationship between the city and the moving image, the question of movement and mobility, and, by extension, that of time and 'rhythmicity' (Wunderlich 2008), reinforces the essentially dynamic, affective and 'emotional' (Bruno 2002) properties of urban space. Equally, Roland Barthes' observation that it is not so important to multiply the surveys or the functional studies of the city, 'but to multiply the readings of the city' (Barthes 1997 [1967]: 171) provides a critical acknowledgement of the limited value of technocratic modes of urban representation, pointing to the need to develop more 'fuzzy' and multi-layered semiotics of space, place and urban memory.

Taking reference from the above and other propositions by spatial and cultural theorists, this book will invite the reader to place themselves in the position of a filmmaker who engages with spatio-urban formations through a comprehension of cinema, film language, narration and editing. Arguably, this unusual approach would provide a new meaning to Gidieon's statement that 'only film can make the new architecture intelligible' (Gidieon 1995 [1928]: 176).

Postmodern Spatial Montage

Contemporary architectural practices have approached the question of cinematic architecture by showing an attachment to structuralist, poststructuralist, and deconstructivist theories and, by extension, to the work of notable theorists such as Saussure, Barthes, Derrida, Foucault and Deleuze. Interestingly, regardless of how much architects see (like Eisenman, Agrest and Gandelsonas, Tschumi or Nouvel, their argument rooted in linguistic formalism or its decomposition), they all show a deep fascination for the fragmented, composite quality of contemporary urban spaces, and the expressive nature of architectural form and function. The consequence of this is that theories related to film, film editing and cinema have permeated the process and articulation of architectural and urban design. This journey through linguistic and montage theory, and their relevance to architectural practice, will start with a quote by Elliot Gaines in which he addresses the question of space in traditional semiotics.

> The study of space as a semiotic phenomenon suggests that the meaning of space, as a sign, is generally understood in relation to other concerns. Communication draws attention to the content of messages while space contributes to the meanings of those messages with being obvious about its role in constructing meaning.
>
> (Gaines 2006: 173)

Gaines insightful text highlights that, in semiotic terms, there is relatively little consideration for the study of space, since it is often seen as a 'background to other objects and relationships' and not necessarily as a sign (ibid.); hence I approach this problem from the direction of *déjà vu* explored in Part I. From an architectural perspective, however, space can be defined by the objects by which it is surrounded. Architects differentiate between solid space and void (or open) space. For instance, when describing a city square, the former encloses and hence fundamentally influences and defines the character of the open space. Open space is more than just a background for the surrounding objects. Solid and void relate to each other and can stand in a dialogue, which begins to describe space in ways that come closer to how Charles Sanders Peirce (founder of the pragmatic and systematic theory of semiotics) defined categories of signs (Peirce 1960–66 [1903–4]: Vols 1, 5, 8; see also Gaines 2006: 173). Peirce sees a triadic relationship between sign and objects and defines it as *firstness*, *secondness* and *thirdness*, which Gaines cites as an example of the relative qualities of space. It appears to be common sense that space can have meaning, yet compared to other forms of communication that we recognise in our everyday lives, space plays a relatively minor and inconspicuous role in the way we construct meaning (Gaines 2006: 173–5), for instance when walking through urban space, and is, therefore, less obvious or palpable than visual advertisement boards.

One architectural practice that works in this area, and stands out for its long-lasting and strong relationship between theory and practice and its keen interest in textual articulation of space, is the office of Diana Agrest and Mario Gandelsonas Architects in New York. Anthony Vidler points out that, in their work, 'an applied semiology [has] been replaced by an extended discussion of the nature of the architectural signifier, and of architecture and urbanism as complex system of signs' (Vidler 1995: 10). While being engaged in structuralist analysis of their theories during the 1970s (and thereby running the risk of manoeuvring architectural design into a rigid and inflexible system of signs), Vidler highlights that 'their work has been consistently suspicious of reified analogies, finding in poststructuralism, rather, a mode of setting architecture in motion' (ibid.). Thus, they see architecture not as a form of language *per se*, but instead as a form of writing, or to quote Gandelsonas, 'as an area of production where the subject works in transgressive way with the notion of rules as a limit' (ibid.; Gandelsonas 1979: 28). Both see architecture and urban spaces as elements in a cultural system that, on the one hand requires a semiotic or textual approach, but on the other hand incorporates movement. From this position, Agrest and Gandelsonas quickly arrived at film and montage theory as influential for their practical work.

Inspiration for this comes from Soviet theoretical and practical discourses on montage, in particular the film work of Sergei Eisenstein, Dziga Vertov and Vsevolod Pudovkin, all of whom were influenced by Lev Kuleshov, the great theorist of Soviet cinema. Eisenstein established the basic rationale for his montage theory in the 1923 manifesto *The Montage of Attractions*, which, in the first instance, he discusses, not in the context of film, but of photomontage, the work of Alexandre Rodchenko and George Grosz (Christie and Taylor 1993: 195). Eisenstein's basic definition of montage describes an enunciative phenomenon that arises through the collision of two independent pieces (ibid.), which is sufficiently wide to be related to modern, as well as postmodern urban, phenomena. Playing to the strength of film montage to connote meaning from two unrelated images, Agrest and Gandelsonas note that their *150 Wooster Street project* (1989) in New York City 'presented the opportunity to inspect the possibility of generating formal arrangements and configurations that allow an exotic theme to be read without resorting to direct representation; instead a strategy of metonymic montage was used throughout the project' (Agrest and Gandelsonas 1995: 204). Therefore, montage is seen as a spatial method of juxtaposition that, whilst originating in the context of images, has the power to transform three-dimensional spaces.

Filmic montage is widely regarded as a mode of production and expression that shows considerable affinity with the perceived spatial conditions found in turn-of-the-century modern cities. Not only have architects and planners begun to view the physical environment of cities, through a process of historical evolution, industrialisation, and/or warfare, as being disjointed, they also view its inner structure, in social, political and economic terms, as fragmented or even shattered. Simmel's assertion that the metropolis can have adverse effects on the psychosocial health of its inhabitants shows a surprising analogy to filmic montage theory: 'Man is a creature whose existence is dependent on the differences, i.e. his mind is stimulated by the difference between present impressions and those which have preceded' (Simmel 2010 [1903]: 103).[11] Indeed the city symphonies of Vertov or Walter Ruttmann make explicit use of montage editing techniques to show a cross-section of clashing and incongruous urban conditions in 1920s metropolises. On this subject, Allen and Agrest note that 'The early modern metropolis produced a new subject: the montage eye, capable of constructing a new reality out of the barrage of fragmentary, contradictory, and obsolete information that characterises the modern city' (Allen and Agrest 2000: 27). Therefore, if seen in the context of urban and filmic construction, the notion of montage has obtained a simultaneous double connotation, as remarked by Beller: 'Montage as fragmentation and montage as the connection of fragments are at once the condition of modern life and the condition for the production of meaning in modern life' (Beller 2006: 39).

As mentioned earlier, Sergei Eisenstein explored the phenomena of sequentiality and montage in paintings. He uses the term *cinématisme* for the particular forms of visual articulation he found in paintings, and argues that these are indeed linked to the art of cinema (Bois 1989: 112–3). A similar methodical approach is taken by Davide Deriu, whose notable study on Sigfried Giedion's book *Building in France, Building in Iron, Building in Ferroconcrete* (Giedion 1995 [1928]) sets out to link the visual illustrations of Giedion's book with Eisenstein's theories. He argues that Eisenstein's montage theory, and the concept of *cinématisme* in particular, were 'not only the implicit method but also a latent object of Giedion's operation', which means that his 'understanding of architecture revealed a distinctively cinematic conception of space' (Deriu 2007: 55, 50). If this is accepted, then such a convergence between space and cinema – in the context of twentieth century architectural modernity – is once again evidenced through an image-based practice.

It is therefore not only through a series of well-known narrative films, such as *L'Inhumaine* (1924), *Le Vertige* (1926), *L'Agent* (1928), *Le P'tit Parigot* (1926), *Le Diable au Coeur* (1928), *Le Nouveau Messieurs* (1928), *A Nous la Liberté* (1931) or the semi-documentary film *L'Architecture d'Aujourd'hui* (1931) promoting the work of Le Corbusier, but also through more subtle visual means found in print media that architectural modernism was related to the mobile gaze of cinema. Yves-Alain Bois notes in the introduction to *Montage and Architecture* that 'Cinematographic montage is, too, a means to "link" in one point – the screen – various elements (fragments) of a phenomenon filmed in diverse dimensions, from diverse points of view and sides' (Bois 1989: 111). Thus, cinematic montage infuses in us not only the recognition of multiple dimensions with regard to the perception of architectural space, but that space itself is presented in more than one dimension, including that of architectural space. While montage theory is rooted in the theory and practice of the early twentieth century, and in particular to concepts of spatial articulation and perception linked to modernity, the same theories are found to be relevant in a discourse of contemporary architectural practice today. Allen and Agrest provide an interesting analogy between filmmaker and architect, in the sense that both are essentially builders:

> It is no accident that Vertov uses the language of the builder to describe the operations of montage. Montage is revealed construction. It utilizes instrumental procedures, but its products are not exclusively instrumental. The engineer-*monteur* is an architect who builds images. Montage does not pretend to reproduce natural vision. It works on the surface, constructing new objects (and subjects) out of new relations of image to image.
>
> (Allen and Agrest 2000: 28)

Apart from Berhard Tschumi and Jean Nouvel, who have been discussed above, Rem Koolhaas has been a further prominent architectural force whose theoretical and creative design work shows a clear affinity to theories of montage and editing, and hence to a discourse with film and cinema. The critically-acclaimed architect, theorist and urbanist has been outspoken about the influence that his previous education as a scriptwriter and work as a screenwriter had on his work in the architectural profession. Koolhaas, whose intellectual affinity to cinema and montage theory is well illustrated in such writings as *Delirious New York: A Retroactive Manifesto of Manhattan* (Koolhaas 1978) and *S, M, L, XL* (Koolhaas *et al.* 1995), indicates that his experiences in the film profession have informed his thinking and work in architectural and urban design: 'I think the art of the scriptwriter is to conceive sequences of episode which build suspense and a chain of events … The largest part of my work is montage … spatial montage' (cited in Toy 1994: 7). This shows that he sees montage as an element in story telling that is no longer limited to a two-dimensional surface, but seeks a manifestation in three-dimensional space. Evidence of the correlation between architectural practice and film are particularly well illustrated in the Kunsthal, Rotterdam (1993), Seattle Central Library (2004) and the Casa da Música (2001–2005) in Porto, where the notion of montage cannot only be traced in the way that the buildings are situated within an urban context, but are also presented in the organisation of spaces inside the building.

KEY CONCEPTS

> The pro-filmic refers to everything placed in front of the camera to be filmed. It includes things such actors (and therefore casting decisions and performance style), lighting, set design, selection of locations, and selection of props. … Therefore, as narrative discourse the pro-filmic embodies a series of choices and reveals a narrative intention behind the choices.
>
> (Gunning 1991: 19)

Narrative and Space

I argue in this book that architectural spaces and urban landscapes can have narrative qualities which link them with film and cinema. What exactly does the term *narrative* mean? It has become something of a buzzword, freely adopted – if not to say overused – in almost every field of research, including history, anthropology, gender studies, psychoanalysis, sociology, cultural studies, media studies, and even management studies and law. However, it is worth being reminded that the study of narrative has its origins in linguistics, where it began life as a structuralist pursuit for a formal system and was subsequently adapted to other fields, such as film studies. The following discussion will address the rationale for the study of narrative in the context of urban landscapes, before looking at narrative mechanisms with regard to screen space and on-location space (spaces where films are shot), as well as how these can have a presence in actual urban spaces.

The term narratology, coined by the Franco-Bulgarian philosopher Tzvetan Todorov in his *Grammaire du Décaméron* (1969), denotes a field of research that considers narrative to be a discourse in its own right, and in which narrative communication undergoes a more-or-less scientific study. Key scholars in this field, such as Algirdas Julien Greimas (1966), Gérard Genette (1966, 1972, 1982) and Roland Barthes (1997 [1967]), have advanced an understanding of *narrative* from a semiotic position in which language is seen as signifiers (*sjuzet*) and signifieds (*fabula*) (Rudrum 2005: 196; cf. Altman 2008: 5). This approach has been called into question by a poststructural shift, such as one in the field of deconstruction by Jacques Derrida (1979: 72–3) and Jonathan Culler (1981: 170–2). Edward Branigan recalls a similar shift taking place in the field of film studies where, in the mid-1960s, film theory began as 'an object-centered epistemology (where the goal was to present numerous methods by which to segment and analyse the parts of a film)' before repositioning itself to a 'subject-centered epistemology (where the goal was to investigate the actual methods employed by a human perceiver to watch, understand, and remember a film)' (Branigan 1992: xi). While it is useful to understand semiotic origins behind the study of narrative, as we embark on a journey in which a cinematic gaze is adapted to architectural spaces and cities, it is equally important to understand the limits of applying a formal structure to a system that is as complex as that of architectural and urban spaces. Hence, the semiotic reading of spaces and places in the context of film and architecture is seen to be useful only to a limited extent.

My other concern lies with the term 'narrative' itself, whose meaning is debated, if not contested, to a considerable degree. Not only can the term can be used as an adjective (which qualifies a noun that is concerned with narration) as well as a substantive (that is often confused with 'story' or 'plot'),[12] an issue recognised by experts in the field and that can lead to misinterpretations (see, for instance, Coste 1989: 4), but also the term's varied definitions also give only a limited understanding of it, as Rudrum (2005) and Altman (2008), for instance, have noted in recent years. While most scholars would agree that an 'event' is an important constituent of a narrative, it is less clear as to how many of these events are needed so that we can speak of a narrative. Genette notes that 'one will define narrative without difficulty as the representation of *an* event or sequence of events' (Genette 1982 [1966]: 127); Gerald Prince states that a 'narrative is the representation of at least *two* real or fictive events in a time sequence, neither of which presupposes or entails the other' (Prince 1982: 4); and Onega and Landa declare that 'narrative is a semiotic representation of *a series* of events' (emphasis added) (Onega and Landa 1996: 5). The concept that a series of events or actions are fundamental to the formation of a narrative deserves a closer look and will be examined later in the book. For now, it is important to note that the definition of narrative has expanded from an initially confined investigation of the inner structure to, more recently, outward-looking implications. Scholars such as Monika Fludernik have begun to question the salient role of 'sequences of action' for the formation of a narrative, and define the essence of narrative as the 'communication of anthropocentric experience – the experientiality which is inherent in human experience and feelings, and depiction perceptions and reflections' (Fludernik 2009: 59). Accordingly, narrative is seen not simply as a sequence of events, but renders such sequences, and, through it, 'narrative' itself, as an integral part of human experience.

This shows that considerable intellectual baggage accompanies the use of the term which, when applied to non-textual or verbal forms of communication (such as through an engagement with urban landscapes as proposed here), faces the danger of becoming more convoluted and problematic. Nevertheless, it seems fruitful to borrow an understanding of narrative from such disciplines as the basis for further discussion wherever possible. Importantly, this discourse contains a key point – the universality of narrative – which is not only recognised by the majority of scholars, but also informs my argument in terms of the importance of considering the narrative properties and potential of urban spaces and cities. H. Porter Abbott points out that narrative is not limited to traditional modes of storytelling, but that 'narrative is also something we all engage in, artists and non-artists alike', which means that narratives advance into every aspect of our everyday lives: 'we make narratives many times a day, every day of our lives' (Abbott 2008: 1). Consequently, we must consider that narratives are present in nearly all human dialogue, which means that theorists have placed the study of narrative alongside language as an essential human trait, and used it as a distinctive strategy to make sense of the world around us (see ibid.; Branigan 1992: xi; cf. Altman 2008: 1). This perspective is particularly recognised in postmodern literary criticism, such as in the texts of Fredric Jameson (1981: 13) and Jean-François Lyotard (1984: 19), who are concerned about the impact of postmodernity on the human condition (see Abbott 2008: 1). If we consider that narrative is part of 'all human dialogue', then this seems to open up the possibility of including *spatial characteristics* in general, as well as cities and architectural spaces in particular, as active agents in a narrative discourse. Even Barthes had to widen his initial structuralist position with regard to the existence of narrative as evidenced in *Image, Music, Text*:

> The narratives of the world are numberless. Narrative is first and foremost a prodigious variety of genres, themselves distributed amongst different substances – as though any material were fit to receive man's stories. Able to be carried by articulated language, spoken or written, fixed or moving images, gestures, and the ordered mixture of all these substances; narrative is present in myth, legend, fable, tale, novella, epic, history, tragedy, drama, comedy, mime, painting (think of Carpaccio's *Saint Ursula*), stained glass windows, cinema, comics, news item, conversation. Moreover, under this almost infinite diversity of forms, narrative is present in every age, in every place, in every society; it begins with the very history of mankind and there nowhere is nor has been a people without narrative.
>
> (Barthes and Heath 1977: 79)

It could, of course, be argued that cities and urban situations are filled with signs, images and forms that contribute, to some degree, to what might be seen as an architectural language, which would mean that it might fall into the formal, semiotic designation of narrative in line with the spirit of Barthes' early work. However, taking into consideration Barthes' all-inclusive position as quoted above, such a contestable theoretical stance is made obsolete. This argument follows, in essence, what Robert Altman demands when saying that a 'new definition of narrative, open to a more inclusive range of texts and experiences' is necessary today (Altman 2008: 2). If narratives exist, as Barthes and others conclude, as a written, oral, visual discourse in an 'infinite diversity of forms', then architecture and cities become agents that can be studied for their narrative significance in a represented or mediated form (e.g. film) as well as unmediated existence (e.g. actual space).

For nearly forty years, considerable research has been dedicated to the study of *narrative* and its relationship to *space* in the context of *film*. Stephen Heath's work on *narrative space* made a key contribution to this field, and it is probably fair to say that ever since the publications of 'Narrative Space' (Heath 1976) and *Questions of Cinema* (Heath 1981), the study of film has become unimaginable without a consideration of spatial narrative dimensions. While Heath's work has arguably influenced principal scholars with regard to the three levels that define the 'pro-filmic' – namely everything in front of the camera; the enframed image; and editing (Gunning 1991: 19) – or a process that called 'narrativization' as argued by Stam *et al.* (1992: 112), Heath's contribution to film studies is also seen critically (cf. Andrew 2000: 343). Mark Cooper notes that the 'essay's virtue ['Narrative Space'] … lies in its refusal to define either "narrative" or "space" apart from cinema's conventional manner of relating the two' (Cooper 2002: 144). Heath, who is concerned with the relationship between spectator and screen sees the 'Renaissance perspective as the defining model of modern space', which is an intellectual starting point that has since been contested, as remarked by Cooper's discerning revisiting of the original text (Cooper 2002: 145). Setting this aside, Heath demonstrates the dynamic correlations of narrative and space, which draws attention to one of the reasons why cinema differs from Renaissance painting with regards to the perception of space (Heath 1976: 83; cf. Cooper 2002: 139). He argues that 'one of the narrative acts of a film is the creation of space, but what gives the moving space its coherence in time, decides the metonymy as a "taking place", is here "the narrative itself" …' (Heath 1976: 92). Heath, alludes that 'film makes space, takes place as narrative, and the subject too, set – sutured – in the conversion of the one to the other' (ibid.: 107). In doing so, the concept of *narrative space* does not foreground the narrative qualities of film space, but the notion of film as narrative space (ibid.: 75), which can perhaps be summarised as a hypothesis that says that film forms a dynamic space that is held together by a narrative (ibid.: 75).

Other scholars, while perhaps not wholly agreeing with Heath's arguments, have adopted the term *narrative space* for their investigations. Scholars whose research is rooted in classical Hollywood cinema, as well as many others thereafter, have used the term and added important dimensions (cf. Bordwell 1981: 37–69; cf. Bordwell 1985: 203, 214–30; cf. Haralovich 1990: 57–72). In the most basic terms, such research was pursued along two principal lines. First, it was felt that there is a need to study the *spatio-temporal organisation of narrative*. Edward Branigan notes that narrative is in itself 'a way of organizing spatial and temporal data into a cause-effect chain of events with a beginning, middle, and end' (Branigan 1992: 3). More recently, scholars have begun to see the relationship between film narrative and new media and have expanded their research interests from linear to non-linear story telling techniques. Maureen Thomas takes this discourse of the 'spatial organisation of narrative' from the field of film studies and expands it into the digital world, where the computer game environment presents us with a series of new ways of understanding space (Thomas 2003: 51–134). Second, a proportionally larger body of researchers, to which I will frequently refer throughout this text, place their attention on the *spatial representation of narrative* in film. It is remarkable to see how many international conferences, symposia, screenings and publications have been dedicated to the study of *space* in film, although it is not always clear that people are referring to the same meaning of this very popular term.

This raises the question of whether the dialectic above discussed between space and narrative is one that not only applies to the study of film, but also to the study of architecture and urban space. There seem to be enticing parallels between Stephen Heath's notion of a *narrative space*, in terms of a spectator/space relationship, and our bodily engagement with physical urban space, some of which seem applicable, while others are less convincing. Therefore my attempted summary of Heath's position (that film forms a dynamic space that is held together by a narrative) is one that shows considerable overlaps with the argument for an understanding of cities as cinematic cityscapes outlined here. We, as occupants of urban space, can form a dynamic relationship with that space, which is, crucially, held together by narratives that are attached or stitched into the spaces we inhabit. With regard to such an extended thought model, the presumed rules of engagement with space changes considerably from those envisioned by Heath. While his observation is largely based on the notion of a passive spectator, a cinematic engagement with urban spaces is at the same time an active and narrative immersion that not only brings about a change in mental attitude, but ultimately a change of a *space* into a *place*.

The Filmic Universe of Space

The word *space* is probably one of the most ambiguous and abused terms found in the literature of human geography, film studies and architecture, as well as in other arts and social sciences. The abstractness and universality of the word entices us to a lapidary use, and I am sure that, at times, this text will be no exception. It is perhaps worth reminding ourselves that, in the context of film, there are clearly distinct forms of space. Heath alludes to the fact that photographic vision is able to create a quasi 'ideal space', through an optical mechanism in which the camera apparatus becomes a Vertovian 'perfect eye' that is free from the body (Heath 1976: 79). This perfect space, however, is made up of, and diluted by, a series of other spaces before it arrives at the viewer's end.

In *La structure de l'Univers Filmique et le Vocabulaire de la Filmologie*, Étienne Souriau (1951) talks about the structural analysis of narrative and introduces the term 'diegesis', the imaginary world created by film, to the context of cinema (Souriau 1951: 233; see also Lowry 1985: 85). Years later, Genette in *Frontières du Récit* (Genette 1966), appropriated the concept of diegesis in

Figure I.3   Prague. Filming on location for *Mission Impossible IV*.

a literary studies context, from where it entered mainstream scholarly use (cf. Sipière 2008: 13). Apart from this important input to our understanding of diegesis, Souriau made a valuable contribution to the identification and naming of seven levels of filmic reality (see Buckland 2000: 47; cf. Lowry 1985: 84–6). These levels of filmic reality are related to the way we spatially engage with film. His approach is based on a 'separation of *time* stages in the making of a film and on a *spatial* distinction between the different status of the filmic text and performance' (Sipière 2008: 11). It seems possible, therefore, to transpose some of his well-known definitions into categories of space that are evident in filmic production and consumption, which ultimately aims to give us a more nuanced terminology of space that will be helpful in other parts of this book.[13]

First, Souriau introduces the term *afilmic* reality. In terms of space, this denotes the physical space that exists independently of the filmic reality. In other words, afilmic space is the space that exists before and after film production; it is the spatial setting in which a film is shot, either on a set or on location. Souriau then defines *profilmic* reality, which, when seen in our context, can be defined as the physical space that is photographed and later transformed by the camera. It is the space of the filmic production that exists either as actual space, for instance as a location in the city, or a set in a film studio, or as virtual space in the form of computer generated imagery (CGI). Profilmic space is therefore a manipulated space, used by filmmakers to shape a narrative or plot. It is the spatial basis for allowing us to engage with film, as Benjamin notes in his 1936 essay *The Work of Art in the Age of Mechanical Reproduction*, in a process of optical unconsciousness:

Evidently a different nature opens itself to the camera than opens to the naked eye – if only because an unconsciously penetrated space is substituted for a space consciously explored by man. ... The camera introduces us to unconscious optics as does psychoanalysis to unconscious impulses.

(Benjamin 1968 [1936]: 237)

Profilmic space is the space that, as Thom Anderson asks us in his film *Let Los Angeles Play Itself* (2003), we should not concede to in a process of 'involuntary attention' as it encourages us to blur the boundary between fiction and reality.[14] This space, which takes part in the process of film production, is often a very different to the space that we see on the screen. It has the function to set a scene and thus to articulate what we might call a *filmographic* space as discussed below. Both afilmic and profilmic space are born out of a 'reality photographed by the movie camera' (Lowry 1985: 85). They are considered by Buckland as 'extratextual' (2000: 47) and are positioned outside the filmic text. In our analogy between filmic reality and space, 'afilmic space exists outside the realm of cinema, whereas the profilmic exists inside' (ibid.).

Souriau's next level, the filmographic reality, deals with film as a physical and completed object. Filmographic space, which could also be called *filmic space* or *film space*, is then the space that is seen in the finished film and which is constructed from 'all techniques, such as editing, which affect the film as material object' (Buckland 2000: 85). It is neither a physical space nor a manipulated film space that the camera captures, but the sum of its parts bound together by the film. The fourth level could be described as *screenic* space, which denotes the film-theatrical space that is part of the experience of a filmic projection. Film does not, of course, exist without the filmic environment in which a viewer can observe the projected moving images and it is this space that is important in the formation of a diegesis in the mind of the observer (Sipière 2008: 13). On the final level examined here, Souriau then defines diegetic reality created by a filmic narrative. In this definition, *diegetic space* is the fictive space created by the fictional story of the film in which all narrative action takes place.

In the cinema, diagetic space is created through the act of projection on to a screen. However, what is seen on the screen is incomplete and requires a dialectic exchange with the spectator in the cinema. Furthermore, a diagetic boundary of the screen image is not as easily defined as it first seems. There is the space seen *in* the frame, which is often used as the object of a sociological or architectural study, and which by itself is full of layers and depth. Then – and arguably equally importantly – is a film's ability to suggest an *off*-screen space; an illusory, non-visualised space outside our field of vision: 'the frame, the scene, the mask, the hidden, the absent' (Heath 1976: 91).

It is evident from the above that there are many spatial phenomena that can be related to the production and experience of film. In the most fundamental terms, it seems useful to principally recognise that film-generated space is highly composite in nature. A film creates in us, through the experiences gained when watching it and those we already possess, a *narrative* or *diegetic space* that is generated by the interplay of a *physical exteriority*. This, the environment in which film is produced (on location, in the city, virtual) and experienced (e.g. theatrical space), is combined with a *media interiority*, or screen space, which comprises of visible and/or invisible components relating to the frame of the picture. This raises the question of how this narrative or diagetic space is shaped. Certainly, films commonly have an underlying narrative structure which, as considerable research in recent decades has demonstrated, is of fundamental importance to the development of a plot and subsequent reading of the film (cf. Dudley 1984; Burch 1973; Chatman 1978; Heath 1981; Metz 1974; Scholes and Kellogg 1966; Bordwell *et al.* 1985). However, it is not just the narrative structure of the story or plot that shapes a narrative space, but also stylistic and spatial properties found in the film that contribute to a comprehension of the film. It seems, therefore, equally important to recognise that the framework of fictional storytelling in film relies, to a considerable extent, on a represented *film space* which, in turn, can have its own narrative quality. This film space can be meaningful and memorable, and – as the following chapters demonstrate – can be essential to the physical probing of architectural and urban spaces.

STRUCTURE OF BOOK

This book is organised into three main parts, with a final conclusion. Part I concentrates on the way in which 'Film, Mind and Body' are interconnected constituents that make up the existential and experiential qualities of space. This part begins by highlighting the spatial and tectonic qualities of a series of films that have a particular affinity to memorable experiences of cities and have proven to have created them. It then explores the various ways in which we can encounter filmic narratives, thus highlighting the importance of film locations in experiential and economical terms. Furthermore, I will emphasise film's capacity for an embodied perception of architecture and spaces seen in film, and will show how this is related to the construction of an image of the world by which we are surrounded. Looking at the perception of space beyond its visual dominance, this part ends by revisiting key existential and experiential theories with regard to dialectical relationships between the human body and space, such as those of Martin Heidegger, Otto Friedrich Bollnow, Jean Baudrillard, Maurice Merleau-Ponty, Christian Norberg-Schulz and Juhani Pallasmaa.

Part II, entitled 'Cinema, Architecture and the Everyday', begins by following the idea that some aspects of film language – such as its most basic film editing strategies like 'continuity' and 'montage', and editing techniques like that of a 'cut' and 'dissolve' – could perhaps be used to interpret architectural and urban settings, not only in terms of their abstract representation of spaces, but also in its hidden layers of everyday social spaces and practices. I will then survey several theoretical and practical concepts that share a common ground, or what I call 'shared space', between film and architecture, such as the notions of *sequences and events* and *movement and passage*. This part concludes by questioning whether we can regard architecture and urban form as instances linked to the idea of a *cinematic apparatus*. In doing so, I hope to shed light on what could be meant by saying that a particular architecture or space has a 'cinematic quality', and to do so, it will be necessary to look closer at a series of architectural tactics and mechanisms allied to narrative, optical and other film-related characteristics of space.

Part III focuses on 'Urbanity and Image', and investigates urban phenomena that show how still and moving images have permeated cities and urban spaces and thus have become an integral part of place-making. This part starts by highlighting how product advertisement is inseparable today from urban design and the appearance of cities. It explores the challenges that planners face when considering the 'image of the city', and examines notions of architectural iconography and more recent forms of architectural signs. Rising financial costs and risks for Hollywood movie productions means also that sophisticated marketing approaches now play a vital role for the success or failure of a film. The chapter ends with examples of popular Hollywood productions that have used complex marketing strategies that physically engage with architectural and urban spaces, thereby beginning to dissolve the long-established boundaries between film and urban space.

The concluding chapter, 'The Near Future of Cinescapes', begins (paradoxically, yet intentionally) with a quantum leap back to the year 600 BCE, before highlighting examples of latest research and practice in terms of cinematic concepts of space. The journey begins with two established ideas. The first is that cities can be regarded for their *theatrical qualities*, for which I will briefly survey the key components of the Athenian *Agora*, Renaissance architecture and art, such as the paintings of Piero della Francesca and Francesco di Giorgio Martini, the rise of scenography as an art form in its own right by the north Italian Galli da Bibiena family, and their influence through Richard Wagner on modern theatre. This is followed by an examination of the concept of the city viewed as a *stage*. Referencing Lewis Mumford, I explore the sociological nature of the modern city which Mumford describes as a 'theatre of social action, and an aesthetic symbol of collective unity' (Mumford 2007

[1937]: 185). I then present a new thought model in which I propose that the city can be seen as *mise-en-urbanité*. Building on this, I explore the human geography of our contemporary urban landscapes under the notion of authenticity, pseudo events and staged authenticity, and the associated work of Erving Goffman, Daniel J. Boorstin and Dean MacCannell. The book ends by arguing that, in light of the latest digital developments, such as 3D mapping, 3D screens, responsive architecture, augmented realities, human computation, and unceasing innovation in the ways advertisements and information are shared with us, we are standing at the threshold of an important turning point in urban history. These new technologies will arguably further blur the boundaries between the two-dimensional screen and the multi-dimensional, embodied experience of urban spaces.

Part I

Film, Mind and Body

Chapter 1

Tectonics of Film Space

Cinematographic drama is, so to speak, finer-grained than real-life encounters: it takes place in a world that is more exact than the real world. But in the last analysis perception permits us to understand the meaning of the cinema.

(Merleau-Ponty 1964: 58)

Writing Film Space

In Jean Baudrillard's perceptive travelogue, *America*, in which he conceptualises the emptiness and superficiality of the postmodern age, he concludes that in order to understand the 'secret' of this place, one should not start the investigation with the city and then consider the cinema, but instead one 'should begin with the screen and move outwards to the city' (Baudrillard 1988 [1986]: 56). I would like to follow this analogy with an investigation of what David B. Clarke calls 'a conceptualization of the cityscape as *screenscape*' (Clarke 1997: 1), and thus explore the role of space in film. In doing so, we will look more closely at key spatial moments from the history of cinema, which has arguably had a considerable influence on our perception and imagination of urban landscapes; an argument that will later become quintessential.

Weihsmann describes the portrayal of architecture in film as 'the architecture of the filmic space' (*Die Architektur des filmischen Raumes*), which in its original German text is a particularly appropriate description of the distinct *tectonic quality* of film space (Weihsmann 1995: 9). His words illustrate that film space is, in one sense, a *mise-en-abyme* (to borrow a term from literary and film theory), although this is not on the level of a two-dimensional frame, but rather on that of a three-dimensional space. Weihsmann notes that architecture seen in film is an intrinsic part of *eingebunden*, a complex play between form, meaning and symbol which frames psychological and aesthetic interpretations (ibid.: 56). Film is able to convey meaning with origins outside an immediate optical system, and can thus communicate more than just spatial coordinates assigned to a plot, a phenomenon that is linked by Weihsmann to our subconscious perception. This *space within a space* – cities and urban sites represented in film – reflects, as Aitken and Zonn note, 'prevailing cultural norms, ethical mores, societal structures, and ideologies' (Aitken and Zonn 1994: 5). However the question remains how, in cinema, such a conscious, or for that matter subconscious, 'reflection' is achieved and what role this phenomenon might play in our perception of actual city spaces. We will return to this in a moment, but not before briefly examining the different meanings of the term *space* in the context of film. What, then, are the characteristics that contribute to the *tectonic quality* of film space?

> The effect of film is neither absolutely two-dimensional nor absolutely three-dimensional, but something between.
>
> (Arnheim 1957: 12)

Rudolf Arnheim's study of the art of film alludes to the fascinating transgressive dimensional nature of film, and seems particularly relevant to a study of how film communicates spatial and architectural properties. For Heath, who shares Arnheim's fascination, it is the spatially-ambiguous character that the medium of film offers which is responsible for 'the habitual response to the famous "impression of reality" in cinema' (Heath 1976: 75). Weihsmann once said that 'a film without any spatial bearing is simply unimaginable' (Weihsmann 1995: 55). I would add that film is created by *movement*, and where there is movement there is also *space*. In other words, even the most abstract and experimental films – works of art using only shapes and movement, and omitting traditional pictures, as seen in the films of Viking Eggeling and Hans Richter in the 1920s – have a natural spatial dimension. When it comes to feature-length narrative films, where the pictures are shot on location or on purpose-built stage sets, the amount of spatial information embedded in moving pictures and spatial relationships, true or imagined, is inconceivably high, and in its totality is perhaps beyond the capacity of our sensory apparatus.

As a prelude to my journey through architectural moments in film, I would like to briefly diverge from the topic of filmic spatial perception and focus attention on urban filmmaking practice. Giuliano Bruno observes 'The physicality of the street and of the social epidermis materialized into fiction as a formalized architectural aesthetic in postwar Italian neorealism' (Bruno 2002: 30). She highlights that the Italian neorealist cinema of the mid-1940s to early 1950s made a key contribution to a mobilised screen-engagement with urban landscapes and the drama occurring within them. Bruno quotes André Bazin, who commented that Vittorio De Sica's classic masterpiece *Ladri di Biciclette* (1948, aka *Bicycle Thieves*) is 'the story of a walk through Rome' (see ibid. and Bazin 2005 [1971]: 55). Bazin's remark indicates a shift in Italian, and subsequently other, cinematic productions from being predominantly being shot in the studio to being shot on location. Roberto Rossellini's landmark production, *Roma Città Aperta* (*Rome, Open City*, 1945), was shot only a few months after the surrender of the Italian Campaign of World War II. However, Italian neorealist cinema was only the beginning of a

Figure 1.1   Screenshot. *Bicycle Thieves*. © Produzioni De Sica (left). Screenshot. *Rome, Open City*. © Excelsa Film (right).

new filmic vocabulary that was lost in the studio era of the 1920s to the 1940s. The French New Wave cinema was better connected to a critical discourse concerning modern urban conditions and, as such, it arguably placed an even greater focus on the centrality of shooting on location in cities and urban landscapes. Commenting on the opening shot of Alain Resnais' *Hiroshima mon amour* (1959), Richard J. Neupert notes that:

> The camera travels slowly down the empty street; the opening clarinet music ends, and the viewer studies the street as if it were a starkly beautiful photograph, as deserted as an Atget photograph, come to life.

(Neupert 2007: 61)

This quote draws attention to the way in which the camera can capture the distinct spatial quality of urban settings, and to a film movement that made particular use of urban space, thereby marking a decisive moment in film history. Neuper's description of Resnais' film is a description of how filmmakers aimed to perfect a type of filmmaking in the late 1950s and 1960s which used the *real* city as a spatial and meaningful setting for their films. This is intellectually linked to theories and critical positions on film propagated by, for instance, Bazin and the magazine *Cahiers du Cinéma*, a group of filmmakers which included François Truffaut, Jean-Luc Godard, Éric Rohmer, Claude Chabrol, Jacques Rivette, Agnès Varda and Jacques Demy. These were part of a movement and spirit of the time that not only saw political revolts on inner-city streets, but also the development of the art of filmmaking. The French New Wave saw their film practice linked to what Alexandre Astruc called, in 1948, the new age of cinema as an age of *camera-stylo* (camera-pen), using new forms of cinematography, more mobile filming technology and real locations as mechanisms for the development of a new film language. Film, which has

Figure 1.2   Screenshot. *L'Avventura*. © Cino del Duca.

historically undergone a transformation from fairground attraction to a means of representation in boulevard theatres, was finally seen to be on its way to 'becoming a means of expression, just as all the other arts have been before it, and in particular painting and the novel' (Astruc 1968 [1948]; cited in Graham 1968: 17). Similarly, Monaco describes the French New Wave as a 'tertium quid – a cinematic *écriture* that combines "language" and "style" and is "written" with a Caméra-Stylo' (Monaco 2002: 19). Importantly, this newly-found consciousness of film as a medium promoted a series of stylistic expressions, which spread from France to other countries in the world. Films that are today recognised as milestones in film history, such as Michelangelo Antonioni's *L'Avventura* (1960), Federico Fellini's *La Dolce Vita* (1960) and Ingmar Bergman's *Virgin Spring* (1960), were notably European offshoots of the French New Wave (ibid.: 20), although the movement's influence was also felt across the Atlantic.[1]

It is this notion of the cinematic *écriture* that I believe to be important in the filmic act of rendering the essence of architectural qualities in movies. Some readers may have experienced, as have I, *cine-spatial moments* – in other words, moments in which portrayed architectural settings have left an imprint in their cinematic memory. In my case, some of these cinematic impressions were so powerful that they began to shape the boundaries of lived reality (see also Pallasmaa 2001: 23), and I have reason to believe that this experience is not mine alone. When teaching film and architecture, I tend to ask students who have not been to the United States to give me a spatial description of New York. I have yet to meet someone who could not

Figure 1.3   Screenshots of *Taxi Driver*. © Columbia Pictures Corporation.

give an impression of the sort of spaces one would find in that city, the sort of urban activity that would take place there, and how it would feel to live in it. These imagined impressions come to a great extent from the fact that they have seen countless films set in New York which have contributed to the construction of a cinematic montage of spatial impressions in their minds. How is this achieved? To answer this question, it is worth a closer reading of a particularly iconic city film, Martin Scorsese's *Taxi Driver* (1976), with Robert De Niro, Jodie Foster, Albert Brooks and Harvey Keitel in the leading roles. I will not so much concentrate on the plot of the film (an approach that resides in the field of film studies), but rather I will focus on some of the film's *cine-spatial* articulations, namely their textural, haptic, acoustic and other properties that, communicated through *audio-visual* media, contribute to a sense of space.

Traditionally, the opening shots of a film set the scene and are, therefore, particularly rich in spatial information. *Taxi Driver* is no exception to this rule. The opening credits show steam rising from the city's underground canal system, which is accompanied by Bernard Herrmann's moody saxophone musical score, produced shortly before his death. After briefly being introduced to our main protagonist, Travis Bickle (Robert De Niro), through an extreme close up (ECU), the blurred lights of the city materialise through the rainy windscreen of his taxi, using point of view (POV) shots as if filmed from inside the vehicle. Slow motion shots give us brief glimpses of people crossing a busy street in night-time New York, before the camera leaves the steam and mist behind and follows Travis as he enters the office of the taxi agency. The following internal shots, which frame a conversation between Travis and his prospective employer, are remarkably rich in architectural texture. The ringing of a traditional American telephone bounces off the walls of unrendered concrete block-work, and broken light switches, florescent light fixtures, squeaking doors and poorly-painted walls further create a spatially-tight architectural setting for Travis's famous line: 'I'll work anytime, anywhere'. As Travis makes his way out of the office again, he traverses a half-indoor, half-outdoor space that vocalises 'New York City' across every inch of the screen. The camera pans over a poorly-lit garage that is filled with a fleet of incoming and outgoing iconic yellow New York City cabs. Travis's third space, finally filmed as a wide shot (WS), gives a brief respite from the previously claustrophobic places. It permits an acoustic and visual glimpse of New York's roads and sidewalks, before changing the spatial setting once again from the anonymity of the street to the intimacy of his apartment. Pallasmaa remarks elsewhere that 'Architectural imagery and the articulation of space create the basic dramatic and choreographic rhythm of any film' (Pallasmaa 2001: 32). This is certainly the case in *Taxi Driver*, where a carefully choreographed sequence of what Tom Gunning (1991) describes as 'pro-filmic' spaces begin to form an emotional map of Travis's mind and the spaces he occupies both cognitively and physically.

The deconstructed analysis of *Taxi Driver* outlined above exemplifies the richness of a cine-spatial moment which, in real-time, only lasts a few minutes. It is intended to illustrate the spatial depth of the film that we do not all see. Film provides us with an infinite amount of spatial information, which we can never process in its entirety when watching a film for the first time. Watching a movie requires us to select information, and the magic of film lies in the fact that our brain fills in the blanks, just as it does when in real life urban scenarios. Furthermore, it creates spatial impressions without the need of a nuanced analysis of all the spatial information that unfolds in front of us. Pallasmaa notes that 'A street in a film does not end at the edge of the screen; it expands all around the viewer as a network of streets, buildings and life situations' (Pallasmaa 2001: 21), and the same is also true when watching a film about New York. Although we might never have physically been to New York ourselves, we seem to know the city, and can make connections between the spaces we see and the filmic narrative. This enables us to draw conclusions, not just with regard to spatial relationships in the city, but also to the structure of social relationships linked to a place.

Instruments of Spatial Communication

Ever since the earliest days of filmmaking, pioneers such as George Méliès (who used painted stage sets to create an illusion of place) were concerned with the manipulation of a screen space. He recognised, as have many others who followed him, that the spaces and places represented on the screen are part of a *narrative composition* that rely, in its most basic terms, on visual motifs, light, colour and sound, as well as their many respective subcategories.

Figure 1.4   Screenshot. *Citizen Kane*. © Mercury Productions.

During the last century, many technical developments in each of these fields changed the way that space is produced by the industry and perceived by the audience. In fact, it is remarkable to see how particular innovations dealing with film space, such as miniature models, mirror techniques (*Schüftan-Verfahren*), back projection or camera tracking, were internationally borrowed and adopted. Such milestones in the history of film were achieved in, for example, Orson Welles' *Citizen Kane* (1941), with its space-penetrating, deep focus photography, or the French *Nouvelle Vague* that contributed to an entirely new articulation of urban space in city films through direct sound recordings, mobile cameras and long takes. In fact, the preoccupation with space in film practice is far from over, and is still showing a striking liveliness whilst constantly evolving. With the advent of the digital revolution, from which lightweight and inexpensive optical recording devices, inexpensive digital editing stations and much more emerged, filmmakers have gained more control over their final pictures and the space they portray than ever before. Filmmakers today can choose from an extensive vocabulary that allows them to tune their narrative composition of space in every way imaginable – or at least as far as their budget permits. This includes the manipulation of *mise-en-scène* (e.g., positions, surfaces, textures), cinematography (e.g., light, motion control systems, depth of field), and postproduction (e.g., colour grading, digital compositing, motion tracking, sound design); all of which employ a wide range of specialists, subcontractors and freelancers.

Filmmaking was once an art that a single person could pursue. The digital revolution has, to some extent, brought back the days when a filmmaker was able to carry his camera on to the streets, develop and splice the film, and show it to an audience the same evening.[2] An understanding and recognition of film space (in terms of how it is constructed as part of the filmmaking process and its representation by the medium) is, in my view, fundamental to understanding actual space, which can then be used to develop a more nuanced understanding of architecture and cities. A library of knowledge relating to film space can also become an instrument of spatial communication, with (for example) architectural practice being a point of reference when discussing the qualities of planned or realised spatial situations. Finally, paying attention to filmic articulations of screen space can sharpen our perception, and enrich our experience, not only of the spaces represented on the screen, but also those found 'on location'.

Chapter 2

City in Our Mind

Where is the cinema? It is all around you outside, all over the city, that marvellous, continuous performance of films and scenarios.

(Baudrillard 1988: 56)

Urban Narratives and Cinematic Constructs

Interestingly, it was film studies and the social sciences, rather than other disciplines, that more naturally aligned with architectural space, and which recognised that an understanding of narrative is relevant in the context of cities. Urban spaces, either *represented/mediated* or *actual/perceived*, were important, not only as expert studies of literature, but also for the study of popular culture regarding aspects of everyday life. While the concept of narrative space is well established for the study of motion pictures, this understanding is less present in the study and design of architectural space. This is surprising, and it is evident that, when it comes to the study of *spatial* narratives in *time-based* media, film scholars and practitioners, with their long traditions of analysing screen space, have much to contribute to the cinematic debate of cities proposed here.

Certainly, the history of architecture is full of examples that demonstrate a careful consideration of the narrative properties of their designs, but, with notable exceptions, there is little regard for investigations into the narrative properties of actual architecture or cities as systems of communication or sources for impact or quality. Research contributions into narrative and space have come from human geography and its related fields of cultural geography, sociology and media studies, all of which recognise that, as noted by Sallie Westwood and John Williams in *Imagining Cities* (1997: 12), 'novels, poetry and film provide us all, and sociologists and cultural theorists in particular, with a never-ending commentary on the city, the urban, city people and institutions, the "real" and the fictive more and more woven together in intertextual discourses'. This is then applied to the discourse of spaces and cities, with regard to their historical and narrative significance, in the noteworthy architectural text, *Strangely Familiar: Narratives of Architecture in the City* (Borden *et al.* 1996). Further groundbreaking research has also come from James Donald (1992, 1997, 1999), whose book *Imagining the Modern City*, as well as some of his previous texts, offers much insight into architecture and the city, and its filmic representations and visions as narrative text with which we engage in our everyday lives and, therefore, deserve to be closely examined.

As we saw earlier, the definition of narrative can vary to some degree. However, most definitions allude to the *spatial* and *temporal* characteristics of narrative, which is a direct result of the aforementioned 'series of events' or 'sequences' that are essential for a narrative. This suggests a natural affinity to architectural and urban studies, where cities have long been seen as not only spatial, but also, crucially, temporal constructs.

> In the city, time becomes visible: buildings and monuments and public ways, more open than the written record, more subject to the gaze of many men than the scattered arte-facts of the countryside, leave an imprint upon the minds even of the ignorant or the indifferent.
>
> (Mumford 1938: 4)

Mumford notes, in *The Culture of Cities* (1938), that 'Cities are a product of time'. He defines the city as a congealed and hardened mould in which human civilisation has imprinted itself; in other words, the city is seen as a *temporal* form (ibid.). Today, we would perhaps say that cities are much more dynamic in their character; perhaps even themselves a form of *time-based media*. Just like time and space have ceased to exist as absolute measures, so has the city. Cities can be bent, stretched and compressed, both in physical terms and in terms of the images that we have formed of them in our own minds. Mumford's argument makes the important point that the city is a mental construct that, whenever we visit it, either consciously or subconsciously leaves narrative traces in our minds. These traces play a role in our spatial perception when revisiting the city, creating an internal cycle of images and impressions that form our view of it. They contribute to a confirmation or revision of narratives known to us from previous visits. 'A simple narrative is a series of episodes', Branigan notes (1992: 20), and as we walk or drive with open eyes through cities today, we make our way through sequential configurations of space, and can recognise that urban spaces are full of pockets of activities that are apparent in the spatial practices presented on the ground, and that linger as filmic memories. Viewing the city from this perspective, it becomes a cinematic construct that is made from a hybrid system of screen spaces and filmic *on location* spaces, in which episodic and situational narratives render the actual urban sites into narrative expressive spaces.[1]

Visit the Scene: Encountering Cinematic Spaces

Popular tourist destinations, such as New York, Washington DC, Los Angeles, London, Paris and Vienna, offer bus or walking tours to famous film locations.[2] Visiting *on location* settings shows a conscious attempt to

Figure 2.1   Paris. Grocery store on Rue Lepic. © Kate Stevens.

Figure 2.2   Paris. Café des Deux Moulins.

revisit a cinematic experience, and has become increasingly popular in recent years. One film that contributed considerably to this phenomenon was Jean-Pierre Jeunet's movie hit *Amélie* (2001), with Audrey Tautou in the lead role. Every year, thousands of visitors to Paris visit the grocery store on Rue Lepic and the Café des Deux Moulins further up at the junction of Rue Cauchois in Montmartre, simply because they want to have a *spatial encounter* with this film. Reading online tourist blogs gives a fascinating insight into what attracts people to visit the café, with evidence suggesting that they want to experience the spatial quality of (what was) a film set. Most cineastes might not care too much for the quality of the food there,[3] although this is perhaps not entirely true in the case of *Amélie* as some fans of the film come to the café to listen to the cracking noise of the caramelised sugar crust on the *crème brûlée*. However, I would see this as a *spatial act* rooted more in the film than in the space itself. It seems that there is an underlying desire for a haptic experience which allows visitors to connect visual memories with concrete spaces. Clearly, cities are full of cinematic sites such as those described above, although it has to be said that not all of them have

Figure 2.3 *Fontana di Trevi*. © Bodow (left). Fishing for coins. © Lalupa (right).

been advertised to the degree that *Amélie's* café and grocery store have (with corresponding smaller economic impact).

Rome, the Eternal City, is blessed with extraordinary architectural monuments that millions of visitors come to see each year. One site, amongst many in the city, that has a special link to the world of cinema is the *Fontana di Trevi* in front of the *Palazzo Poli*. Completed in 1762 and the largest Baroque fountain in Rome, the structure is not only a landmark of the city, its culture and history, but also a cinematic device in more ways than one. In 1730, in the reign of Pope Clement XII, an architectural competition selected Nicola Salvi to build the fountain at a place where, a few years earlier, the owners of the Palazzo Poli had demolished the buildings on either side. Salvi proposed an entirely new design for the Palazzo's south façade, the design of which is attributed to Luigi Vanvitelli. In technical terms, this meant that Salvi had to place a second, non-load bearing, artificial façade in front of an existing building which today forms the backdrop to the famous fountain (Sullivan 2006: 156). The resulting visual architectural setting has transformed the piazza into a theatrical space, with the screen-like façade of the Palazzo Poli sitting in front of the kinematic action that derives from the fountain and its visitors.[4]

The fountain and its backdrop is a centuries-old architectural marvel that is known well beyond the city's boundaries for its architectural and artistic merit. However, what made it arguably the most famous fountain in the world, and indeed *eternalised* it, was the role it played in (as I am sure most readers have guessed) Federico Fellini's *La Dolce Vita* (1960). It is worth lingering near the fountain for some time, watching the re-enacted urban acts of Fellini's films played out by visitors to the fountain. Women putting their hands into the water and gliding them through their hair; couples posing and kissing in front the fountain; and the occasional utterance of 'La Dolce Vita' in many different languages. All of these acts are references to Anita Ekberg

Figure 2.4   Screenshot. *La Dolce Vita*. © Riama Film.

and Marcello Mastroianni, and thus to the film, which renders a visit to the fountain a cinematic experience par excellence.[5] Returning to the economic impact discussed in relation to *Amélie*, it might be worth noting that the fountain is emptied daily of coins by the city council, who allegedly collect thousands of Euros on busy days.

Of course, the list of cities with a strong cinematic heritage is long, and I would like to move on to another European city with many astonishing cinematic sites. Vienna, the Austrian capital, has a long tradition of studio productions from the silent and early sound era, through to companies such as the Sascha-Filmindustrie (later Tobis-Sascha-Filmindustrie AG) and Vita-Film, which laid the foundations for a flourishing period for film production from the 1930s to the 1950s. Whilst film productions today are less important in Vienna than in those earlier years, the city promoted outstanding film talents and movies. In addition to having been thematically treated in studio productions, as a city, Vienna has featured in a number of more recent films, such as Nicolas Roeg's *Bad Timing* (1980), John Glen's *James Bond: The Living Daylights* (1987) and Richard Linklater's *Before Sunrise* (1995).[6] These films established places, such as the opera house (*Volksoper*), the central cemetery (*Zentralfriedhof*), the Hotel Sacher and the fairground Ferris wheel at the Prater as recognisable place-specific cinematic icons. No other film, however, is more closely linked to Vienna than Carol Reed (director) and Graham Greene's (screenplay writer) masterpiece *The Third Man* (1949), with Orson Welles, Joseph Cotton and Alida Valli in unforgettable lead roles, and voted in 2000 as the best British film of the twentieth century by a British Film Institute (BFI) poll.[7] Filming in the city in the 1940s was difficult for numerous reasons. First, the supply of equipment (e.g. large film lights) was difficult to organise, and much had to be flown in from abroad.

Figure 2.5   Screenshot. *The Third Man*. Holly Martins chasing after Harry Lime. © London Film Productions.

Second, the rebuilding of the city after significant war damage was still underway, therefore the locations for filming had to be carefully chosen. Reed's film was not only the first post-war film to be shot on location in Austria, but no other film has subsequently managed to portray Viennese urban spaces with more architectural texture and spatial depth. Orson Welles might have been the Hollywood star hired to ensure that the film was an international success, but it was the city that is remembered as one of the main protagonists of the film. When walking through Vienna's streets today, providing one has seen the film, the city invites us to travel back in time to a post-war version of itself and a place in which Holly Martins is still chasing after his friend Harry Lime. The architecture of Vienna's historical inner city has been visually and acoustically preserved to such an extent that the nocturnal, expressively-lit streets become narrative spaces which can be transformed in our minds into a near-identical filmsetting of the 1940s. However, it is not just the streets of Vienna that left an imprint on our filmic recollection. Some of the most memorable chase scenes take place in the underground sewers of Vienna, leaving palpable traces of visual, sonic and olfactory filmic sensations in our mental archive of spatial experiences. The fascination of the film is so considerable that, even today, people still enrol for guided tours of the sewers of central Vienna where parts of the film were shot.[8] Interestingly, these tours also include underground screenings of

Figure 2.6 Screenshot. *The Third Man*. Harry Lime in the sewers of Vienna. © London Film Productions (left). Still image taken during *The Third Man* sewer tour. © Alfred Diem (right).

relevant film scenes, which amounts to a conceptually-fascinating overlapping of screen space and film location that comes with all the sensual experiences (sight, sound, smell) one would expect from being in a sewer, thus leading us, in spatial terms, deep inside an exceptional cinematic experience.

These examples from Paris, Rome and Vienna have shown that cities contain cinematic points or zones (hotspots) in which *on location* space is intertwined with a cinematic space from our memory. This can lead to a hybrid cinematic experience that lingers in our mind long after we have seen the film. The making of films, which has a history of over a century of filming in cities, also has a history that relates to the shape and design of cities. In other words, we have built up an archive of cinematic urban experiences, which plays a part in the processes of comprehending and constructing the urban world in which we live. This makes a series of interesting points. The framing of a space (cinematography) in films as popular as the ones discussed here can detach the space from its mundane – even repellent – natural setting, turning it into a cinematic place that becomes attractive to certain people. There are thousands of cafés in Paris, but *Amélie* made the Café des Deux Moulins unique; similarly, it was *The Third Man* that turned the wastewater canals under the Girardipark near the Karlsplatz into a space that contributes to the fascination of being in Vienna. It is through film that these urban sites have gained a *Dasein* – a term to which I will return later in this chapter – and the camera serves, in these cases, as more than just a recording device.

In the context of literature and geography, we seem to have a good understanding that the representation of spaces and places can have a creative element through engagement in the process of reading and writing. James Donald draws attention to the important relationship between novels and the city, and concludes that it is not only one of representation: 'Writing does not only record or reflect the fact of the city. It has its role in producing the city for a reading

Figure 2.7   Screenshot. *The Man with a Movie Camera.* © VUFKU.

public' (Donald 1997: 187). This is echoed by Phil Hubbard, who alludes to the fact that, from a geographers' perspective, it has become increasingly important to consider the 'representation of a city' in literature and what this representation might do for the creation of urban identities, and through this 'the ability of a text to create reality' (Hubbard 2006: 74). In the context of the literary works of Dostoyesvky, Juhani Pallasmaa notes that the 'images of places, created by a reader, are not detached pictorial images, they are experiences of embodied and lived space' (Pallasmaa 2001: 21). The concept of a 'cinematic' *écriture* (in which film is seen as 'text') has been explored by, amongst others, Barthes, Metz and Truffaut, and is therefore well recognised in the sphere of film studies. However, the idea of a 'spatial' *écriture* is arguably not as pronounced in studies of cinema and cinematography. This is surprising as early filmmakers recognised film as medium that can transform our sense of perceived place. Dziga Vertov famously stated: 'I am kino-eye. I am a mechanical eye. I, a machine, show you the world as only I can see it' (Vertov and Michelson 1984: 17). This points to the generative power of the camera and the distinct place-making capability of cinematography itself. In fact, Vertov's film *The Man with a Movie* Camera (1929) was produced from images shot in at least three different cities (Moscow, Kiev and Odessa) at different times. Consequently, his film is not a city symphony of a particular place, but a generic utopian vision of Soviet urban modernity. Evidently, film is able to create a new realism of fictional space that, in this case, even seems familiar to the eye of the beholder.

Cinematography can provide an extraordinary *spatial intimacy* with the locations shown in a film. Locations known from watching *The Third Man* and other films are, in the first instance, a product of the way in which the camera captures the sites. The power of film lies, in part, in the cropping of the image, and therefore, the cutting away of the spatial context of the site. This increases the viewer's degree of engagement with a particular space, and begins to shape the perceived narrative of the film and actual space. On visiting the location, the perception of the spatial setting is often quite different – if not a little disappointing – because the effects described above contribute to the magic of a film. Why, then, are these cinematic sites so frequently visited? Certainly, people come because they want to visit the location where a film was shot, but this does not alone explain why a location is so attractive. One explanation is that these seemingly ordinary urban sites are nodes that are linked to a narrative, and by visiting the spaces and places seen in a film, people also revisit places that tell a story.[10] In addition, these cinematic urban sites present themselves as expressive narrative spaces, stitched into real urban landscapes, and uniting fragments that are otherwise dispersed in the perception of our highly-mediated world. The discussions above show deliberate encounters with cinematic spaces that are embedded in urban sites, and entail the visiting of actual locations where a film was shot. The *re-visiting of scenes* can, of course, also occur in places that are independent of and different to the location of the film's production; quasi *déjà vu* situational encounters that can happen at any place in cities where stored spatial information is retrieved by our filmic memory.

Secret Cinema: Tell No-One

The following examines Secret Cinema, a relatively recent urban phenomenon which has infused new life into the existing cinema landscape of the UK. Secret Cinema is a spinoff project of Future Cinema and Future Shorts, founded in 2003 by creative director Fabien Riggall. Against the British film establishment, Riggall and his team gave young film professionals a platform and community for their talent to be showcased and shared. The Secret Cinema project is unusual in that it strikes against the disappearance of cinemas in city centres and offers an alternative to the ordinary popcorn-sales-driven cinema multiplex experience. In fact, it is fair to say that, in some ways, this new urban cinematic venture revitalises some of the unpredictability and flair of the fairground from which cinema arose in the early twentieth century. This extraordinary cinematic experience is best explained with an extract from the organiser's Facebook site:

> Secret Cinema is a growing community of all who love cinema, experience and the unknown. Secret audience. Secret locations. Secret worlds. The time is now to change how we watch films. Whisper only amongst yourselves. Tell no-one.
>
> (Secret Cinema)

With over 60,000 followers and more than a 125,000 'likes' from around the world, Secret Cinema has successfully built a large audience in a relatively short time. Once an interested person has signed up to their social network, they receive sporadic electronic messages, giving them clues as to where,

Figure 2.8 Secret Cinema, *Blade Runner* event. Still taken outside Canary Wharf Station. © Mike Massaro.

when and what is going to be screened; and, in some instances, even what they should bring or wear at the next event. Consequently, the cinema-goer becomes one of the central figures in the event and, by extension, a part of the filmic experience on the day. One of the monthly screenings in 2010 took place under the premise of Ridley Scott's classic *Blade Runner*, which was only gradually revealed to the people taking part in the event. Attended by airhostesses from *Utopia Airways*, people were transported by bus from Canary Wharf Tube station to a nearby warehouse district, where they found a spatial and theatrical reenactment of the film by real actors, referring to Los Angeles' China Town in the year 2019, as seen in the original film. After about 800 cinema-goers, some of whom were dressed as Rick Deckard and replicant Rachel, found their way to the *Blade Runner* scenario at its secret location, the film was screened to a cheerful audience who did not simply watch the movie, but actively took part in a cinematic happening. Instead of screening the film at the actual location, the location was substituted by a theatrical atmosphere of the original cinematic space, which was sufficient to allow the audience to enter into a mindset infused with film. *The Guardian* described the event as 'a truly innovative fusion of film and live action';[11] an active cinematic experience in the truest sense, where the cinema-goer is on the move (through space) and is moved (emotionally), thus blurring the boundaries between reality and fiction, actual and filmic spaces, urban and filmic narratives. Secret Cinema is an example par excellence which renders urban space into a cinematic landscape;

a fusion of film, mind and the body. Pallasmaa describes this mental and spatial phenomenon as follows:

> Place and event, space and mind, are not outside of each other. Mutually defining each other, they fuse unavoidably into a singular experience; the mind is in the world, and the world exists through the mind.
>
> (Pallasmaa 2001: 22)

What is interesting with Secret Cinema is the role that the location plays for the cinematic event, with the location kept a mystery, which becomes part of the anticipative and overall experience, but also has a significant marketing effect. However, this is not where the story ends, either literally or metaphorically. Secret Cinema could hire any multiplex cinema, announce a screening through their social networking site, and screen the film in a traditional way. Instead, the organisers choose a location, fill it with movie props and actors, thus giving the audience the impression of embodying the film. The organisers tend to show film classics, creating a unique cinematic *déjà vu* experience for those who have already seen the film, both in terms of the space and the film. Consequently, the location of the film screening within the city is of considerable importance.

Mitchell approaches the notion of meaning and space from an embodied perspective, which gives an interesting insight into the reading of the Secret Cinema phenomenon. He observes that the organisation of architectural and urban spaces can provide tangible, visual references and hence play a role in the construction of the 'meaning of the speech that unfolds within them' (Mitchell 2005a: 4). Later in his text, he includes other faculties of our sensory apparatus, and states that what we 'see, hear, smell, or touch may make you think of something else', emphasising the close relationship between mind, body and space. In other words, the physical objects and spaces we encounter in our daily activities, as well as in the staged cinematic events described above, can carry associations and evoke memories, thus constructing narratives (ibid.: 8). The 'surrounding scene may serve as a link to memories of past events and distant places, to narratives that you have heard, and to facts that you have learned' (ibid.: 8). Mitchell proposes that such connections derive from 'reflexes' operating through 'resemblance, visual metaphor, metonymy, or synecdoche', which seems conceptually similar to the spontaneous situational encounters that we know from commonly-experienced *déjà vu* moments. Elsewhere, Mitchell draws attention to the work of stage and film directors and their intentions with regard to playwrights and *mise-en-scène* (ibid.: 4), which implicitly positions his considerations of space close to the cinematic ones outlined here. Architecture and urban spaces can act as spatial agents which 'construct a virtual mise-en-scène on the substructure of the immediate physical one' (ibid.: 8). To stay with the previous example, visiting a location that is dressed up with elements from *Blade Runner* means we not only occupy a physical space, but also enter a cinematic space and, therefore, cross the boundary between objective and experienced reality.

Film Locations and Economic Impact

The United States, with its long history of film production, has gained a strong foothold on both its East and West Coasts, and is a prime example of how a nation has understood the enormous economic force and impact of shooting films in cities. The State of New York and New York City stand out from others. The State prides itself of having the largest film and television production industry in the United States after California, and the city of New York proudly promotes itself as the country's premier filmmaking centre, formed before the development of Hollywood (DiNapoli and Bleiwas 2010: 1–2). Some city councils and marketing organisations – certainly those in Manhattan – have recognised the various ways in which film productions shot in the city have a positive effect on the local economy. Most obviously, there is the immediate and increasing profit from the planning and shooting of a film on location, through the employment of local people and services related to the production. In 2008, for instance, the film industry in New York paid more than $3.3 billion in direct wages, which amounts to a 33.8 per cent increase on 2004 (ibid.). To support this trend, New York City – like many other cities in the US and elsewhere that have followed the same path – operates a dedicated film office, which aims to proactively promote and facilitate the shooting of films set in the city.

The City of New York Mayor's Office of Film, Theatre and Broadcasting offers, through tax credits, film grants and other initiatives, a range of incentives to production companies and studios that choose New York City as a film location. These efforts seem to pay off. According to the Governor's office, the New York film production credit system has generated $6.98 billion in economic activity since 2004 (ibid.). To ensure long-term financial growth, the state is now considering passing legislation that would extend the current tax programme through the 2014–15 fiscal year, and which would not only lengthen the tax credit programme, but also increase it from $350 million to $420 million per year (ibid.). Despite these impressive figures, even a state and city like New York cannot afford to relax in its market-leading position, as it fears the shrinking of income margins by other competing cities. DiNapoli and Bleiwas explicitly warn that forty-two other states, Washington, D.C., and eleven Canadian provinces are also 'aggressively' seeking to expand their marketing initiatives as film locations by offering tax-based and other incentives (ibid.).

Indeed, other cities have recognised the economic potential of film and have begun to promote their cities as cost-effective, high-rise alternatives to the market leader. Toronto has made a name for itself in recent years, benefiting from a blossoming film production industry; but it is other American cities with smaller populations, such as Chicago (2.85 million residents) or even Seattle (630,000), which have jumped on the 'brandwagon' and are now perceived as a threat.[12] For instance, the Seattle Mayor's Office recently published a report on the economic impacts of film and video productions in its city. It concludes that film and video productions supported 4,991 jobs and that, as a result, Seattle enjoyed over $471 million in additional economic output (Seattle Mayor's Office 2003: 1). This sends a clear message that the city intends to expand its engagement with the film industry. It comes as no surprise that, in response to this 'increased competition', New York has recently 'expanded its tax credit from 10 percent to 30 percent of the production cost for qualified feature films and television episodes, pilots, and movies or miniseries' (DiNapoli and Bleiwas 2010). Furthermore, The City of New York Mayor's Office has launched the trendy 'Made in NY' merchandise programme, which sells T-Shirts and trousers depicting an appealing logo and gives film professionals and tourists alike the opportunity to take a piece of a *cinematic NY* with them when they leave the city. This latest attempt to promote the city leads us to the second, less immediate but equally important revenue stream: film tourism.

> Everywhere, picturesque natives fashion paper-maché images of themselves. Yet all this earnest picturesqueness too often produces only a pallid imitation of the technicolor motion picture which the tourist goes to verify.
>
> (Boorstin 1992 [1962]: 107)

This unforgiving quote stems from Daniel Boorstin's study of North American culture, *The Image: A Guide to Pseudo-events in America*, first published in 1962. It shows his concern that tourists are travelling to site attractions constructed as products and places made solely for tourist consumption and defined by so-called 'pseudo-events'. He argues that American travellers face the danger of favouring an artificial and safe reality, while disregarding the real outside world (ibid.: 103; see also Urry 1990: 7). Boorstin's ground-breaking work was well ahead of its time, especially as it anticipated, in part, Baudrillard's later notion that signs and symbols are replacing all reality (Baudrillard 2008 [1981]). Baurillard argues that people are drawn to sites that they seem to know through media such as film, and that America is essentially *cinematic*. In his book, *America*, he famously notes:

> Is it not the least of America's charms that even outside the movie theatres the whole country is cinematic? The desert you pass through is like the set of a Western, the city

a screen of signs and formulas. It is the same feeling you get when you step out of an Italian or a Dutch gallery into a city that seems the very reflection of the paintings you have just seen, as if the city had come out of the paintings and not the other way about. The American city seems to have stepped right out of the movies.

(Baurillard 1988 [1986]: 56)

These, and other provoking texts, have stimulated a rich debate. Since the 1990s, a significant amount of research has been undertaken in measuring and evaluating the promotional value and, ultimately, the economic impact of film-induced tourism. O'Connor *et al.* (2008) point us to two areas within this field that are of particular relevance, namely 'film-induced tourism as a destination motivator'[13] and 'film-induced destination marketing'[14]. This push towards a place-based marketing of filmic sites is specifically and particularly well addressed in Sue Beeton's book, *Film-induced Tourism* (2005), in which, among other areas, she looks at the destination marketing of film locations (ibid.: 43–66) and the promotion of film place (ibid.: 67–96). Additionally, and more recently, academic journals, such as the *International Journal of Tourism Research* (John Wiley & Sons) and *Tourism Planning & Development* (Routledge), have shown an increased interest in the impact of film and other visual media on tourism, the latter having recently run a special issue on *Film Tourism* (Volume 7, Issue 1, 2010). This demonstrates there is a distinct link between film, place and tourism. It is evident that people show an appetite for places where film or television series have been recorded, as referred to in the earlier examples of *Amélie*, *La Dolce Vita* and *The Third Man* (see also O'Connor *et al.* 2008: 424). Film, in other words, has become an instrument for the destination-related *branding* of real settings, such as cities, and can play a part in strategic marketing campaigns (see also Riley 1994; Stewart 1997).

A remarkable campaign dealing specifically with *place marketing* recently emerged from the United States. In 2004, the U.S. Department of Commerce unveiled a multi-million dollar advertising campaign that was designed to promote the United States as a travel destination for the UK market, and later, to other countries around the globe.[15] The campaign was created by M & C Saatchi and focused on the United States as it is seen through film and television, and thus, on America's biggest export: the entertainment industry. The slogan that M & C Saatchi developed, 'You've Seen the Films, Now Visit the Set', which featured in television advertisements and on outdoor billboards, showed easily-recognisable cinematic glimpses of films, including *Maid in Manhattan*, *Chicago*, *L.A. Story*, *Beverly Hills Cop II*, *Viva Las Vegas* and others, and aimed to invite tourists to visit the locales where these films were shot.[16] An independent study assessing the results of the UK campaign in the first year reported that the advertising campaign returned a staggering $117 per $1 invested, resulting in approximately two million more British travellers visiting the United States during that period.[17] Receiving such results from the UK, the U.S. Department of Commerce decided that it could do more to support its $100 billion international travel and tourism industry. In collaboration with several private-sector partners, it launched similar advertisements in Japan, again based entirely on popular film clips (e.g. *Forest Gump* (1994) and *King Kong* (2005)) to promote the United States as a tourist destination.[18]

Alongside these government-sponsored efforts, the public sector has also learned that it can capitalise on the desire of tourists to visit movie locations. As stated above, many cinematic cities offer bus and walking tours to famous film locations, and countless websites and blogs (some of which are sponsored or linked to local tourist boards) have sprung up to share the latest gossip on which film location to visit. The online magazine *Empire* provides its readers with advice on how to 'follow in Harry Potter's footsteps' with a link to a handy travel guide.[19] For London's serious cineastes and tourists, Tony Reeves offers a printed guide called *Movie London* (Reeves 2008) that contains 192 pages of systematic 'film-by-film' information on movie locations. Furthermore, as an adjunct to his *Worldwide Guide to Movie Locations* (Reeves 1999), he provides an online database which is regularly updated with newly-released films, as well as an interactive, country-by-country, district-by-district map for popular movie locations worldwide. Since its launch in 1999, the site has been visited by over 2.55 million Internet users.[20]

In the light of evidence of the influence that moving images have had as instruments of place marketing, one wonders what underlying forces are at play that apparently draw so many people to the places they have seen in films. Bazin notes that 'Photography and the cinema … are discoveries that satisfy, once and for all and in its very essence, our obsession with realism' (Bazin 2005 [1967]: 12). However, how does this obsession for realism find application, or validity, in the context of space, place and cities? Furthermore, how is our sense of the reality of a place formed and satisfied? Where do popular visual media draw the line between realism and fiction in terms of urban space, especially in light of cataclysmic events such as in New York City on 11 September 2001, which fundamentally shifted our sense of on- and off-screen reality? Again, taking our cue from Baudrillard, in terms of our spatial imaginary, what happens when the real coincides with the image? Although the special constraints of this book will not enable an exploration of such complex paradigms, it will hopefully offer some insight into the mechanisms that define what we call urban reality, and how we can *see* cities and *inhabit* films. On this topic, Boorstin asks:

Is the Trevi Fountain in Rome really like its portrayal in the movie Three Coins in the Fountain? Is Hong Kong really like Love is a Many Splendored Thing? We go not to test the image by the reality, but to test reality by the image.

(Boorstin 1992 [1962]: 116)

There seems to be some truth in the proposition that contemporary society is saturated not with the real, but with images that have become yardsticks of what we believe to be real. We acknowledge and test what we think constitutes our *being in* urban space with a plethora of film emitting devices. Moving images or film do not form a contained reality by themselves, as they perhaps did to a greater extent in the early days of cinema when 'going to the movies' meant going to a fairground or theatre, and, as such, part of a distinct spatial event or act. Digital film images today are passively consumed in university food halls, hotel lobbies, medical surgeries, on the street, and even during times when we ourselves are on the move, on busses, trains and aeroplanes. It is in this ambiance of *spatial ambivalence* (multiplicity), where representations of spaces and places on the screen are interwoven with our physical existence, that we find comfort in moments of comparative *spatial unity* (singularity), which are paradoxically found more frequently on the screen than under our feet. We seem to perceive some cities in film, framed and edited by a screen language, with a narrative clarity, definition and structure that is apparently so attractive that we are drawn to intentionally visit the places they depict. We find it reassuring and gain pleasure from turning our spatial experience from the screen, our memory and imagination into a corporal and thus complementary reality, which is paradoxical to what we normally associate with entertainment, gaming and other media, and not the actual space which offers us a corresponding existence.

Chapter 3

Existential and Experiential Notions of Space

The city as we imagine it, the soft city of illusion, myth, aspiration, nightmare, is as real, maybe more real, than the hard city one can locate on maps, in statistics, in monographs on urban sociology and demography and architecture.

(Raban 2008 [1974]: 2)

Limits of the Euclidean Space: Being in Time and Space

If we were asked to describe a particular city or urban space, then, in the most basic terms, we might resort to a description or mapping of the physical properties of the city. We can form an image of a city, and thus begin to define it, from the perspective of natural sciences. The city could be described as a space that consists of a matrix of fixed and moving coordinates, which operate within physical, biological and other natural laws. Certainly, the city is seen and studied along these valuable lines, but such an approach requires expert knowledge and offers a specialised point of view. This fragmentary description is of a place that, in real terms, is amalgamated and which, within the sphere of those sciences, is often looked upon as lacking humanity. Such an abstract view of urban space has been called into question by Lefebvre, being seen as a non-human space of planners and architects (Lefebvre 1991 [1974]); an argument which draws attention to an assessment that cities cannot rely on the study of a Cartesian space, but must include the concept of social space, which has been echoed and specified by other critical thinkers (cf. Harvey 1989; Soja 1989; Norberg-Schulz 2000: 67, Hill 2006: 52–5). Cities certainly have a physical form and can be differentiated from each other by this form. They leave a three-dimensional fingerprint in the topography of the natural landscape. However, an attempt to define the city by the most basic natural phenomenon of its size would be not only near impossible,[1] it would also miss the point. The city we all know is, as Jonathan Raban eloquently points out, present as an illusion, myth, aspiration and nightmare, where it can become 'more real, than the hard city one can locate on maps'. Raban alludes to the fact that a considerable amount of our perception of self and the environment in which we live takes place on a cognitive level. This raises the question of the relationship between the inner space of our mind and our bodily sensation of external physical space. Ali Madanipour notes: 'The

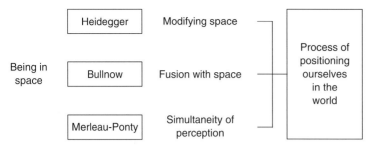

Figure 3.1   Examples of theories relating to the process of positioning ourselves in spatial environments.

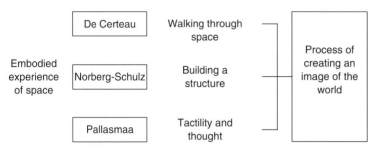

Figure 3.2   Examples of theories relating to the process of creating an image of the world around us.

non-physical, inner private space of the mind is thus highly dependent on the body to grasp the physical, outer space of the world', which means that the 'body is the boundary between the two realms. It is the medium through which the two realms are related to each other' (Madanipour 2003: 8). A number of key twentieth- and twenty-first-century theorists and philosophers dedicated their thoughts to similar questions, and the limits of Euclidean space was seen as the only measure of defining reality and our existence in space (see Figures 3.1 and 3.2). The following brief excursion into this vast territory is intended to offer a theoretical grounding for the argument of the overlapping spheres between physical and filmic reality seen in this and subsequent chapters.[2] Such graphical representations risk a lack of context and an oversimplification of the complex information and arguments hidden behind arrows and symbols. However, the simple charting of key scholars and selected concepts they discuss shown above identifies two categories of 'being in a space' and an 'embodied experience of space' that might be a useful way to understand some of the relevant themes relating to this deliberation of the city and the cinema.

Martin Heidegger questions the notion of a mathematical space in architecture as the 'construction of manifolds with an arbitrary number of dimensions'. In other words, it creates a meaningless shell that 'contains no spaces and no places' (Heidegger 1971 [1951]: 155). In his essay *Building, Dwelling, Thinking* (1971 [1951]), first presented at the *Darmstädter Gespräch* under the title of *Mensch und Raum* and organised by the German Werkbund in 1951, he makes explicit reference to the housing problems in Germany at the time, and the response of architects to them. Heidegger criticised the modern movement in architecture for being more concerned about formal and functional principles, rather than what the term dwelling (*wohnen*) really meant in terms of human spatial relations and inhabitation (see also Sharr 2007: 37). By referring to houses that are 'well planned, easy to keep, attractively cheap, open to air, light, and sun', he points to the ideological principles of Le Corbusier, Hilberseimer, Taut and others, before asking the critical question: 'do the houses in themselves hold any guarantee that *dwelling* occurs in them?' (Heidegger 1971 [1951]: 146).[3] Heidegger uses a bridge in his essay as an example with which to argue that architectural elements are essentially *things*, and 'a location comes into existence only by virtue' of such things (ibid.: 154). An interesting picture emerges if we substitute the variable of the bridge with that of the city. In this context, a city becomes a *location* through the things 'for which room has been made'; and these things become expressions and, ultimately, symbols (ibid.: 153–4). Heidegger highlights that 'spaces receive their being from locations and not from "space"' (ibid.: 154),[4] and this raises the question of what sort of things we make *room* (space) for in our everyday perception of cities that are not purely based on mathematical space. In Heidegger's native language, German, as in other languages, the making of room (*Raum machen*) is also used in the context of 'thinking' (*denken*). This opens up the opportunity to relate his argument to the filmic spaces that we carry with us when we walk through cities.

Heidegger argues that our thoughts about locations and spaces are not limited by geographical distance; '*in itself* thinking gets through, persists through, the distance to that location' (ibid.: 156). If we accept that the act of thinking of a physical space recalls a sensation in us that is similar to that of thinking of a space we remember from seeing it in a film, then we are closer to that filmic space than we might expect. 'From right here we may even be much nearer to that bridge and to what it makes room for than someone who uses it daily as an indifferent river crossing' (ibid.: 157). Heidegger observes further, 'I am never here only, as this encapsulated body; rather, I am there, that is, I already pervade the room, and only thus can I go through it' (ibid.). Here he relates our entire existence to our *occupation* and *taking up* of space (*Raum einnehmen*), which is somewhat confirmed in *Being and Time*, where he notes that 'Dasein takes space in; this is to be understood literally. It is by no means just present-at-hand in a bit of space which its body fills up' (Heidegger 2005 [1962]: 419; cf. Malpas 2006: 74).

If we look at Heidegger's relationship between the body and space, it becomes apparent that he did not see man and space 'as though man stood on

Figure 3.3 Porto. *Ponte Luís I* in the city centre.

one side, space on the other' (Heidegger 1971 [1951]: 157). This sheds an interesting light on the radical extent to which he saw the interdependence between *being* and the *space* one occupies. This important point was further explored by German philosopher Otto Friedrich Bullnow in his essay (relatively unknown due it not being translated into English) *Der Mensch und der Raum* (Bullnow 1963). He alludes to a possible misinterpretation of Heidegger's analogy between man and space, in the sense that the spatiality (*Räumlichkeit*) of the being (*Dasein*) does not simply mean that our body extends into space, but that man, in his existence, is determined by a *reference to space*.[5] This far-reaching definition is further clarified by Bullnow's notion of the 'identification' of the human body and mind with the space by which one is surrounded. He argues that architectural space can become some form of an extension to the body (*erweiterter Leib*) with which man identifies himself as if it was his own (Bullnow 1963: 506). The result of this, according to Bullnow, is a reciprocal relationship in which space exercises not only a modifying (*modifizierend*) function on a human being, but also that they achieve a sense of being through unity with the space by which are surrounded (ibid.: 507).[6] He disagrees with Heidegger on the question that man has been placed in a foreign and potentially uncanny space, and argues instead that we are affiliated with or fused (*verschmolzen*) to space in an incarnation-like existence (ibid.: 501, 512).

A constant theme in Heidegger's thinking is the deliberation of the essential nature of human existence in time and place, which he explores through the tropes of 'place' (*Ort*), 'situatedness' (*Befindlichkeit*), 'nearness' (*Nähe*), 'distancelessness' (*Entfernung, Entferntheit*) and 'being there' (*Dasein*) (Malpas 2006: 224–25). Some people might find it difficult to engage with the essence

Figure 3.4   Liverpool. People gathering in Anglican Cathedral.

of his text, which is exacerbated by Heidegger's own linguistic ambiguities. Furthermore, his concepts are interwoven in a network of shifting meanings. For example, Heidegger considers that the term 'closeness' or 'nearness', in the context of his concept of *Dasein* (see Heidgegger 1971 [1951]: 177–8), takes on multiple meanings ranging from a measurable distance to the tactility of existential space (Heidegger 2005 [1962]: 98, 130–142). However, it is evident that Heidegger held some concern for the 'loss of nearness' that arose from the technological ordering of the modern world (see Malpas 2006: 73). 'The frank abolition of all distances brings no nearness … Everything gets lumped together into uniform distancelessness' (Heidegger, 1971 [1951]: 165–6). On these remarks, Malpas comments that 'Technological ordering thus involves, as Heidegger puts it in "The Thing," a loss of "nearness" to things in the rise of a "uniform distancelessness," a loss of nearness, and so also of "place," and an essential "homelessness" (Malpas 2006: 297). In other words, modernity might have overcome the problem of distance, but its technological advancements undermine and to some extent destroy a fundamentally human necessity, namely space and all of its epistemological connotations. Sharr notes that Heidegger's concept of nearness is a 'fundamental aspect of human experience' and nearness may be experienced through 'tactile, cognitive and sociological familiarity of things' (Sharr 2007: 35). It is this concern for the 'loss of nearness' and 'uniform distancelessness' that gave rise to a series of existential explorations into multisensory experience of architectural spaces. As such, in essence, his work underpins Kenneth Frampton's concept of a 'Critical Regionalism', which deserves to be revisited in a longer quote:

> In this way, Critical Regionalism seeks to complement our normative visual experience by readdressing the tactile range of human perceptions. In so doing, it endeavors to balance the priority accorded to the image and to counter the Western tendency to interpret the environment in exclusively perspectival terms. According to its etymology, perspective means rationalized sight or clear seeing, and as such it presupposed a conscious suppression of the sense of smell, hearing and taste, and a consequent distancing from a more direct experience of the environment. This self-imposed limitation relates to that which Heidegger has called a 'loss of nearness'.
>
> (Frampton 1983: 29)

In 'The Visual versus the Tactile', Frampton emphasises the importance of tactility as a measure of perceiving built form (ibid.: 28). He is concerned with how, in the wake of Postmodernism, architects have begun to see architecture and cities as a commodity, and thus resort to a design position that is either 'pure technique or pure scenography' (ibid.: 19). The notion of scenography is one that we will come across later with regard to *urban advertisement* and *sign structures*, and which is here attributed to the postmodern architects' irresponsible 'feeding [of] the media-society with gratuitous, quietistic images' (ibid.). Frampton defines the function of Critical Regionalism as a mechanism to 'mediate the impact of universal civilization with elements derived *indirectly* from the peculiarities of a particular place', a synthesis between universal civilisation and world culture (ibid.: 21). His proposed strategy against 'placelessness' (ibid.: 26) draws on the work of architects such as Mario Botta, but also on Scandinavian architects, such as Jørn Utzon and Alvar Aalto. What is common to their stance on architectural design is that they see architectural sites as *Ort* (place) filled with cultural, material and technological specificities, and which require a site-specific architectural response. They are known for producing work that shows an emphasis on the choice of materials and the way these are used, emphasising experiential dimensions that are multisensory, and overcoming the limits of purely visual features.

A Phenomenology of Space: Limits of Visual Perception of Cityscapes

The brief excursion into the territory of Heidegger and Bullnow was intended to underpin and sharpen our perspective on how body and space are fundamental parts of the cognitive processes that define our being. Following on from this, I will examine the position that, despite an assumed visual dominance in the human experience of urban landscapes, our sense of space comes from a *multisensory* engagement that is grounded in phenomenological and existentialist arguments. This will lay the foundation for posing the question as to what extent we can or cannot disconnect film and cinema from an embodied experience. Furthermore, to turn the argument around, can we say that our perception of urban space cannot not be disassociated from those presented to us through film and cinema?

The fused relationship between the body and space, as described by Bullnow, is particularly relevant for this excursion into the phenomenology of real and cinematic spaces, as his concept transgresses the boundaries between physical and filmic space, and opens up a discussion of a multisensory reading of urban spaces. Logically, the notion that cities are perceived by more than just one sense derives from the fact that a considerable amount of scholarly writing highlights and disapproves of the visual dominance of postmodern landscapes, particularly if they have theatrical or inauthentic qualities as discussed below. This confirms that even the most visual form of our culture – cinema – is based on a multisensory experience. Here is one example:

> In the contemporary city of spectacle, all that remains of the drama of architecture and the city is pure visual form. We no longer question the performance, for there is no moral argument, logical narration, or centred community to link the drama and the spectators in dialogue. Visually enthralled, we submit to the theatricalised show, suspending critical judgement.
>
> (Boyer 1994: 75)

Boyer's quote challenges this modern concept and argues that, in the context of the postmodern 'city of spectacles' (ibid.), often-cited theatrical qualities arrive merely in the form of images at the receiver's or citizen's end. Analogously, the perceived form of cities is increasingly defined by images, hence relying on an inherently unstable medium. Published in the same year as Boyer's text, Paul Virilio's landmark book, *The Vision Machine* (Virilio 1994), also highlights that the visual dominance of postmodern landscapes overpowers all other senses. Intriguingly, Virilio relates the appearance of postmodern city centres to that of optical, cinematic *apparati*, which could hardly better describe the physical fusion between the city and cinema.

> From the town, as theatre of human activity with its church square and market place bustling with so many *present* actors and spectators, to CINECITTA and then TELECITTA, bustling with *absent* televiewers, it was just a short step through that venerable urban invention, *the shopwindow.* This putting behind glass of objects and people, the implementation of a transparency that has intensified over the past few decades, has led, beyond the optics of photography and cinema, to an optoelectronics of the means of

television broadcasting. These are now capable of creating not only window-apartments and houses, but window-towns window-nations, media megacities that have the paradoxical power of *bringing individuals together longdistance*, around standardised opinions and behaviour.

(Ibid.: 65)

I will return to the notion that architecture and cities have optical and cinematic qualities in the next part of this book. For now, what I want to concentrate on is that Boyer and Virilio's arguments echo Baudrillard's critique in *America* (1988 [1986]) of the American metropolis and the notion that cities are visually consumed through media. Baudrillard describes large American cities as 'desert-like banality' that are 'not at any stage regarded as places of pleasure or culture, but seen televisually as scenery, as scenarios' (1988 [1986]: 9). Furthermore, in *Simulacra and Simulation*, Baudrillard (2008 [1981]) places his focus on the hypothesis that all reality and meaning, including that related to urban space as well as many other phenomena in our society, is replaced by a system of signs and symbols. Many of these signs and symbols, such as advertising images, are visual by nature, which is where Baudrillard's argument ends, and mine begins.

My following point may seem somewhat contradictory, as it directly follows on from Baudrillard's account, yet it is important to underscore that our awareness of space does not wholly rely on optics. In fact, our perception of space, regardless of whether it is physical or screen-based, is never purely visual. When watching a movie at the cinema, we are acoustically and visually consumed by the dark space of the theatre. The physical setting in which we watch a movie can determine how quickly we suspend our awareness of the space we inhabit. As movie-goers, we sometimes forget that we are in actual physical space, and drift with our subconscious into the cinematic spaces that the film offers us. A related phenomenon occurs when we walk through urban environments that remind us of scenes from a film. Certainly, to say that the sensation of a filmic *déjà vu* matches Bullnow's notion of the 'affiliated' or 'fused' (*verschmolzen*) would go too far. Instead, it is perhaps more useful to describe such as sensation as a momentary double reality in which the physical and spaces from our filmic memories begin to overlap. Yet again, this filmic sensation is multisensory, in that the visual impression, the acoustic quality and the sense of smell of a space work hand-in-hand to trigger our cinematic memory. In any case, Bullnow would probably view both instances as defining phenomena of our human existence: 'man is determined in his existence by his reference to space',[7] and if this reference comes from our previous perception of filmic space, then that bears as big an impact as any other space would.

Maurice Merleau-Ponty made important contributions to the phenomenological examination of space and its relation to the body, which is relevant to the study of both architectural and filmic space. His book, *The Structure of*

Figure 3.5   Nanning, China. People having lunch in a street restaurant.

Behavior (Merleau-Ponty 1963 [1942]), is a complex critique of aspects of behavioural psychology and the study of physiology, and addresses the concept of a 'Cartesian dualism of mind and body' (Mallgrave 2011: 109).[8] He aligns himself with the Gestalt theory of Max Wertheimer, Wolfgang Köhler and Kurt Koffka of the Berlin school of the 1920s. One of their arguments indicates that our human experience is not 'broken up into atomistic units called "sensations", but were structured wholes in which the meaning of individual elements depended on their relation to the whole' (Matthews 2006: 2). Although Merleau-Ponty quickly moved on to produce other, arguably more widely-recognised work, this early text lays strong foundations for a conceptual re-evaluation of an experiential framework that is set in place when studying the perception of space, regardless of whether it is a physical or cinematic experience. Three years later in 1945, Merleau-Ponty published, in French, his widely-admired and later translated book *Phenomenology and Perception* (Merleau-Ponty 1962 [1945]). In this, he further concretises how the human body interprets and relates to space. With regard to the embodied subject, he observes the essential distinction between 'physical space' and 'geometrical space' that is necessary to understand the interrelationship between object and subject. Merleau-Ponty notes that *physical space* is related to '… my body and things, their concrete relationships expressed in such terms as top and bottom, right and left, near and far, may appear to me as an irreducibly manifold variety …' (ibid.: 284). This can be interpreted as the measurable space, a space that is based on hard sciences, a space that is inescapable, and the physical basis for a direct embodied experience. Merleau-Ponty's *geometrical space* has been described as 'space as thought, rather than space as directly experienced'; a space that is reflected rather than physically perceived (Priest 1998: 103). He suggests that geometrical space has 'interchangeable dimensions', such as 'homogeneous and isotropic', by which he means that 'a pure change of place which would leave the moving body unchanged, and consequently a pure *position* distinct from the *situation* of the object in its concrete context' (Merleau-Ponty 1962 [1945]: 284). In doing so, Merleau-Ponty establishes a phenomenological position that emphasises an embodied perception of space that cannot be seen in isolation. Mallgrave sums this up by saying that 'there is for everyone "an autochthonous significance of the world," one that is always and everywhere conditioned by our essential incarnate existence and therefore accessible only through our embodied dealings with the world' (Mallgrave 2011: 110). The notion of embodiment is applicable to our perception of space in architecture and cities, and in film, or in the words of Merleau-Ponty:

> We cannot remain in this dilemma of having to fail to understand either the subject or the object. We must discover the origin of the object at the very centre of our experience; we must describe the emergence of being and we must understand how, paradoxically, there is *for us* an *in-itself*.

> (Merleau-Ponty 1962 [1945]: 82–83)

Understanding these concepts has great relevance to the way we conceptualise our engagement with space in architecture and film, and architectural space is as much 'physical' as it is 'geometrical' space, to use Merleau-Ponty's terminology. This might, at first, sound like a daring statement, but we must consider that our perception of the physical world relies on stimuli coming from our optical apparatus – our eyes – as well as stimuli coming from our other senses (smell, touch and hearing). Furthermore, if we consider the amount of interpretation required from our computational centre – the brain – to process incoming data on the basis of our past experiences in order to form a 'true' representation of the world, then we might begin to understand that space is a highly individualised 'reflection' and, therefore, not an absolute.

Our visual sense cannot be disconnected from our other senses. Merleau-Ponty describes this through an experiment in which a person wears special glasses for a period of time that reverses the effect of the lens; that is, it flips an upside down projection of images on to our retina, providing serious perceptual challenges (Merleau-Ponty 1962 [1945]: 284–6).

> … it [the world of touch] can no longer coincide with the visual world so that the subject has two irreconcilable representations of his body, one given to him by his tactile sensations and by those 'visual images' which he has managed to retain from the period preceding the experiment.

> (Ibid.: 286)

Accordingly, the human brain has the capacity to gradually attune itself to this disengagement between our visual and other senses, and begins to synchronise its visual and tactile fields of perception, showing how intrinsically they are linked. Consequently, our visual perception of a space is intertwined with a series of other senses that cannot simply be isolated or switched off. Elsewhere, Merleau-Ponty discusses the psychology of film, and speaks of the multiplicity and simultaneity of perception.

> My perception is [therefore] not a sum of visual, tactile, and audible givens: I perceive in a total way with my whole being: I grasp a unique structure of the thing, a unique way of being, which speaks to all my senses at once.
>
> (Merleau-Ponty 1964: 18)

This illustrates not only the way in which we physiologically engage with physical space, but also how the space is represented by visual means, e.g. through moving images. Therefore, the perception and reading of spatial representations in film are also linked to our tactile experiences and understanding of geometric space (see also Bruno), which sheds an interesting light on the filmic *déjà vu* moments. This aforementioned phenomenon relates to Merleau-Ponty's notion of geometric space, in the sense that this space of thought constitutes 'a pure change of place which would leave the moving body unchanged' (Merleau-Ponty 1962 [1945]: 284).

Following the Scandinavian tradition of looking at architectural space as an experiential space (established by Danish architect and urban planner Steen Eiler Rasmussen with his book *Experiencing Architecture* (1959)), the Norwegian architect, architectural historian and theorist Christian Norberg-Schulz was one of the driving forces behind the introduction of phenomenological thought to architectural theory and practice. It is surprising that he is sometimes overlooked in books that regard the relationship between mind, body and space. No less than twelve of his books have been translated into English, of which *Intentions in Architecture* (Norberg-Schulz 1979 [1963]), *Genius Loci: Towards a Phenomenology of Architecture* (Norberg-Schulz 1980) and *Architecture: Presence, Language, Place* (Norberg-Schulz 2000) are perhaps the best known. His rich oeuvre has influenced many other architectural thinkers and practitioners alike. The design work of architects such as Alvar Aalto, Juhani Pallasmaa, Peter Zumthor and Steven Holl cite his influence, either in terms of the sensory dimension of architectural design or the special consideration required to achieve a distinct sense of space. Norberg-Schulz draws inspiration for his theories on existential space from those provided by Merleau-Ponty, Bachelard, Bullnow and Heidegger. He echoes Heidegger when he says that architecture should not be seen as isolated aesthetic constructs, but instead should be read as a manifestation that is relative to situations (ibid.: 85). Furthermore, he is influenced by the writings of developmental psychologist and philosopher Jean Piaget, notably *The Child's Construction of Reality* (Piaget 1955), in which Piaget argues that 'the true nature of space does not reside in the more or less extended character of sensations as such, but in the intelligence which interconnects these sensations' (Piaget 1955: 212; cf. Norberg-Schulz 1971: 17). Space, then, is inseparable from the body. In fact, it is a 'product of an interaction between the organism and the environment' (Piaget 1955: 212). Norberg-Schulz builds on and extends this thought by calling for an active mode of perception. He argues that 'Perception, therefore, is anything but a passive reception of impressions. We may change the phenomena by changing our attitude' (Norberg-Schulz 1979 [1963]: 31).

Norberg-Schulz does not apply his theories to film, but his theories can be used to inform our understanding of film and cinematic space, both those on the screen as well as those in real landscapes. If we were to apply his last quote to the world of cinema, we could say that moving images cannot only change our perception of cities and urban landscapes, but also our active engagement with them. Furthermore, if we take one of Norberg-Schulz's central claims, that 'man gradually constructs the image of a structured world, in which the notion of space, that is, *existential space*, forms an integral part' (Norberg-Schulz 1988: 29), similar assumptions could be made about our reading of film. It is well established in film studies that the representation of a film space on the screen plays a vital part in the reading of the film. However, it is not just the profilmic space that plays a considerable role when watching a film. The space in which we watch a movie, what Souriou called 'screenic space', has an impact on the immersive qualities of watching a film. If we recall for a moment my earlier proposition that cities are cinematic constructs, that is, environments that are full of movement, signs and narratives, then we come to the conclusion that urban landscapes can be seen as a form of screenic space, namely theatrical settings that play an integral part in the formation of an existential space. Our brain does its best in filtering incoming information, comparing it with other known experiences, searching for and building narratives, thus engaging in processes which lead to the formation of what we often refer to as *sense of space*. In equal terms, and turning this argument on its head, our perception of space when watching a film is connected to our perception of space based on physical laws and reality. Our reading of spaces and landscapes on the screen is informed by what Elsaesser and Hagener evocatively refer to as 'tacit knowledge' (2010: 167), namely unconscious bodily experiences that we all have stored in our brain. We cannot disassociate ourselves from previous physical or corporal experiences, therefore urban landscapes and architectural spaces, taking into account Norberg-Schulz, play an 'integral part in the process of building an image of a structured world'. This position is similar to that taken by Pallasmaa, examined below, who sees parallels in the 'modes of experiencing architecture and cinema', as both operate on the basis of a kinaesthetic experience and exist in an experiential realm (Pallasmaa 2001: 18).

Juhani Pallasmaa has earned recognition not only for being a distinguished Finnish architect, but also as an intellectual force in existential debates in the field of architecture. His numerous publications, including *The Architecture of Image: Existential Space in Cinema* (Pallasmaa 2001), *The Eyes of the Skin: Architecture and the Senses* (Pallasmaa 2005), *The Thinking Hand: Existential and Embodied Wisdom in Architecture* (Pallasmaa 2009) and *The Embodied Image: Imagination and Imagery in Architecture* (Pallasmaa 2011), cross disciplinary boundaries with regard to issues surrounding the representation and perception of architectural space and design, the human body, and film. Pallasmaa sees many parallels between architecture and cinema, and he advocates what he calls 'embodied thinking', as well as 'embodied memory and thought' (Pallasmaa 2009: 107). His ideas are closely aligned to those of phenomenologist and existentialist thinkers, not least Merleau-Ponty and Norberg-Schulz. His work is therefore relevant to the concepts of the cinematic engagement of space explored both here and in other chapters. Among his numerous insightful contributions, Pallasmaa's notion that 'visual perceptions are fused and integrated into the haptic continuum of the self' is one that is particularly thought provoking and of considerable relevance to the study of cinema's reciprocity with urban landscapes (Pallasmaa 2006: 137). He argues that all our senses, including vision, are 'extensions of the tactile sense', and that 'all sensory experiences are modes of touching, both literally and metaphorically, and thus related to tactility' (ibid.). The human body is, for Pallasmaa, an essence that is responsive and exists in space and also, crucially, in time. This becomes apparent when he describes the human body as a 'site of reference, memory, imagination and integration' (ibid.) which is capable of responding to external stimuli. Applied to our bodily experience of cities, his argument illustrates that we cannot disconnect ourselves from our cinematic experiences, in the same way as we cannot detach our mind from the physical experiences outlined above. Both spheres are part of our experienced spatial memory, and form an archive that is stored in our mind.[9]

Pallasmaa makes an interesting remark on the creative processes involved in the planning and realisation of architectural spaces: 'In the same way that cinema is a mode of cinematic thinking, painting as means of articulating painterly ideas, … architecture is a means of philosophising about the world and human existence through the embodied material act of construction' (Pallasmaa 2009: 114). However, Pallasmaa rejects the notion that the reduced lessons learned from cinema, such as its emphasis on the image, should inform contemporary architectural practice. He is highly critical of the spectacularisation and fictionalisation of built architecture, and warns of an enticing and seducing architecture of the 'commercialised image' (Pallasmaa 2011: 22). He proclaims that 'the task of the critical, profound and responsible architect is to create and defend the sense of the real', and 'the duty of responsible architecture is to defend the authenticity and autonomy of human experience' (ibid.: 23). This is where he draws an important line between the superficial application of images, for instance in architectural design, and the importance of images as part of an imaginative cognitive process that can drive culture and innovation. Pallasmaa, citing Charles Baudelaire, notes: 'Imagination created the world' (ibid.: 37). Images play an essential role in our imagination and hence for Pallasmaa and many of us, a considerable role in the world in which we live.

Part II

Cinema, Architecture and the Everyday

Chapter 4

Spatial Editing

Regardless of the historically prevailing view of imageless and essentially verbal thought, seminal theories of pure visual thinking, such as those of Paul Klee, Wassily Kandinsky, György Kepes and Rudolf Arnheim, have decisively expanded the understanding of the realm of thought and creativity.

(Pallasmaa 2011: 34)

A New Perspective

The previous chapter explores a series of critical theories, such as those of Heidegger and Bullnow, with regard to dialectical and existential relationships between the human body and urban space. Looking at the perception of space beyond its visual dominance, we have considered the phenomenological discourses of Merleau-Ponty, Norberg-Schulz and Pallasmaa, which show that our sense of space is intrinsically linked to a sense of embodiment. Crucially, this spatial proposition finds application in the context of architecture and urban landscapes as well as film and cinema, a field that is more prone, in the arts, to visio-centricity. In the above quote, Pallasmaa alludes to the fact that visual theories are transgressive and have influenced our thinking and practice, particularly with regard to the notion of space. His assessment of contemporary urban culture is also noteworthy, because he is one of a number of practicing architects who declare that film and cinema have had a momentous impact on their professional life. Other well-known architectural practices discussed below, such as those of Jean Nouvel, Bernhard Tschumi, Diana Agrest and Mario Gandelsonas, Elizabeth Diller and Ricardo Scofidio, and Rem Koolhaas, have expressed a similar sentiment towards visual theory and have made an explicit connection to film. However, what does this mean in terms of architectural and urban design? If visual theories, film and cinema influence the design of spaces, does this not suggest that we should consider the use of film and cinematic principles as a natural instrument to facilitate engagement with architectural spaces? Having worked with moving images in an academic and professional context for a considerable number of years, I continue to be astonished by the transformative power of the camera; in other words, film's ability to focus on a particular space and distil, from ordinary everyday situations, dramas that would otherwise be consumed by an open urban landscape.

Figure 4.1   Prague, Czech Republic. Courtyard in the Prague Castle.

Anthony Vidler's discerning book *Warped Space* references Walter Benjamin to illustrate, as part of an approach towards a new modernity, how filmic techniques were considered appropriate to render or construe 'a version of reality that might otherwise go unrecorded' (Vidler 2002: 113). Benjamin notes in *The Work of Art in the Age of Mechanical Reproduction* that the 'camera introduces us to unconscious optics' (Benjamin 1968 [1936]: 237), which, according to Vidler, can be seen as a form of perception-based analysis in the context of urban space that conforms with Freud's *Psychopathology of Everday Life* (1901) (Vidler 2002: 114).

> By close-ups of the things around us, by focusing on hidden details of familiar objects, by exploring commonplace milieus under the ingenious guidance of the camera, the film, on the one hand, extends our comprehension of the necessities which rule our lives; on the other hand, it manages to assure us of an immense and unexpected field of action.
>
> (Benjamin 1968 [1936]: 236)

Since Benjamin recognised that the camera is a powerful means by which we can gain a new perspective on architectural and urban spaces, the natural question is whether moving images are particularly pertinent to capture the 'aura' or spirit of places and cities. Benjamin seems to believe so, because, as Vidler notes, his unfinished *Passagen-Werk* was 'written out on hundreds of single index cards, each one letter-, number-, and color-coded to cross-reference them to all the rest', so that they could be put together as a filmic montage of the city (Vidler 2002: 114). The enthusiasm with which he applied the idea to making a film of Paris is shown in the following:

> Could one not shoot a passionate film of the city plan of Paris? Of the development of its different forms [*Gestalten*] in temporal succession? Of the condensation of a century-long movement of streets, boulevards, passages, squares, in the space of half an hour? And what else does the flâneur do?
>
> (Benjamin 1974–89, Vol. 5: 135)

Vidler asks further: 'If, as Benjamin intimates, the model of the film director was to be found it the figure of the flâneur, how might this figure translate his essentially nineteenth-century habits of walking and seeing into cinematographic terms?' (Vidler 2002: 116). Vidler expresses here an idea that I would like to explore further. Can we, as ordinary people, place ourselves in the position of a cinematographer and view the city through cinematic lenses? The flâneur is a nineteenth-century male, rooted in a particular social milieu of that age, making it difficult to transpose him into contemporary times. However, if we consider for a moment the equivalent of a flâneur, for instance a contemporary stroller, who commonly reads urban landscapes through the screen of a digital phone camera, capable of instantly editing clips, and uploading them to a mobile social network, it becomes clear that his or her visual point of reference is not that of the picturesque writings of Baudelaire, but of narratives and images that we have seen in screen-based advertisements and motion pictures.

> There is a growing body of evidence and argument that our culture is, in fact, deeply visually literate, recognising and interpreting a complex mass of images with extreme sophistication, and that this sophistication is growing with the spread of advertising and television culture.
>
> (Rattenbury 1994: 36)

As the above quote underlines, we have learned to mentally select and process the flood of moving images to which we are exposed every day. All of us in the western world are film literate, and most learned to view and interpret moving images in childhood. So, as we are so familiar with film practices, do we not already naturally gaze at architectural spaces and cities as if we were a filmmaker ourselves; not as Benjamin proposed in his *Passagen-Werk*, but in terms of reading the city cinematically? What lessons have we learned from the rich cultural and practical discourses of film and cinema, for instance how films are put together; a practice that reaches back well over a hundred years, and can we apply this knowledge to our understanding of architectural spaces and cities? These and other questions are explored further below in considering the city as a signifying body full of filmic references.

> The city is a discourse and this discourse is truly a language: the city speaks to its inhabitants, we speak our city, the city where we are, simply by living in it, by wandering through it, by looking at it.
>
> (Barthes 1997 [1967]: 169)

This quote references Roland Barthes' hypothesis that the urban spaces we inhabit in our everyday life stand in steady dialogue with their inhabitants. However, unlike Barthes' discourse on urban semiology, the filmic engagement with urban landscapes that I highlight here does not require an understanding of the city as having a distinct language, author or reader. Instead, the *cinemantics* of a city can be understood without the linguistic knowledge of units, syntax and grammar. It regards the city as a layered, multifaceted system that is open to interpretation; a poststructuralist sphere that is shaped and understood by more than just functional programme, economic constraints, environmental concerns and social impacts (the measures that normally lie at the fingertips of architects and planners when considering urban interventions). Instead of trying to define a linguistic understanding of urban space, it builds on an existing and habitual system of film language through which we might be able to view, and interpret, urban spaces. What follows will, therefore, test whether it is possible to apply simple aspects of film language (such as the most basic film editing strategies of 'continuity' and 'montage' as well as editing techniques like those of 'cut' and 'dissolve') and use them to interpret architectural and urban settings. The aim here is to borrow and investigate cinematic terminologies and practice-based principles, and apply them to a reading of spatial settings in order to, as suggested by Benjamin, open up potentially unexpected perspectives on architectural and urban forms. As the basis for such an unconventional analysis, this serves not only the visual, signifying nature of the city, but also other hidden layers of everyday social spaces and practices.

Urban Continuity

A classical editing technique applied to most mainstream narrative films, and often associated with Hollywood, is 'continuity editing'. The principle objective of this editing style is to sustain 'a sense of uninterrupted and continuous narrative action within each scene' that maintains 'the illusion of reality for the spectator' (Blandford *et al.* 2001: 56). This is normally achieved by assembling the individual fragments of the film consisting of wide-shots, mid-shots and close-ups, in a chronologically and spatially consistent order, for example

Figure 4.2   Tallinn, Estonia. Urban continuity in the old town of the city.

by means of: 'motivated cuts' (when an actor looks in one direction and the camera cuts to what the actor sees); 'cuts on subject movement' (when an actor turns his or her head in a wide-shot and finishes the movement in a mid-shot); 'shot and reaction shots' (when the camera cuts from a person speaking to a another listening to see the person's reaction); and 'eyeline matches' (when the eyelines of two engaged characters are framed). Transposed into the sphere of urban environments, a 'continuity edit' relates to a city that postulates an ideal, yet seldom achieved scenario. Its material reality would need to demonstrate, to a large extent, a spatial and temporal consistency that is, with the exception some medieval towns,[1] a rarity in European countries today.

When applied to cities, the term 'continuity edit' is not understood as an urban space that only allows for one-directional growth. Rather, such cities consist of many different fragments – solids and voids that have been built, demolished and replaced over time. However, this has to be done in a way that makes these fragments appear to have been 'cut on the action' – fragmented and replaced consistently with the underlying socio-economic and architectural structure of a particular time and place. Continuity cities have to attest to a nearly uninterrupted development, a city in which the political, mercantile and industrial phases of its evolution have been harmoniously linked to one another (Lefebvre 2003 [1970]: 15), and where every building stands comprehensively and proportionately to others. In such cases, the physical properties of the city clearly articulate a plot or identity, one that can be ascribed to the particular trade, industry or occupation of its inhabitants.

Figure 4.3   Liverpool. New and old buildings at the Liverpool docks.

The majority of cities have long since lost their spatial coherency, however. Indeed, one of the absurdities of some cities today is their aspiration to return to a utopian or at least pseudo-ideal scenario. Debord sees the artificial homogenisation of spaces from one generation to another as a trivial by-product of postindustrial society which undermines 'the autonomy and quality of *places*'. 'Capitalist production has unified space, breaking down the boundaries between one society and the next. This unification is at the same time an extensive and intensive process of *banalization*' (Debord 2002: 94). In terms of the planning of cities, we might want to ask ourselves the question as to how far are we willing to go to 'regenerate' an illusion of reality. Some cities struggle as they seem to see the marketing of heritage, entertainment and leisure as the only commercially viable options for growth. However, it is clear that, while it might be possible to impersonate a cultural past in architectural terms, it is impossible to reinstate the socio-economic tissue that defined the character of historical buildings and street patterns. Cities undergo a natural evolution of growth and decline. Like the seasons in a year, cities and places blossom and fade. It goes without saying that as long as cities are inhabited, they are in constant flux and dialogue with the present, which becomes problematic when we try to mould them into formulaic and primarily static regeneration strategies.

Urban Montage

Around 1918, the Russian film practitioner and theoretician Lev Kuleshov conducted a famous film experiment 'whereby one image crosscut with another would give the impression of simultaneous or consecutive actions' (Gillespie 2000: 22). Using this powerful and effective means of juxtaposing two unrelated shots to create a new meaning, known as the 'Kuleshov Effect', he quintessentially influenced the thinking and work of Soviet avant-garde artists, such as Sergei Eisenstein, Vsevolod Pudovkin and Dziga Vertov. Eisenstein, who admired this technique for its reliance on the audience's active engagement with the subject matter, was keen to apply it to and expand it in his own theatrical work. Eisenstein's *Montage of Attractions*, first published in 1923, devises an aggressive, disruptive narrative strategy that should stimulate the sensual apparatus of the audience and encourage it to perceive a certain ideology (Eisenstein 1974: 78). Crucially, Eisenstein did not depend on the *real* units of time and space, but made use of the 'discursive function of cinema and its potential to reorganize reality' (Cook 1999: 319); a reality that is principally generated in the eyes of the beholder. One wonders what would happen if Eisenstein's theory, which he later extended to film practices and referred to as *dialectic montage*, were viewed in the context of contemporary architectural practice. Eisenstein intended to liberate 'the theatre from the weight of the "illusory imitativeness" and "representationality"' (ibid.: 79), virtues which, I would argue, find parallels in many cities today.

Not unlike the traditional theatre referred to by Eisenstein, some cities have lost their original sense of self, not least because the progression of time (social, political and economic changes), becoming at best an imitation of a lost identity that lies somewhere in the past. They often compete with each other on a representational level, whereby city councils resort to employing *landmark architects* to create *landmark buildings* as a universal remedy for diseased urban landscapes. Like a sequence of images that are interrupted by one another as part of a montage, a sequence of buildings can be interrupted by a piece of arbitrary freeform architecture that, when viewed on a surface level (as image) has no relation with its surrounding context. Both filmic montage and landmark architecture can serve as powerful underlying instruments of a political and ideological agenda. However, in architectural history, only in isolated circumstances, such as the Eiffel Tower in Paris (built for the 1889 World Exhibition) or the Sydney Opera House (completed 1973), has this led to the synthesis of a new identifying image for an entire city.

The editing of a film using montage operates under the assumption that an individual shot is free from the relational constraints of *space* and *time*, since it does not intend to uphold the illusion of their continuity. As mentioned above, when inserted into an established urban matrix, landmark buildings have no obvious relation to their surrounding context. However, this assertion is not entirely accurate. While, on a representational level, the isolated *image* of the signature building may have no relation to its context, the point

Figure 4.4 Casa da Música, Porto. Urban montage.

remains that any insertion into a sequence has semantic consequences. The term *relational editing* refers to the 'Kuleshov Effect', which is a process whereby the meaning of one shot, such as a smiling face, bears a significant relation to the following shot, which may be (a) a child playing, or (b) a dead body. From this we might conclude that if architects of iconic architecture were to apply the concept of montage correctly, they would be less concerned with the formal and material aspects of the building itself, and more concerned with the (image-) context in which their building is to be placed, since, as Kuleshov has shown, it is that placement that has profound consequences on the meanings that are collectively generated.

A completely different approach to the notion of urban montage is offered by the Berlin-based group Raumlabor. Instead of aiming to create architectural iconographies through landmarks, this interdisciplinary group uses subversive tactics to change the function, perception and meaning of places. As with Tschumi's concept of defamiliarisation, superimposition and cross programming outlined in *Architecture and Disjunction* (Tschumi 1996), the temporary installations of Raumlabor built up spatial conflicts that, montage-like, create a new room for associations in a triangular relationship between space, events and people. For example, they transformed a metro station between Essen and Mülheim situated between two highway intersections into a performance space for operas, and transformed Erich Honecker's former *Palast der Republik* in Berlin into a temporary alpine hotel. Similarly, in New York, they used a 'space-busting' van from which an inflatable structure would emerge to create space in the most unlikely locations, intervening in film screenings, dance events, workshops and other functions.

Figure 4.5   Raumlabor's 'Space Buster' under an archway in the Dumbo Improvement District in NYC. © Alan Tansey.

Urban Cuts

The most fundamental method of joining two shots is by means of a cut. Splicing and rearranging the running order of a film print or digital footage on a timeline is the most basic yet simultaneously the most powerful editorial tool of a film practitioner. The quality of editors is measured by their ability to assemble the footage in accordance with the script and storyboard (so that the editing is in line with the strategy of the narration), as well as their artistic skill (or ability to either disguise or emphasise the cut so that it supports the narrative structure of the film). Cuts can shape an edit by omitting the least important information and thus tighten the narrative flow of a film. Cuts allow the editor to jump in *time* and *space*, which can, depending on the placement of the cut (for example, a cut on action), hide or reveal gaps in the spatio-temporal unity of the sequence. Stanley Kubrick's *2001: A Space Odyssey* (1968) contains perhaps one of the most famous examples of a *cut on visual match*, in which a new scene opens by framing an object of similar tone, movement, size and background to the object framed at the end of the previous scene. In the film, we cut from a bone thrown by an ape to a space ship orbiting the earth – objects that are vastly different from each other in terms of time and space. Cuts are important ways of determining the pace and rhythm of a film. They allow the editor to condense and expand the perceived time, and are therefore an important means of attracting and keeping the viewer's attention. In today's filmic perception, long scenes without any cuts are often seen as difficult to watch because, depending on the movement of the camera among other factors, they become either too boring or too

Figure 4.6   Macau. Nocturnal street scene.

demanding. Finally, in terms of the present discussion, cuts influence the emotional connection of the viewer to the scene.

Cuts in urban architectural terms can, of course, be seen as the material joints between two adjacent buildings or districts. However, as demonstrated by Lefebvre among others, this is not the only level and dimension at which we engage with a perceived spatial urban reality. Cuts (as well as *dissolves*, which will be discussed in the following section) can occur in a city's topological, socio-economic or political form. They can also arise when sudden and distinct changes in social dispositions, economic drivers or activities take place, although this cut might not be particularly apparent in the appearance of the landscape itself. On a recent trip to Macau, for instance, I noticed near the Lisboa Hotel on Avenida Almeida Ribeiro and Avenida Horta e Costa a sequence of mixed retail outlets and restaurants of a similar size suddenly cut into a part of the urban fabric that is dominated by a distinct form of retail, in this case jewelry shops. Although there is little variation in the form of the landscape itself, when walking along the sidewalk, one gains a sense of passing a threshold in terms of the buildings or spaces that both parts occupy.

When examining the composition of contemporary city centres, we sometimes have the impression that architects and planners try to avoid strong or pronounced architectural cuts, especially if the building and spaces are located within a historically sensitive context. Despite the fact that heritage and preservation authorities increasingly favour clear distinctions between historic and new structures, it is still common design practice in these areas to retreat to what is perceived as *safe ground* – a superficial duplication of previous building materials and methods. To simply blend into the critical urban landscapes, regardless of the planned function developed for inhabitants behind those façades, misses the opportunity to create a distinct *cut* and thereby a stimulating influence on the pace, rhythm and narrative of the city. Rather than relying on an architectural and spatial vocabulary of what is commonly perceived as either acceptable or unacceptable urban language, perhaps we could view this question from the perspective of movie editing, and ask whether it is relevant for the *story of a place* to disguise the *spatio-temporal break* between buildings or spaces, or whether this should be emphasised? Just as a narrative film tends not to be constructed from one cut alone, so architectural and urban cohesion does not come from the treatment of a single join. Typically, it is a sequence of shots/buildings that build up a narrative, although a single cut both in architectural and filmic practices can be an important means of engaging with the public. Cuts bring structure to urban sites just as they do to film. Furthermore, they provide the potential to form and prescribe new relationships between adjacent socio-spatial situations, and are distinctly different from the *dissolves* discussed below.

Urban Dissolves

In filmic terms, dissolves are a method of gradual transition between two images, by which one image fades out while the other simultaneously fades in. Compared to cuts, dissolves are relatively rare in the professional editing of motion pictures. Film editors often see dissolves as a last resort in cases where a cut would break the narrative flow. Although dissolves are sometimes applied in important moments of the plot, in most cases they serve to make the transition between two unrelated shots (passage of time and/or space) as discrete as possible. Particularly when used at regular intervals, dissolves commonly become unnoticeable links between shots, and, I would argue, fail to take advantage of the suggestive power of the cut. Whereas distinct cuts in a montage provide an opportunity to create associative meanings that are independent of the two adjacent shots, dissolves leave relatively little room for imagination by the viewer. As a result one might go so far as to say that dissolves are, in comparison with cuts, a more imposing means of engaging the viewer with a narrative.

So, how would we explain dissolves in the context of real space? In their most basic form, architectural dissolves might be present in situations where there is no distinct material separation between two adjacent buildings. This draws attention to the conjoined character of buildings within parts of a city that attempts to act in harmony; a trend that, paradoxically, might increase the risk of creating spaces that lack identity. Architectural dissolves can also occur

Figure 4.7   Liverpool. Residential apartment buildings with brick façades matching empty
warehouses from the turn of the twentieth century.

on a social level, where two or more social activities or interest groups share
an overlapping common space. The need for spaces and places that allow for
a social, economic and ethnic mix is now widely accepted as good practice in
architectural and planning circles,[1] and we could therefore conclude that permeable urban dissolves are an appropriate strategy for new housing developments, for example. In other words, neighbourhoods in spaces and places are
constructed in a way that the low-income social groups, who might want to
rent apartments, can naturally mix with the high-income groups who might
want to purchase a property. The concept of dissolves seen in an architectural
context, then, is reflected in the choice of design, form and materials used in
such projects. This blended approach is already practiced in many places,
particularly across Europe, where tactics are employed to avoid the development of ghettos in which one particular social norm dominates, such as a
population with only one ethnic, social or age group. Consequently, we might
want to view well-executed architectural or urban dissolves as instruments to
provide social *continuity*, which is not the same as a technique that creates a
lack of expression as suggested in the aforementioned architectural approach.
In fact, in order to ensure a sustained social balance within mixed architectural systems, it is equally important to pay attention to a degree of definition
and clarity, the physical quality of adjacent spaces (shots) or, in Lynch's words,
the 'imageability' of individual components when planning such neighbourhoods (Lynch 1960: 9–10). Despite a desire to 'dissolve' social boundaries, a
truly soft design strategy will need to give room for distinct social, cultural,
religious or other activities. They must permit the maintenance and cultiva-
tion of different identities, which ultimately means they need to become
'permeable spaces' in which interaction with other groups can take place.

This thought model, which considers urban design as a form of spatial editing, is, of course, far from perfect, being fuzzy and open to personal interpretation. On the other hand, one wonders if the culturally- and socially-diverse postmodern places and cities that we inhabit today require a mode of engagement that is exactly that: one that is less precise and allows multiple readings. Therefore, a soft cinematic perspective might be seen as a complementary approach to the harder and more statistical methods that commonly dominate our professional discourse in architectural design and city planning. My students find it natural to share their ideas through modes of communication they are familiar with; that is, through cinema and moving image (film and animations). One wonders, therefore, if future generations will find film and cinematic editing techniques provide a more acceptable frame of reference, valid and fruitful in its ability to engage us with the architectural and urban design questions we will face in the future. Furthermore, it is interesting that we can already see many people in possession of a basic knowledge of film language and hence with an understanding of the difference between cuts and dissolves. This suggests that looking at architectural and urban designs through a filmic lens can lend a voice, even to non-experts in planning and design. Consequently, using film as a tool of communication corresponds with Dziga Vertov's aspiration to harness the potential universality of filmic language through basic editing techniques, including montage, which could close the circle between the history of film and contemporary architectural practice.

Chapter 5

A Shared Space

[A]rchitectural form relates to the form of film as one text to another, in terms of a structure composed of so many patterns, or rather fragments of structure or language, organized in time and through space. Film becomes analogous to the modern perception of a city, continuous sequences of space frames perceived through time.

(Weihsmann 1997: 9)

Sequences and Events

The following explores a number of theoretical and practical concepts that share common ground between film and architecture. I will begin by considering the notion of sequences and events. From production to screening, film is a sequential art form. A film crew shoots a movie shot-by-shot and scene-by-scene, hence it is normally produced in a sequential and not a chronological order. Film stock records and stores pictorial information in a sequential order. One foot of 35mm film normally has 16 frames. If a film is shot at 24 frames per second, 1,440 sequential frames are shot per minute. This means that every minute produces 90 feet of film, which amounts to 8,100 feet (about 2.5 km or 1.5 miles) for a 90-minute film; if unrolled on the streets of Los Angeles, this would reach from Grauman's Chinese Theatre eastwards on Hollywood Boulevard to across the Hollywood Freeway. The digital age is gradually changing the sequential recording of image information, and while various digital tape formats still store information sequentially on magnetic tape, new digital cameras use built-in hard discs or flash cards to store units of information in a more randomised order. The editing of film stock is the art of selecting and combining different shots in a sequential order, a process that is fundamentally important for the plot and narrative structure of the film. Digital editing stations have largely kept a linearly-organised interface. However, instead of moving film stock across a cutting table, the editor now moves digitised sound and image sequences across a timeline. Once edited (by whatever means), copies are made (as rolls of film or tapes) and distributed for projection.[1]

With regard to space, sequences and events are deeply rooted in human culture. Whether in the form of journeys and routes in Chinese classical gardens,[2] or the Stations of the Cross in Christianity, we have long since known spaces in which a processional movement of the body has been used to detach stories that have been sequentially stitched into a place. In the fourteenth century, for instance, the Franciscan Order helped to spread the idea of a processional commemoration of the Passion of Christ to many countries, where it has since been extended to up to fifteen stations that depict the final hours of Christ (*Leidensweg*). This sequential reenactment of events is also used in design, with frescos (e.g. inside churches) or sculptural relics (e.g. outside, along footpaths) serving as visual aids that underpin the narrative behind the journey. Equally, architecture manifests itself and is perceived in linear arrangements. From antiquity to the present, architectural design has relied on the repetition of elements, in particular on sequences expressed through the composition of building forms, the arrangement of openings or the position of columns.

Sequences in architecture, whether they comprise of openings in a Renaissance façade or row houses, are more than functional expressions or design arbitrariness. Mitchell notes that architects tend to 'organize space along circulation routes to present sequences of views, or to create staged transitions from public to private space, or perhaps from profane to sacred' (Mitchell 2005a: 6). He compares the simultaneity and unfolding succession of sounds with the interconnected spaces of a city, where the 'synchronic effect of simultaneously visible elements and relationships and the diachronic effect of elements and relationships presenting themselves sequentially to moving observers' (ibid.: 6–7). Furthermore, Tschumi highlights that the 'sequences of space, *configurations-en-suite*, *enfilades*, spaces aligned along a common axis – all are specific architectural organizations, from Egyptian temples through the churches of the quattrocento to the present' (Tschumi 1996: 155). Mario Gandelsonas describes sequences as an important means by which architecture denotes social and cultural conventions, and which ultimately 'constitute[s] the system that in most times provided the logic for architectural form' (Gandelsonas 1998: 205). However, it is not just solid forms that express a sequence in architecture, but also the voids – the spaces it frames and articulates. Gandelsonas again alludes to the notion of sequences in the structural organisation of architectural space:

> A house is not just a place where one opens a door, enters, and remains. It is a system and a sequence of elements that provide a fine gradation of public, semi-public, and private spaces, separated and connected sequences which go from purely public – the entrance door – to purely private.
>
> (Ibid.)

Another aspect that deals with spatial sequences is the way in which architectural spaces are perceived. Together with Kevin Lynch's *Image of the City* (1960) and Jane Jacobs' *The Death and Life of Great American Cities*

Figure 5.1   Berlin. The *Altes Museum* (Old Museum) built by Karl Friedrich Schinkel between 1823–30. © Keith Hamilton.

Figure 5.2   Porto, Portugal. Architectural sequence.

(1961), Gordon Cullen's book *The Concise Townscape* (2005 [1961]) is one of a series of influential texts on urban design published in the early 1960s that remain an inspiration to anyone who is interested in the ways we perceive urban landscapes. What unites all three books is that they look at urban design and the city from eye level, instead of the top-down, planning-approach manner that dominates many later texts. Lynch queries the navigability and legibility of cities through people's memory, and Jacobs critiques modernist planning policies by examining neighbourhoods and communities. Cullen, on the other hand, studies the design quality of the city through the eyes of people walking through urban spaces and thus sets an important subjective and empirical counter-perspective to the rationalist doctrine and study of spatial paradigms (cf. Walters and Brown 2004: 85). Seeing the city from a point of view that recalls visual impressions known in Renaissance perspective paintings, Cullen insists that urban spaces are almost entirely perceived through our faculty of vision (Cullen 2005 [1961]: 8), a hypothesis that can, of course, be challenged. This aside, Cullen's work gives a fascinating insight into the sequence of experiences that people encounter when walking through a city, a phenomenon for which he coined the term *serial vision*.

> The significance of all this is that although the pedestrian walks through the town at a uniform speed, the scenery of towns is often revealed in a series of jerks or revelations. This we call SERIAL VISION.
>
> (Ibid.: 9)

The approach outlined in Cullen's book values early twentieth century philosophies of Garden Cities and garden suburbs for their emotional qualities of space; these were developed and proliferated by Raymond Unwin and Barry Parker who were influenced by the nineteenth century urban theories of Camillo Sitte (Walters and Brown 2004: 85). By studying the city through visual analysis, Cullen's approach shows a natural affinity to moving images; in fact he appears to apply principles that are fundamentally tied to filmic production. First, Cullen applies a point of view (POV) for his drawings and photographs which are similar to those of a subjective camera POV. His visual study places a virtual camera in space, thus allowing him to study urban space through a visual abstraction (drawings, photographs), omitting everything that is outside the frame and his chosen field of vision, achieving an effect that is known from filming urban space with a camera. Second, Cullen studies urban space as *city scenery* in which every POV is deliberately framed. Although his approach is one that aspires to visually *freeze-frame* the city as it is, his hand drawings in particular look as if they: (a) are carefully composed; (b) capture a space that is carefully lit (demonstrated by his indication shadows); and (c) frame a city at just the right angle. Each of these helps to achieve the maximum dramatic effect, and the impression we get is of a visual storyboard of a city. All these are methods that show the trademarks of a *cinematographer* or *set-designer* working in urban spaces, and whose responsibility it is to make the best use of the atmospheric and scenographic qualities of a city. Finally, Cullen argues that his serial vision of urban space is taken at fixed temporal

Figure 5.3   Exhibition of Eduardo Souto Moura's work at FAUP in Porto. The work is mounted in the form of a visual storyboard.

intervals, which clearly links to one of the core principles upon which the accurate recording of movement in film is based. While a camera exposes individual frames on a film medium (in the case of 35mm film stock at a speed of 24 frames per second), Cullen captures his frame by drawing a space by hand. While he has no intention to compete with the speed of a camera, his timed spatial snapshots give the impression of movement through space. If we imagine flipping through his drawings in consecutive order, as some of us have done with 'thumb cinemas', the resulting image sequence would stitch spaces together and thereby create the illusion of filmic movement.

Many of the visual methods and thinking strategies of architecture and urban space that Cullen outlines in his book (although not the conclusions drawn from them) can be related to Tschumi's concept of spatial deconstruction. Cullen's study draws attention to a 'sequence of revelations' (Cullen 2005 [1961]: 17) which denote some form of a visual/spatial event that bears a resemblance to Tschumi's own concept of spatial events. Both like the idea of freeze-framing architectural situations, a practice that can clearly be referenced back to a cinematic tradition. On this point, Tschumi notes that he is 'Examining architecture "frame by frame," as through a film-editing machine' (Tschumi 1996: 165), and it is well known that much of his creative output has evolved from theories of montage and editing, and a discourse of film and cinema. Of note here are projects like *The Screenplays* (Tschumi 1977) or *The Manhattan Transcripts* (Tschumi 1976–81), both of which share the formal resemblance of visual storyboards as mentioned above. As with Cullen, Tschumi is interested in the notion of temporal sequences and their relation to the visual appearance of architecture.

> In literature and in the cinema, sequences can be manipulated by such devices as flashbacks, crosscuttings, close-ups, and dissolves. Are the inclusion of baroque details in the modern architectural sequence … temporary flashbacks?
>
> (Tschumi 1996: 165)

However, his concept of architectural sequence should be understood as more than purely a formal strategy: 'architectural sequences do not mean only the reality of actual buildings, or the symbolic reality of their fictions' (ibid.: 163). Tschumi asserts that the 'meaning of any architectural situation depends on the relationship of the triadic sequence of *Space*, *Event*, and *Movement*' (ibid.: 162) and is thus created by a dynamic that is the shifting of spatial and narrative interpretations between these individual parts.[3] For Tschumi, narratives are a means of exploring architecture's ability to communicate through spatial paradigms and, as such, seek an active engagement between the user and architectural space. Among other places, this is manifested in the *Parc de La Villette* (1983–98), the first of the projects that led to his international reputation, and reason enough to look closely at the notion of architectural events.

As we have seen previously, a narrative is often defined as a sequence of *events*; it has a structure that is based on time, cause and effect. Indeed, it seems that various interpretations of the concept of events provide a theoretical framework by which it is possible to link *verbal* narrative with *non-verbal* space. Tschumi recalls that a series of 1970s literary projects have formed the basis for his investigations of the 'dialectic between the verbal and the visual', which subsequently impacted on his own creative work (ibid.: 145). Inspired by texts such as Italo Calvino's *Invisible Cities* (2009 [1972]), Franz Kafka's *The Burrow* (1991 [1923]) and Edgar Allan Poe's *Masque of the Red Death* (1842), he began to see 'parallels between narrative and spatial sequences' (Tschumi 1996) and formed the question: 'If writers could manipulate the structure of stories in the same way as they twist vocabulary and grammar, couldn't architects do the same, organizing the programme in a similar objective, detached, or imaginative way?' (ibid.: 146). Devising architectural programmes along such provocative lines led to a disjunction between architectural form and use (ibid.: 147) which traditionally lie at the root of a rational modern planning approach. The purposeful design of conflicting spaces is related to what Tschumi calls 'shock', a didactic element that is also seen in theatrical tradition. However, the difference lies in the motivation behind the creation of such shocks. In the mid-1920s, for the epic theatre, Bertholt Brecht developed the stylistic device of a pedagogical 'shock' (*Erschütterung*) and the related concept of 'dis-illusion' (*Entzauberung*). Whilst these are aimed at offering a 'thought-provoking surprise', and thus provide encouragement to 'the audience to see the contradictions between ideology [including those created by the theatre itself] and actual social conflict with the intention to provoke to change the world off- as well as on-stage' (Kruger 2004: 43; see also Carney 2005: 112–15),[4] Tschumi argues 'that "shock" must be manufactured by the architect if architecture is to communicate' (Tschumi 1996: 149). This suggests that he sees the shock concept in architecture as a dramatic instrument which underlines the non-verbal narrative function of architectural form and space, and brings it into line with film and montage theory that is more specifically addressed below.

Tschumi sees 'the concept of space and the experience of space' as two disjunctive, contradictive and exclusive terms (Tschumi 1996: 16). He criticises that 'the making of architecture had generally focused on the formal or physical aspects of buildings and cities, rarely raising the question of the events that took place in them' (ibid.). Architecture, he notes elsewhere, 'is as much about the events that take place in spaces as about the spaces themselves' (Tschumi 1994: 13). This led Tschumi to highlight (echoing Lefebvre's critique on abstract space) the disparity 'between ideal space (the product of mental processes) and real space (the product of social practice)' (Tschumi 1996: 31; cf. Kaye 2000: 42–43). His writing suggests that, although he sees the concept of 'events' as linked to the programmatic dimensions of 'cross-programming', 'transprogramming' and 'disprogramming' alluded to in *Event-Cities* (Tschumi 1994: 13), they are, of course, also linked to the human activity that takes place in urban spaces, and which provides a theoretical affinity to early filmmaking practices. For Tschumi, events often lie at the centre of his architectural attention, just as early film pioneers are often focused on the filming of events, such as in the form of 'actualities'. In fact, even the screening of the film (the gathering of people and their interaction with each other as well as interaction with the screen) can become an event in itself. Tschumi notes that 'Events "take place." And again. And again' (Tschumi 1996: 160), and these events can lead to a cinematic chain of *cause and effect* that is manifested on the screen as well as in meaningful architectural space. The danger lies in the fact that we have become a society of the spectacle, and that we turn into an event-*Gesellschaft*, surrounded by highly communicative architectures yet with ultimately questionable meanings attached to sequences of space, event and movement.

Movement and Passage

Cinema that is based on the use of the medium of film is inherently compounded by the concept of movement. In the most basic terms, film captures movement in live action and replays it through a mechanism that requires movement. In fact, the motion picture process would not have been invented, had not been for the fascination of people like Étienne Jules de Marey and Eadweard J. Muybridge with photographically capturing and reproducing movement; an argument that, in visual terms, finds beautiful expression in the dances of Loïe Fuller, captured on camera by the Lumière Brothers in the 1890s, and of Annabelle Moore, filmed by Edison and Biograph between 1894 and 1897.[5] Most of this is self-evident and well

Figure 5.4   Portrait of Loïe Fuller dancing, c. 1902. © Frederick Glasier.

illustrated in the history of cinema, and therefore I will discuss some less well-documented movement-related tactics employed in early film and architecture.

The representation of cities and urban spaces in early film are a particularly fascinating field of study, as it gives an insight into the nature of urban space in a relatively sparsely mediated form. This is because early films, such as those produced by film pioneers like the Lumière Brothers, Thomas Edison, Mitchell and Kenyon, and Robert W. Paul, are often associated with a type of film practice that predates the notion of editing. The camera was either fixed to or mounted on a moving vehicle, and a hand-cranked camera captured urban space with minimal interference (although the latter point is, of course, not universally true if we consider the audience's lively engagement with the camera in some cases). It is fascinating that, even in these early days, not all filmmakers used the same film tactics when filming in cities. Frank Kessler compares various strategies applied by early film practitioners with regard to their filming of urban space. For the Lumière company he recognises that their films are primarily shot at locations where the cinematographer would find: (a) characteristic, recognisable monuments (landmark buildings); (b) picturesque scenery and backdrops (not necessarily with landmarks); and (c) movement caused by traffic (Kessler 2007). Such location-specific strategies are distinctly different from those of Mitchell and Kenyon who, deriving from practices of travelling showmen, focused more on the inhabitants of a city (often moving towards the camera) than on particular architectural locations. In both the examples cited, early cinema provides a means in which movement adds a spatial dimension to two-dimensional images and thereby adds a vital factor to the perception of a sense of place. Whether it is horse-drawn carriages or people crossing the frame, their movement suggests a depth and continuity of space that goes beyond the frame of the image. Movement offers a contrast to the more static elements in the frame, such as buildings, and opens a gap in our perception that widens the space on the screen. This fascination with movement was not only recognised as a quintessential currency of early film, but also in architecture.

In *Histoire de l'Architecture*, published only five years after the Lumière brothers' inaugural screening in Paris, Auguste Choisy (1899) discusses 'the successive perspective views of the movement of an imaginary spectator on the Acropolis', a statement that draws attention to the importance of movement in the composition of the site and the perception of architectural space (Vidler 1996: 22–3). This important theme reappears in Le Corbusier's *Vers une Architecture* (1927 [1923]), where he repeatedly draws on the work of Choisy.[6] It is this notion of an architectural path (*promenade architecturale*) that provides historians with confirmation of an important link between members of the avant-garde in architecture and film, and by extension a significant conventional parallel between the perception of space through physical architecture and the medium of film. Sergei Eisenstein, in his article *Montage and Architecture* (Eisenstein 1989 [*c.* 1938]), highlights the importance of the cinematic 'path' in films, and compares it with the 'carefully disposed phenomena that he [man, or, in this example, a child] absorbed sequentially with his visual sense' when walking through an architectural space. This analogy must be attributed to the fact that Eisenstein trained as architect and, furthermore, was an admirer of the work of Le Corbusier (ibid.; see Vidler 1996: 22–3). The direct connection between Le Corbusier and Eisenstein's own concepts of the architectural promenade become evident when, in his study, he explicitly refers to the work of Choisy and the Acropolis.

> … I would only ask you to look at it with the eye of a filmmaker: it is hard to imagine a montage sequence for an architectural ensemble more subtly composed, shot by shot, than the one that our legs create by walking among the buildings of the Acropolis.
>
> (Eisenstein 1989 [c. 1938]: 117)

The Acropolis, Eisenstein remarks, 'has an equal right to be called the perfect example of one of the most ancient films'; an assumption that is based on the observation that the temple design comprises a sequential order of spaces which create an architectural path and hence require the movement of a human (or camera) eye across the site in order to engage fully with the depth of the space. In doing so, Eisenstein highlights two distinct yet interrelated phenomena, one that is cinematic and the other that is architectural, at whose centre lies the movement of a 'spatial eye' along a pathway. In Vidler's words, the cinematic path is one 'where a spectator follows an imaginary line among a series of objects, through the sight as well as in the mind' (Vidler 1996: 118), whereas in the architectural path, a person (spectator) moves through a series of 'carefully disposed phenomena' which he observes sequentially with his visual sense (Eisenstein 1989 [c. 1938]: 116). While it is important to recognise that, as observed by Davide Deriu (2007: 38), Le Corbusier's idea of the *promenade architecturale* differs from Eisenstein's notion of montage, the idea of 'movement and passage' is of central importance to both arguments and thus creates a common alliance between the concepts. As established above, movement in relation to early film is essential if we are to *capture* and *represent* space in cinema, and the same seems to be the case in the field of architecture. Just as film creates space through movement, it is movement in architecture that *reveals* the cinematic quality of space, through which it *creates* a cinematic experience of architectural space. Jean Nouvel offers a practice-based perspective that emblematises both aspects of 'sequences' and 'passage'.

> Architecture exists, like cinema, in the dimension of time and movement. One conceives and reads a building in terms of sequences. To erect as building is to predict and seek effects of contrast and linkage through which one passes. ... In the continuous shot/ sequence that a building is, the architect works with cuts and edits, framings and openings. ... I like to work with a depth of field, reading space in terms of thickness, hence the superimposition of different screens, plans legible from obligator joints of passage which are to be found in all my buildings.
>
> (Nouvel quoted in Rattenbury 1994: 35)

Architectural design and our reading of it, as Nouvel remarks, is intrinsically connected to the imagining of a moving body in and passage through space, which links cinema and architecture at the level of production and consumption of space, and thus in theoretical and practical terms.

Michel de Certeau's chapter 'Walking the City' in his seminal book *The Practice of Everyday Life* (De Certeau 1988 [1980]), starts with a critique of the way in which we visually engage with the city. Calling into question the prevalent functionalist urban discourse, and believing that it is important to question how we engage with urban spaces, de Certeau asserts that 'the city serves as a totalizing and almost mythical landmark for socioeconomic and political strategies' (ibid.: 95). His argument is influenced by Lefebvre's critique of spatial production and, on multiple levels, by Jean François Augoyard's text *Step by Step: Everyday Walks in a French Urban Housing Project*

(Augoyard 2007 [1989]). Augoyard addresses the problem between conceived and lived space from the position of the inhabitants of densely populated and functionally planned architectural environments as being essentially 'captive of an overly complex network of functional operations' (ibid.: 9), and then continues by giving perceptive accounts of the modes of human inhabitation and pedestrian movement in everyday spaces and situations. De Certeau, on the other hand, clearly differentiates between 'strategies' and 'tactics'. The first deals with the political, economic and architectural rationality of a place, which involves the ruling, governing and shaping of an institutionalised subject, in this case the city. 'Tactics', on the other hand (in which he is far more interested) can subvert the previously described space by opportunistic and spontaneous spatial practices or acts. De Certeau is consequently fascinated by a 'lived space' and the mundane activities of everyday life that take place in it. He argues that these are either overlooked or are regarded as an 'obscure background of social activity' by those who are more interested in the technocratic or systematic conceptions of power (De Certeau 1988 [1980]: xi, 96; Stevenson 2003: 67), which again applies to architects and planners. One of these everyday 'tactical' behaviours deals with walking through urban spaces, and is particularly relevant in this excursion into the question of space creation through movement.

De Certeau regards what he calls 'lived space' as a place of 'tactile apprehension and kinaesthetic appropriation'; a territory in which the seemingly unremarkable pedestrian movement begins to actively shape spaces in the city (De Certeau 1988 [1980]: 97). This creative act, which is normally reserved to spatial strategists, is linked to the enunciating power of the body in space. He makes a noteworthy analogy between the movement of pedestrians and the act of speech: 'The act of walking is to the urban system what the speech act is to language or to the statements uttered' (ibid.). De Certeau alludes to a triple 'enunciative function' that is connected to the act of walking: the appropriation of space and spatial elements, the acting-out of place and the implying of relations (ibid.: 98). Hence, the pedestrian engages in a process of appropriating the topographical system which consists of almost endless choices.[7] The walker is, therefore, selective; one chooses a path and brings certain architectural elements to the forefront while at the same time omitting others. This means that the walker 'transforms spatial signifiers into something else' (ibid.); in other words, the walker creates space. De Certeau states that 'Walking affirms, suspects, tries out, transgresses, respects' thus creating a passage with a trajectory that 'speaks' (ibid.: 99). Where else is this more evident than in film? It is no coincidence that de Certeau illustrates his point by citing Charlie Chaplin and his behaviour in space on the silver screen. Spatial narratives, which we follow with interest, not at least because of the protagonists' decision-making in response to space and the situation in which they are presented, are key elements of filmic plots. The history of cinema is also the history of enunciative action and places, and it could perhaps be argued that there are parallels between de Certeau highlighting the 'rhetoric of walking' and cinema culture. Not only does the pedestrian in the actual city walk and stroll through spaces, but so too do their filmic equivalents. In fact, one of the legacies of film is its creation of a rich cinematic archive; a filmic depository built up with examples accentuating the rhetoric of spaces and their related tactics. In this respect, it could perhaps be argued that the planning of spatial strategies in the real world should direct some of its attention to over a century of the cinematic production of space. Spatial appropriation through movement is an essential cinematic practice, whether acted out in the movies or in real life.

Occupying a similar intellectual position to Lynch, Jacobs and Cullen, for de Certeau it is a question of perspective, in both metaphorical and literal terms. The 'imaginary tantalizations produced by the eye' (ibid.: 91–3) determine the nature of space. By placing an urban analysis on the level of sidewalks and streets, these studies are positioned at the same level as many cinematic POVs. Not only do they share the notion of a filmic perspective, but also that of a common central character, which in the case of Lynch, Jacobs and Cullen is the person on the street and in movies. I am thinking here of street films, including those discussed in Part I (*Taxi Driver*, *Amélie*, *The Third Man*) and the protagonist that occupies that space. It is on street level where de Certeau's 'spatial stories' unfold (ibid.: 115–30); stories that are played out in real as well as screen space, and stories that ultimately determine the narrative quality of cities. He notes that it is the spatial practices that we act out in our everyday tactical engagement with urban landscapes that are the 'beginnings of a story the rest of which is written by the footsteps' (ibid.: 115–6). Consequently, our movement through streets and urban spaces, which are 'geometrically defined by urban planning' (ibid.: 117), has the enigmatic capacity to 'transform the scene' (cf. ibid.: 102), a principle that applies to the physical as well as filmic space. For de Certeau, 'space exists when one takes into consideration vectors of direction, velocities, and time variables', and it is 'composed of intersections of mobile elements' (ibid.: 117). It seems reasonable, therefore, to suggest that a movement- and time-based medium such as film is pertinent when exploring architectural strategies with a particular emphasis on spatial tactics.[8]

Whilst architects, planners and geographers use maps to engage with the city in rational terms, and Lynch sought to map mental images of the city, members of the Situationist International movement – Guy Debord, Asger Jorn and Michèle Bernstein in particular – were interested in alternative forms of mapping that investigated the relationship between language, narrative and cognition in urban landscapes that were spoiled by capitalism and bureaucracy (Sadler 1998: 60). This was exemplified in their 1957 project *The Naked City*, inspired by Jules Dassin's 1948 semi-documentary film of the same name, in which a psycho-geographic map depicted a disconnected, disorientated and fragmented city suffering from the ills of urban redevelopment and renewal programmes, automobile traffic, public anonymity; in short, a space that is unavoidably hostile to pedestrians and its inhabitants (ibid.: 61; Boyer 1996: 72). Using similar street-based tactics to de Certeau, Debord developed the idea of 'drifting' (*derivé*), the playful strolling through urban spaces which was seen as a form of surveying of the psychogeographic conditions of the modern city in order to reveal its hidden delights (Debord 1958 quoted in Knabb 2006; see also Sadler 1998: 69). It could be argued that, since drifting is an engagement with the 'psychogeographical contours' of a city (ibid.), and since these contours show traces of film and cinema, such tactics could lead to useful explorations of the cityscapes in which we live. In another context, Ian Sinclair recommends a similar tactic when he suggests that the best way to understand a city is through purposeful drifting through its streets:

> Walking is the best way to explore and exploit the city; the changes, shifts, breaks in the cloud helmet, movement of light on water. Drifting purposefully is the recommended mode, tramping asphalted earth in alert reverie, allowing the fiction of an underlying pattern to reveal itself.
>
> (Sinclair 1997: 4)

This quote (discussing London) makes reference to Situationist International and de Certeau, as mentioned above, but what is so interesting for me here is the notion that fiction or another form of narrative content is somehow inscribed into a landscape and can be released through our body and the act of walking.

Framing of Space

The Renaissance is recognised as an extraordinary period of history, in which painterly and architectural art worked hand-in-hand to establish the notion of stage-like theatrical spaces. Furthermore, the achievements of the Renaissance, such as the conception of central perspective, helped to place the spectator at the centre of the frame, in terms of both painterly and spatial practices. Renaissance art and architecture helped to establish a scopic regime in which the frame becomes a visual trope in the dialectics between object and onlooker; a powerful visual agent that is loaded with meaning. The magnificent paintings of ideal cities and other visualisations of Renaissance urbanity attributed to Piero della Francesca, Francesco di Giorgio Martini and Fra'

Figure 5.5   Francesco di Giorgio Martini, *Architectural View*, *c.* 1477.

Carnevale demonstrate the importance of architectural frames in paintings, as well as the framing of urban space in general. In Martini's *Architectural View* (*c.* 1477), the visual illusion positions the viewer in such a way that one looks through an architectural colonnade crossing an urban square surrounded by buildings on both sides, before the gaze strays into perspective infinity. In doing so, and by playing to the imagination of the onlooker, Martini invites us to see architecture and urban spaces as optical devices that pre-date and anticipate cinema.

The concept of cinema as a frame or window is well established in film theory, and Charles F. Altman goes so far as to say that the entire history of film criticism and theory can be seen as a dialectic discourse between the two screen metaphors of *window* and *screen* (Altman 1977). This is echoed by Thomas Elsaesser and Malte Hagener, who give a good account of how the various theoretical strands of *formalist* or *constructivist* film theory on the one hand, and *realist* film theory on the other, are manifested in cinematic debates (Elsaesser and Hagener 2010: 15). Beginning with Rudolf Arnheim's classical text, I will provide a practice-based reading of the meanings of the 'framing of space' within the fields of film and architecture. Building on the work of Gestalt theorists such as Ernst Mach (1838–1916) and Christian Ehrenfels (1859–1932), Arnheim established, through his seminal text *Art and Visual Perception* (Arnheim 1954), the notion of *perception* as 'a subject for analysis within art-historical discourse, laying down criteria for how and why we perceive the visual field as we do' (Meecham and Sheldon 2005: 124). In his section on 'frames and windows', Arnheim studies the function of the frame

Figure 5.6   Prague, Czech Republic. Entrance to courtyard in the Prague Castle.

in pictorial art and makes an interesting analogy with architecture and the treatment of façades:

> The frame as we know it today developed during the Renaissance from the façade-like construction of lintels and pilasters that surrounded the altarpieces. As pictorial space emancipated itself from the wall and created deep vistas, a clear visual distinction became necessary between the physical space of the room and the world of the picture. … The frame was thought of as a window, through which the observer peeped into an outer world, confined by the opening of the peephole but unbounded in itself.
>
> (Arnheim 1954: 239)

This quote indicates a natural affinity between architecture and painterly art, which, through the visual device of the frame, is extended into the sphere of photography and film. Arnheim is not alone in relating Renaissance architecture to the notion of the frame in the visual arts. Jacques Aumont remarks that André Bazin's famous concept of the frame as mask is borrowed from Renaissance theoretician Leon-Battista Alberti (Aumont *et al.* 2004 [1983]: 13). In this text, in reference to the limits of the canvas in Jean Renoir's work, André Bazin comments that:

> … the screen is not a simple rectangle but rather the homothetic surface of the view-finder of his camera. It is the very opposite of a frame. The screen is a mask whose function is no less to hide reality than it is to reveal it. The significance of what the camera discloses is relative to what it leaves hidden.
>
> (Bazin and Truffaut 1974: 87)

Aumont's study of 'film space' draws attention to the two material character-istics of the film image with regard to the concept of the border and frame. Primarily, there is the individual photographic still frame on the print, which differs from the projected flat moving image that we see on the screen (Aumont *et al.* 2004 [1983]: 9). Inside the projected moving image frame (on-screen space), frames are once again frequently part of the cinematic sensa-tion; but this time as visual metaphors in the form of, for example, windows and doors. In the context of a classical cinematic style, these can be indicative of the 'complex relations of distance and proximity between film and viewer' (Elsaesser and Hagener 2010: 18). Whatever resides outside the frame (the area that Aumont and Heath calls *off-screen space*) has an altogether different function. The frame cuts off the visibility of filmic elements (*mise-en-scène*) that lie outside the filmographic space, as well as those elements that reveal the mechanisms behind cinematic production, which would inevitably change our cinematic experience. Therein lies one of the magical functions of cinema: a perceived mental space is created by – and depends on – cinema's power to suggest an off-screen space; an illusory, non-visualised space outside our field of vision, with the final product thus comprising 'the frame, the scene, the mask, the hidden, the absent' (Heath 1976: 91).

Altman comments that consideration of the cinema as a metaphorical frame or window threatens to overlook the role of the spectator: '… emphasis is placed on the organization of objects or the movement of people rather than on cinematic process whereby those objects and people are evoked', and therefore the metaphors 'actually share an assumption of the screen's funda-mental independence from the process of production and consumption' (Altman 1977: 260–1; cf. Elsaesser and Hagener 2010: 16). The consumption of film is completed through a two-dimensional screen with the dimension of this interface having an impact on our screen experience. In the context of moving images, the frame of the screen determines the format and therefore the aspect ratio of the picture. Until recently, standard television sets have had an aspect ratio of 4:3 (1.33:1), but newer models have an aspect ratio of 16:9 (1.78:1), which was introduced to match the natural field of vision of the human eye.[9] While television sets are still relatively small and provide a less immersive experience than cinema, the aspect ratio plays a more significant role in the perception of space than when watching a movie on a large cinema screen. During the 1950s, American movie studios began to produce film in widescreen formats, leaving the Academy ratio of 1.33:1 behind and moving towards a ratio of 1.85:1 or 2.35:1 (Pramaggiore and Wallis 2011: 140). Crucial to this development was the fact that the new widescreen format could be achieved with relative ease, and without a change of lens. The CinemaScope and Panavison formats were achieved by shooting with anamorphic lenses and

Figure 5.7   Screenshots. Office scene (left) and architecture as optical device (right).
Playtime. © Jolly Film, Specta Films.

standard 35mm film, cameras and projectors (ibid.). Widescreen ratios have
changed our perception of space on the screen, and whilst smaller aspect
ratios tended to lead spectators to a more focused, forced and, in some
instances, almost inescapable screen engagement (e.g. close-ups), widescreen
format invites viewers to explore the screen in its entirety. A film projected in
CinemaScope format gives the filmmaker the opportunity to break the screen
into segments and thereby permits the unfolding of simultaneous narrative
actions. Consequently, spectators gain power over the image by deciding
which action they want to follow. This is particularly well illustrated in
Stanley Kubrick's *2001: A Space Odyssey* (1968; Cinerama process) and
Jacques Tati's *Playtime* (1967; CinemaScope process), the latter being a further
exception to the rule as it was shot on 70mm film (as used today used by
IMAX). An unforgettable audio-visual feast that illustrates this point can be
seen when Tati's alter ego Monsieur Hulot looks over a glass balustrade into
office cubicles below, and observes the multiple sub-narratives taking place at
the same time.[10] Similarly, in another scene, Tati plays with the idea of modern architecture becoming optical apparatus, and therefore a screening device
in which openings in a building's façade become the monitors for numerous
stories being told at once.

Rhythm and Sound of Space

Scholars and film practitioners often refer to film as a time-based medium.
Indeed, making a movie is always an engagement with time, but it is perhaps
worth being reminded that film addresses multiple categories of time and, by
extension, space. Fundamentally, the filmic production of time is rarely the
same as screening time, unless it is a fly on the wall documentary with no
editing, which is also rare in professional practice. It is more common that
processes in postproduction compress the time of the film into a watchable
format. Film separates the unity between time and space and reconfigures it
in the editing. When filming any space, for instance at 24 frames per second,

it is sliced into layers of time in respect to the frame rate of the movie, each of which is different to the preceding and following frame. Although these frames can appear as almost identical when examining them individually and chronophotographically (such as in cases where there is little visible movement of the camera or object/subject that is filmed), the progression of time means that each frame has captured different spatial information on the medium, even if the difference is small and down to mechanical processes.[11] Once film has dissected space into very small spatio-temporal units (frames), the single continuum is broken and the frames can be controlled and reassembled in an infinite number of ways. This is why the profession of film editor is so highly regarded. The manipulation of sequential picture information – or spacetime fragments – through editing and other effects can either compress or expand the perceived time when watching a film, a concept that I am sure is familiar territory to most readers.

There is something quite architectural in the notion of cuts, as it provides both logic and structure to the film, or, as Sultanik calls it, a 'film's editing unfolds in a progressive, cumulative way: a style of architectonic exposition' (Sultanik 1995: 79). The use of cuts has greatly changed over time, and while in pioneering days, film editing took place (if at all) in the camera by stopping and restarting the film, twentieth century film history can also be told through the way that various editing techniques impacted on stylistic expression. It is difficult to make universal assumptions about the accelerating speed of editing over a period of time, as the shot length of movies can differ widely, but Barry Salt's statistical analysis, *Film Style and Technology: History and Analysis* (Salt 2009 [1983]) and David Bordwell's *The Way Hollywood Tells It: Story and Style in Modern Movies* (Bordwell 2006) give an interesting insight into this phenomenon. Both comment on the Average Shot Length (ASL),[12] which can be seen as an indication of the average editing pace of a film. With notable exceptions, such as D.W. Griffith's *The Avenging Conscience* (1914) or *The Birth of a Nation* (1915), in the pre-war silent era, most Hollywood directors worked with an ASL of 11 to 14 seconds. By 1918, Salt observes that the ASL had decreased substantially to between four and eight seconds (Salt 2009 [1983]: 161), which is a tendency that was put on hold with the introduction of sound. To deviate slightly, the cutting rate of American films in the mid 1960s began to accelerate and often reached an ASL of between 6 and 8 seconds (Bordwell 2006: 121), a development that is quite different to that found on the European continent.

Films produced during the 1950s and 1960s period of Italian Neo-Rationalist and French New Wave show experimental currents with regard to editing and other aspects. This counteracted the formalist paradigms set by Hollywood films. Lengthy takes and the use of mobile cameras set a moderately slow pace for films, and Salt's study, for instance, shows that Jean-Luc

Figure 5.8   Screenshot. *Run Lola Run*. © X-Filme Creative Pool.

Goddard's *À bout de souffié* (1960) has an ASL of 15 seconds. On the other hand, the pace of American movies continuously accelerated during the 1970s, and reached an important turning point in the 1980s due to a number of technical developments, such as the use of handheld steadicams and new editing methods, including the transfer of original rushes on to videotape (Salt 2009 [1983]: 335).[13] With video and MTV transforming film into not only a visual but also a sonic product for a new consumer market, the pace of moving images reached unprecedented heights. Movies like *Pink Floyd: The Wall* (1982), *Tron* (1982) or *Streets of Fire* (1984) show an average ASL of 3 to 4 seconds (Bordwell 2006, 122), although, according to Bordwell, there was only one film between 1961 and 1999 that had an ASL of less than 2 seconds. This film was *Dark City* (1998), although plenty of similarly fast-paced films have been produced since. In the light of music videos edited at a hip-hop pace and rhythm, one wonders today if we have become so attuned to fast-paced mediated environments that, like seeing the word *Lola* in Tom Tykwer's *Run Lola Run* (1998), the only limitation to editing speed is the capacity of human visual apparatus. Notable arguments against this way of perceiving space in moving images in commercial film productions have come from other areas of visual art. Bill Viola, a North American pioneer and innovator of video art, is known for challenging our filmic perception and experience of time and space through slow-motion video art installations in which the picture is formed from a continuous shot with no editing points whatsoever.[14]

   The above shows that there are historical variations in the way that films are edited, and this can be linked to different periods and stylistic preferences.

This is of interest, as the shot length and editing pace are determining factors that influence our perception of film space. This is based on the assumption that the slower the editing pace of a particular film, the more time the viewer has to explore and engage with the space seen in the film. However, it is not only shot length and editing that uphold a perceived rhythm of space when watching moving images. Sound and music contribute in large part to the narrative quality of the moving pictures and the perception of space. Michel Chion notes that there are three aspects that relate to the influence of sound on the perception of time in the image. First, the 'temporal animation of the image'; second, that 'sound endows shots with temporal linearization'; and third, 'sound vectorizes or dramatizes shots', which creates a feeling of 'imminence and expectation' (ibid.: 13–14). Sound gives structure the visual perception of urban environments and architectural spaces, which is a line of reasoning that Chion underpins with the physiological workings of the eye and ear. He argues that the eye perceives more slowly than the ear as 'it must explore in space as well as follow along in time', whereas the ear 'isolates a detail of its auditory field and it follows this point or line in time' (Chion *et al.* 1994: 11). On this point, he coined the legendary phrase 'What we hear is what we haven't had time to see (ibid.: 61). Furthermore, Chion observes that the 'eye is more spatially adept, and the ear more temporally adept' (ibid.), which could, if we accept this position, be relevant to the perception and processing of spatial information when watching a film as well as when being in real urban spaces.

If we look beyond the perceived interplay between the culture of vision and sound, and more closely at the temporal qualities of our built environment, we can perhaps agree that the city is a temporal construct and, therefore, so is architecture. Physically, cities and buildings change and require maintenance, and their performance is evaluated over time. Philosophically, architecture can be seen as a reflection of a particular time and its underlying values, ideologies and belief systems. Formally, we design and regard spaces and places in terms of the way rhythm is expressed architecturally. This applies to a façade, as well as to buildings or the fabric of the city. Tzonis and Lefaivre note that 'Rhythm is one of the most fundamental formal means of composition in classical music, poetry, and architecture. … Rhythm employs stress, contrast, reiteration, and grouping in architectural elements' (Tzonis and Lefaivre 1986: 118). This is the kind of jargon commonly used when designers creatively engage, or critically examine the hard city, visible forms and abstract spaces. But how is rhythm expressed in the deeper layer of our urban realm and beyond compositional architectural terms?

Henri Lefebvre's final book, *Rhythmanalysis: Space, Time and the Everyday*, published posthumously in 1992, points us in a fascinating direction, and partly answers this question. His text offers an insight into the historical and current relationships between time and space, as well as our behavioural role in this matrix. This makes for an insightful reading above and beyond its underlying Marxist perspective.[15] Lefebvre's socio-political argument is that 'Everyday life is modelled on abstract, quantitative time, the time of watches and clocks. Such a concept of time was introduced bit by bit in the West after the invention of watches, in the course of their entry into social practice' (Lefebvre 2004 [1992]: 73). This sets the tone for a dialectic that critiques a capitalist mode of production, whilst also underlining the temporal qualities of everyday urban life, which arguably helps us to understand the city in time-based, cinematic terms. Lefebvre differentiates between 'cyclical' and 'linear' rhythms, the former having a determined period or frequency (such as day and night or seasonal intervals), and the latter being defined by consecutive, almost identical intervals that links to human and social activity (ibid.: 90). He sees the difference between the rhythm 'of the self' and rhythms 'of the other' as coming from personal, familial or group activities that can be either voluntary or imposed by authority, and which might be rooted in ritual, political, religious or other forms of behaviour (ibid.: 99). These are also manifested as behavioural patterns in the city, and the simultaneity of diverse rhythms can also result in contradictions and resistance; polyrhythmic activities and spaces that express the 'struggle between two tendencies: the tendency towards homogenisation and that towards diversity' (ibid.).

Lefebvre alludes to the rhythms of a city that do not necessarily lie in the normal spectrum of our field of vision: 'No camera, no image or series of images can show these rhythms. It requires equally attentive eyes and ears, a head and a memory and a heart' (ibid.: 36). Whilst I do not wholly agree with this assessment, particularly in the light of the technical possibilities that digital film offers today,[16] he draws attention to the important sonic qualities of urban spaces that are normally obscured by the dominance of vision, and which connect to our emotional sense of space. Furthermore, he sees rhythms as a contextual measure: 'the music of the City, a scene that listens to itself, an image in the present of a discontinuous sum' (ibid.). This implied link between architecture and music is one that goes back to Greek and Roman antiquity, where architectural proportions link to harmonic theory in music. In his lectures given in Jena (1802–03) and Würzburg (1804–05), the German philosopher Friedrich Wilhelm Joseph von Schelling declared that 'architecture is actually frozen (*erstarrte*) music'.[17] Schelling formulated an entrancing insight into the inner nature of architecture: 'Architecture, as the music of the plastic arts, thus necessarily follows arithmetical relationships. … It is music in space … in a sense solidified music' (Schelling and Scott 1989 [1859]: 163–6;

original Schelling 1984 [1859]; see also MacGilvray 1992: 87). Similarly, Johann Wolfgang von Goethe calls 'architecture [a] "petrified music". Really there is something in this; the tone of mind produced by architecture approached the effect of music' (Goethe 1829 quoted in MacGilvray 1992: 87). Statements like this have inspired fascinating research. Michael Bright's *Cities built to Music* (Bright 1984), further explores the notion that classical architectural design principles are akin to musical theories. Besides, the study between the relationship of sound and space has clearly gained momentum. Books such as *In the Place of Sound: Architecture, Music, Acoustics* (Ripley *et al.* 2007) or *Essays on the Intersection of Music and Architecture* (Muecke and Zach 2007) consider how musical structure informs architectural form and how the tectonics of buildings and spaces can be thought of as musical instruments.[18]

One of the most interesting pieces of research with regard to the role of sound in spatial perceptions is rooted, as is so much of the work cited in this book, well within the twentieth century. R. Murray Schafer, who coined the term 'soundscape' in the mid 1960s, has become synonymous with an experimental research project entitled *World Soundscape Project* (WSP) that ran at Simon Fraser University in Vancouver during the late 1960s and early 1970s. From this emerged *The New Soundscape* (Schafer 1969), *The Book of Noise* (Schafer 1970) and *The Tuning of the World* (Schafer 1977), which, importantly, look beyond the notion of architectural aesthetics and representation. While Schafer and his team were initially interested in the study of sonic environments and especially noise pollution in the city of Vancouver, they later extended their investigations of soundscapes to rural villages. This pioneering work into the classification of noise, music and everyday sounds stands alongside the recently-released book *Sonic Experience: A Guide to Everyday Sounds* (Augoyard and Torgue 2005 [1995]). This encyclopedic and multidisciplinary textbook provides fascinating links between acoustics, architecture, urban studies and social and cultural theory, and insists on us having a greater acoustic awareness when in and transgressing everyday physical environments. Augoyard and Torgue argue that sonic effects find application on multiple levels with regard to inhabitable spaces. At a psychosociological level, the spaces we are surrounded by can be seen as a 'reservoir of sound possibilities, an *instrumentarium* used to give substance and shape to human relations and the everyday management of urban spaces' (ibid.: 8). Furthermore, at the level of urban planning, the city ought to be seen as a sound *instrumentarium*; in other words, 'constructed space itself shapes many sonic effects' (ibid.), which consequently requires designers and planners to show an awareness of it.

In summary, all of the aforementioned scholars who engaged in the theoretical discourse of the role of the frame in cinema (including Bazin, Altman and Aumont, and also much earlier Eisenstein) recognise the fundamental limitations of the screen, which stems from its two-dimensionality and, therefore, flatness. In the context of architecture and urban form, however, this hurdle is seemingly overcome as the framing of any scenario is always rooted in three-dimensional space. This changes the rules of engagement between the presumed spectator, for instance the walker or drifter, and, when the 'sequences' and 'passage' mentioned above are taken into account, it opens up the opportunity for new insights into the nature of cinematic architecture and urban spaces. At the same time, it is evident that investigations into the sonic quality of spaces lags behind the vast amount of visual studies of cities which either focus on mediated, two-dimensional spaces (in photography or movies) or as three-dimensional phenomena. This is surprising, as non-visual and particularly temporal properties of spaces and places, expressed though sound, rhythms and music, are important carriers of spatial information, and reach into our emotional disposition towards the spaces we encounter in our everyday lives. That the shaping and branding of an image of the city is intrinsically linked to the sonic quality of a place is frequently overlooked by architects and planners, as well as by marketing and place-making specialists. Altman notes that, with regard to a cinematic experience, sound cannot exist in a two-dimensional context because it 'is always recorded in a particular three-dimensional space, and played back in another [so that] we are able to sense the spatial cues that give film sound its personalized spatial signature' (Altman 1992: 5). It seems that much can be learned from these filmic lessons, and we could consider more spaces and places, not only for their visual but also their *sonic-spatial signature*. Film and digital video are undoubtedly useful tools to capture, analyse and generate spaces with clear temporal qualities in architecture in the future. With this in mind, are filmmakers better designers of architectural and urban spaces? This provoking proposition is, of course, nonsensical from a professional point of view, and yet, as we have seen with urban advertisement campaigns, sign-structures and other phenomena, cities are increasingly becoming visual constructs which, as Rattenbury mentioned earlier (1994: 36), are inhabited by a population that is deeply visually literate. It is an intriguing thought that, in the future, we might want to consult film professionals with a track record in the articulation of certain film spaces for comment or advice on how to increase the tactile, sensory or sonic qualities of architectural spaces. I wonder if it is only a matter of time before city councils and marketing executives catch up with this idea, and consult a film producer in questions of architectural design.

Chapter 6

Architecture and Urban Form as Cinematic Apparatus

> The dimension of the event is subsumed in the very structure of the architectural apparatus; sequence, open series, narrativity, the cinematic, dramaturgy, choreography.
>
> (Derrida 1997 [1986]: 325)

William Mitchell is, of course, correct when he says that 'Architecture is not primarily about seeing, but about dwelling and inhabiting' (Mitchell 2005b: 260), and no architect in their right mind would dispute this fact. So some may be surprised by the force with which architecture has been brought into the terrain of 'seeing', both in this book and in other debates. Guy Debord's concept of the 'society of the spectacle', Michel Foucault's notion of 'scopic regimes', Paul Virilio's strategy of 'deception and surveillance', Jean Baudrillard's model of 'simulacra and simulation' and Jacques Derrida's work on the 'La Villette project' are all examples of theoretical thinking produced in recent decades that regard architecture as a body or apparatus with a distinct visual dimension expressed in one way or another. Supported by this history, this chapter proposes yet another unusual perspective: can we view architecture and the city through the lens of a camera? My earlier proposition that architecture and the city can be regarded through film and cinematic concepts (such as 'sequences and events', 'movement and passage' and 'rhythm and sound') might at first glance be seen as a complex position. It is perhaps through practical examples that this hypothesis will become clearer. First of all, it requires a softening of our *hard* understanding of the perception of space and time in traditional architecture and planning, and I want to start by showing that, through film and moving images, we have come to terms with a much *softer* and *fuzzier* concept of space. We have learned to make sense of the spatio-temporal laws of the camera image, and this sense has arguably had a bearing on our perception of real space.

The minute we watch a motion picture, we are subjected to a fragmented reality that is full of temporal, spatial and geographic inconsistencies (creative geographies). These contractions, expansions and shifts of space and time are rooted in the nature of the medium. We readily accepted such ambiguities throughout film history and have, as Elliot Gaines indicates, learned to make sense of the camera image. Our brain stitches these shattered fragments effortlessly and seamlessly together (cf. Gaines 2006: 177). The question then is whether we can relate similar cinematic principles to define not filmic, but physical space. But, why should we bother about a cinematic approach to architecture and urban spaces in our everyday existence? From a design and planning perspective, we might soon need more dynamic thought models to meet the challenges ahead with regard to: urban planning, regeneration and branding; the design of public places and buildings; and a society that desires to inhabit places suitable for individual mass consumption. This requires that we insist on urban spaces that are: imaginative and not formulaic; engaging and formable rather than static; and so enjoyable that we see them as being too important to leave their shaping to public-private partnerships, international consortia and other stakeholders. The language of film and cinema is not only universally understood, but also creates emotions. We might want to ask the question of whether a cinematic approach to the design of architecture and cities – one that captures these emotions and actively engages us with our built environment – would allow us to transform spaces and give us the chance to see our environment through different eyes.

This has led to the notion that architecture and urban form can be understood as cinematic apparatus, which is a concept I hope to illustrate by directly relating my argument to the findings from the previous chapter. The headings that I used – 'Sequences and Events', 'Movement and Passage', 'Framing of Space' and 'Rhythm and Sound of Space' – were deliberately chosen to highlight four elements that are essential in approaching an answer to the question of how cinematic qualities find application in the art of buildings and spaces. Each of the four conceptual areas identifies not only a shared space or affinity between architecture and film practice but also points towards a *spatial quality* found in actual spaces. From this emerges the following simple thought model:

sequences and events	→	narrative qualities
movement and passage	→	spectator qualities
framing of space	→	optical qualities
rhythm and sound of space	→	temporal qualities

Certainly, spaces and places never exist as isolated tropes, and very rarely have only one of these qualities. Instead, we would expect that most spaces and places are made up of a combination of all four characteristics. This means, in practice, that a building or place that is, for example, high on optical qualities can be expected to also have narrative, spectator and temporal qualities (although they might have different weightings). This conceptual model, then, is not meant to concentrate on the boundaries and margins between respective characteristics, but should highlight the interconnectedness between all four areas. This non-exclusive stance implies a that space high in 'narrative quality' can be closely linked to, or indeed share a boundary with, other spatial characteristics. Further, one could also argue that all spaces and places have at least some of the characteristics outlined above and, as such, could be called more or less cinematic. While this is certainly a valid point, I hope to illustrate with the following examples that there are buildings and places in which one or more of these qualities are particularly pronounced.

Narrative Qualities

From classical times, throughout the Renaissance period and up to the present day, architecture has been known for having a communicative function that is often connected to the treatment of architectural form and façade. However, this alone is not enough to speak of a cinematic quality which can also be found more in the programming of spaces or its plan; in short, in the inner organisation of a building or city and its correlation to movement and time. Grounded in concepts of sequences and events (which relates to the work of Tschumi and others), some architectural and urban spaces can have a particularly pronounced narrative quality. It is important to point out here that spaces gain narrative characteristics because they denote social and cultural conventions. This comprises a system that provides logic for our interpretation of architectural form, as noted earlier by Gandelsonas. This means that narratives attributed to spaces are referential and prone to cultural differences, and clearly, spaces are not read by everybody in the same way. Spaces with narrative qualities are often metaphorical or even metaphysical in character. These spaces tell a story that circles around a particular theme. Peter Zumthor's pavilion at Expo 2000 in Hannover was a piece of architecture that pronounced, through its space, a strong underlying narrative. Built as a temporary structure from 2,800m^3 of larch and Douglas pine from Swiss forests and stacked on top of each other, the pavilion was meant to symbolise and represent Switzerland as an environmentally-conscious, sustainable and open country. Visitors were able to enter the pavilion from various sides, and then made their way through the maze-like space, following individual sequences of interventions and small events. Artists climbing overhead and musicians on the ground turned the pavilion into, literally translated, a 'sounding body' (*Klangkörper*) that offered surprises as people walked through the structure. The space, therefore, performed a narrative function as well as serving as a performance space. Zumthor's pavilion, a truly multisensory experience that also incorporated the fragrance of the freshly cut timber, became a storytelling apparatus; a space that created a transitory and ephemeral experience that, more than a decade after visiting, still prompts vivid mental images and thus underpins its cinematic quality.

Figure 6.1   Hannover. Swiss Pavilion at Expo 2000. © Jürgen Götzke.

Spectator Qualities

Spaces that are high in spectator qualities are spaces that tend to create a heightened awareness of the body in space, thereby generating a sense of *being* (*Dasein* in Heidegger's terms). This presence of the human body in space is normally achieved through movement, and is therefore connected to the act of *walking* (de Certeau) or *drifting* (Debord), which are inherently linked to a filmic and cinematic perception of space. At the same time, travelling through space – and this is where it links again to moving images – creates a form of mobile spectatorship, which can transform not only our perception, but also the quality of the space itself. Spaces with spectatorship qualities can be spectacular, but they do not have to be. It is often subtle, reduced and bare spaces that heighten our awareness of the body in space. Iain Borden, for instance, recently discussed the mundane space of the 'Limehouse Link' road tunnel in London's Docklands (Borden 2011). It is interesting to see that he compares the kinetic experience of driving through the tunnel with those depicted in cinema, through films such as *The Italian Job* (1969), *Ronin* (1998) and *I, Robot* (2004).

Spaces with spectator qualities are often linked to *activity*, in the form of bodily movement (e.g. walking, driving) and/or in our thoughts. These spaces become protagonists, in the sense that they inspire a person to *act* or

Figure 6.2   Berlin. Holocaust Memorial. © Keith Hamilton.

perform in a space, which is again a reference to the theatrical and filmic qualities of spaces mentioned throughout this text. In terms of the history of architecture, such spaces are conceptually rooted in the work of Choisy, Le Corbusier and Eisenstein and, as such, the principles behind the idea of the *promenade architecturale*. The world is full of well-known spectator spaces that express this quality to a lesser or greater degree. Frank Lloyd Wright's Guggenheim Museum (1959) in New York, for instance, is a wonderful example of a spectator space that is rooted in architectural modernity. However, for me two contemporary spaces that stand out and which have informed my hypothesis are both found in Berlin: Peter Eisenman's Holocaust Memorial (2004) and Daniel Libeskind's Jewish Museum Berlin (1999–2001). Both spaces create tremendous emotions through the meaning they carry as part of the programme, but also because they transform the social, cultural and political history of Jewish citizens in Berlin into an embodied spatial experience.

This effect was particularly palpable in Libeskind's Jewish Museum just after it was opened in 1999, with none of the exhibition artifacts on display. For little under two years, the building itself fulfilled a narrative function in which the visitors became more than spectators, and therefore an embodied part of the history of Jews in Berlin, communicated entirely through material textures, light, optical illusions, acoustics and the form of space. Unfortunately, only those readers who had the chance to see or rather *kinaesthetically* experience the space without the exhibition being installed can fully relate to the impact that the building had. Libeskind's

Figure 6.3   Berlin. Jewish Museum, interior corridors.

sloped floors, tilting walls, hard surfaces and sparse lighting contributes significantly to a bodily perception of this space. The sequential and illusionistic journey which the museum offers its visitors renders it a cinematic space par excellence. Yet again – and true to the fleeting nature of the cinematic image – these spaces have only endured for a short period of time.

Optical Qualities

Entrenched in theories of visual art and film and, by extension, through the arguments of Arnheim, Bazin and Aumont (as well as others not considered in the above discussion), architectural and urban spaces can have qualities that relate to visual and optical effects. Building components in architectural and urban design, similar to the boundaries and borders around a screen (in painterly as well as filmic art), can act as a frame. In the context of film, this divides the foreground from the background, denotes the difference between on- and off-screen space, and brings the focus of our attention to the content of the screen. The screen, in this metaphor, is liberated from the limits of two-dimensional flatness, as in the case of image-based screen arts, and can freely expand into the realm of a three-dimensional space. What I am proposing is grounded in the relationship between optical and architectural realities of space, as outlined in Vertov's *Kino Eye*; a concept in which the camera and lens that we know as metaphor in and for the film is seen in the context of architectural form and spatial practices. In building terms, optical characteristics tie up the concept of a cinematic

Figure 6.4   Helsinki city centre. An exit of a building frames an incidental urban narrative.

space, and are based on the notion that architecture is, as Beatriz Colomina points out in relation to Le Corbusier's *Villa Savoye*, an instrument for mobile seeing. 'The house is no more than a series of views choreographed by the visitor, the way a filmmaker effects the montage of a film' (Colomina 1992: 114). Moreover, as noted by Deriu, she states that the villa 'might be linked to an optical instrument that turned the mobile experience of space in a kind of editing process' (Deriu 2007: 38; see also Colomina 1992: 114). Such principles, which in this case are rooted in modernity, resonate equally in today's contemporary context. In situations where parts of a city – a gate, entrance or street – turn into a framing device, architectural form becomes akin to an optical apparatus that is filled with incidental narratives of every-day life situations.

In terms of architectural design, one building immediately comes to mind: Jean Nouvel's *Institut du Monde Arabe* (IMA) (1987). Built under the patronage of François Mitterrand as part of his grand scheme for Paris, Nouvel designed an innovative building whose exterior south façade acts as a photosensitive kinetic wall that is inspired by Arab latticework and the lenses of a camera. The building's façade functions as a mechanical aperture, which controls the incoming daylight in ways that technically and metaphorically treat the physical reality outside the building as an image. The High Line project in New York City, which is a collaboration between James Corner Field Operations (Project Lead), Diller Scofidio + Renfro and landscape designer Piet Oudolf, features optical elements in its design that do not require an active mechanism. Opened in 2009, the designers turned a former industrial landmark into an elevated public park that stretches for 1.45 miles along

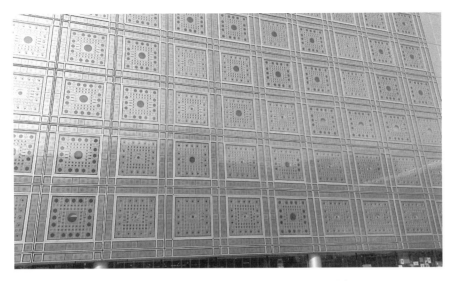

Figure 6.5　Paris. View of façade of *Institut du Monde Arabe*. © Radiuk.

Figure 6.6　High Line, New York City. © Brandon Baunach.

Manhattan's Westside. One section of the High Line features a seating area spanning over and offering views on to the street below which, when sitting inside the structure, functions as a cinematic apparatus that offers plenty of urban narratives. The opening in the structure frames the city underneath in an aspect ratio and high-angle perspective that is otherwise known to us through wide-screen crane shots from the world of cinema. Thus, although people are occupying an outside space, they are viewing the city in a cinema-like environment. Rem Koolhaas' *Casa da Música* (2005) in Porto, Portugal,

Figure 6.7   Casa da Música, Porto. View from inside.

Figure 6.8   Casa da Música, Porto. The entrance forms a wide-screen vista of the city.

commissioned as part of the city's celebration of being European Capital of Culture in 2001, has not only become a landmark for and key performance space in the city, but is also an example that illustrates how a contemporary piece of architecture can become an optical instrument for mobile seeing. The building, which is open to the public most of the time (even when no performance is scheduled), is designed in such a way that a series of rehearsal and other rooms sequentially meander around the large auditorium in the centre. Koolhaas allows the visitor to choose one of several possible journeys through the building, leading from room to room, and to openings in the façade. This carefully composed architectural promenade in a building that is otherwise largely enclosed, invites the visitor to see the city through bright openings, which act as cinematic widescreens through which the city is framed. He plays with further visual effects by using façade systems that at times give the impression of optical filters. The *Casa da Música* employs sinuously-shaped glass panes that distort and animate the view to the exterior in relation to the visitor's own movement along the façade. As if this is not enough in terms of cinematic quality, a visit to Koolhaas' building during a rehearsal or performance demonstrates how the entire building is a sounding body, which links to my next point.

Sonic Qualities

Architectural spaces have an infinite spectrum of sound characteristics. These stem from internal and external noises; sounds shaped by the geometry and surface quality of the space (such as reverberating footsteps inside a church, or music that permeates a building's interior as in the aforementioned case of the *Casa da Música*). Similar assertions can be made when examining the sonic quality of urban spaces. Richard Coyne notes that 'Urban life is saturated by sound, as if lived in continuous immersive soundscapes: the sound of a crowd, the hum of machinery, the roar of traffic', and draws attention to the ambient sound compositions of Iannis Xenakis, Steve Reich and John Cage, whose work provide us with a sense of sonic immersion (Coyne *et al.* 2010: 92). In doing so, he highlights important correlations between urban sounds and music. Chion, on the other hand, calls attention to the fact that cinema is not only an art of the image, but also that of an audiovisual illusion. He speaks of a so-called sound/image synchronism in which sound is an expressive and informative value that enriches the image (Chion *et al.* 1994: 5). He further notes that sound and image work reciprocally, by which he means that 'sound shows us the image differently than what the image shows alone, and the image likewise makes us hear sound differently than if the sound were ringing out in the dark' (ibid.: 21). Can these principles also be applied to the city? Augoyard and Torgue seem to think so and insist that 'no sound can be isolated from the spatial and temporal conditions of its physical signal propagation', which also means that the city's material and spatial characteristics of urban morphology can be related to acoustic instrumentation (Augoyard and Torgue 2005 [1995]: 4). This position is summarised by the concept of a space-specific, urban 'sound signature'.

> Let us listen to our cities. Is it not the very nature of the urban environment to make us hear, whether we like it or not, this mixing of sounds? Dull murmurs, machine noise, the shifting and familiar acoustic racket created by people – every urban moment has a sound signature, usually composed of many sounds together.
>
> (Ibid.)

Figure 6.9   Passers-by in Hong Kong's MTR.

Augoyard and Torgue address our exposure and engagement with ambient or on-location sounds, but more recently sonic influences from other sources are coming to the fore. Chion notes that, for the cinema, 'if a soundtrack resonates in our head by the means of earphones ..., these sounds will be perceived no less as coming from the screen, in spite of the evidence of our own senses' (Chion *et. al.* 1994: 70). This effect of the 'spatial magnetization of sound by image' in the cinema (ibid), arguably also takes place when we walk through urban space listening to sounds on our mobile phones or iPods. We have all observed, on the Tube in London, the Metro in Paris, the Mass Transit Railway (MTR) in Hong Kong or elsewhere on the streets of big cities, that commuters walk and listen to music over headphones at the same time. People often appear to be immersed in the music and seemingly navigate effortlessly, and on autopilot, through urban environments that are filled with other people. In technical terms, many mobile music listeners prefer in-ear headphones that are designed to hermetically seal off the ear from disturbing noises, which has proven to be a dangerous practice indeed.[1] What is interesting here is that when we listen to music on headphones while moving through a streetscape, we are shutting ourselves off from the sync sound of the city. It is this sound that holds important spatial clues; instead, we replace it with music coming from handheld devices. I would argue that this habit introduces a quasi soundtrack to urban spaces in ways that are not dissimilar from a movie experience. Devices such as mobile phones and iPods empower us to do what only film directors can normally do. We can choose the soundtrack that fits a particular space or journey instantly, and thereby create a cinematic experience in which music and urban space form a synchronism that is personalised and controlled by the individual. We know from the cinema what an overwhelming effect sound and music has on moving images and how audio can utterly transform a film. This, in turn, might hold clues to what effect headphones might have on our perception of space, time and its rhythm. Music then, plays an even greater role in everyday life and society. Indeed, it creates 'scenes' that, as highlighted by Tia deNora (2000), can be interpreted in both figurative and cinematic terms as spatial scenes that transform the experience of a perceived physical space.

Part III

Urbanity and Image

Chapter 7

Urban Product and Advertisement

If we talk of images, we mainly talk of figurative images, that is to say that everything is image … architecture itself is image … we understand it through the eye [vision] and it is above all a visual creation.

(Nouvel 2001)[1]

I would like to start this chapter with this sound bite from an interview with Jean Nouvel, in which he underlines his conviction that architecture not only consists of solid form but is equally defined by the immaterial or (as in this quote) is akin to an image altogether. He later substantiates his strong remarks by relating them to the role of urban advertisement in cities such as Tokyo: 'It is incredible to see so many neon publicity signs with bright, hyper-realist images crowning the city's tall buildings. This is a very strong reintroduction of image into a city' (ibid.). He uses the term *reintroduction*, which seems to refer to an ancient relationship between architecture and the image that arguably could be traced back to earliest cave drawings, Egyptian hieroglyphs, or the treatment of façades in the more recent history of architecture such as the Renaissance. Indeed, the assimilation of architecture and image – in other words, between the structure of the building and any ornament (pictorial or non-pictorial) applied to its surface – has been the cause for longstanding debates in architectural theory.

While Renaissance architect Leon Battista Alberti recognised the importance of the ornament in the context of the public secular building by saying that the 'graceful and pleasant appearance, so it is thought, derives from beauty and ornament alone' (Alberti 1988 [1452]: 155), he also established a principal hierarchy by saying the ornament is subservient to the building in the sense of being 'attached or additional' (Tschumi 2000: 171). In the nineteenth century, the notion of a structural rationalism began to permeate architectural debates. Led by theorists like Eugène Emmanuel Viollet-le-Duc and Auguste Choisy, they began to see architecture as a series of independent building parts. According to this line of thought, the architectural wall was considered a composite of non-load-bearing and load-bearing functions, dissolving it into cladding and support, which led to a rethinking of how ornamentation was seen in architectural design. In modern times, this architectural

Figure 7.1   Porto, Portugal. Large advertisement replaces building in an architectural sequence.

dialectic went as far as to completely question the right of the ornament to exist. We recall the Viennese pioneer of modern architecture Adolf Loos (2000 [1908]), for example, who drew attention to the unethical and backward-looking nature of ornament in the context of an exploitative bourgeois society. This context of social responsibility, as well as the availability of new building materials and methods of mass production, brought Peter Behrens, Walter Gropius, Le Corbusier and other protagonists of the Modern Movement to the ideological viewpoint that classical ornamentation on buildings was redundant.

Later in the twentieth century, with the rise of postindustrial consumer culture and its spread into the sphere of architecture, postmodernist theories (such as those put forward by Venturi and Scott Brown) redefined the relationship between architecture and signage. In stating that the 'graphic sign in space has become the architecture of this landscape' and by coining the term 'decorated sheds', they identified a strategic form of architecture in which buildings are reduced to being mere signs (Venturi *et al.* 1977: 88). While this assessment of so-called 'commercial vernacular' architecture (ibid.: 6) was developed in the context of the casino and motor car culture of 1970s Las Vegas, it resonates with the reality of many cities today, where the signage on buildings (e.g. outdoor advertising) can be seen as a form of ornamentation or, in some cases, the very purpose of the building.

As Warnaby and I have highlighted elsewhere (Koeck and Warnaby 2012), Turok's (2009) discussion of urban place differentiation identifies the built environment and amenities as an important set of place attributes that can contribute to urban distinctiveness in an increasingly competitive environment. This distinctiveness can stem from aesthetic appearance, functional utility or experience for users, and Turok reasons that physical structures 'are potent sources of differentiation given their obvious contribution to the character and sense of place, as well as its functionality' (ibid.: 23). However, this contribution will arguably be minimised if the structures themselves are partially or totally hidden or obscured in some way, for example, by large billboard advertising. Indeed, contrasting perspectives on – and approaches to – the obscuring of urban architecture by outdoor advertising can be seen with reference to the cities of Venice and Sao Paulo, which could be regarded as opposite ends of a spectrum in terms of the ideological and design principles relating to this aspect of the urban environment.[2]

In Venice, numerous historic buildings have been covered by giant advertising hoardings which hide scaffolding erected for restoration work (Kington 2010). In order to generate revenue for the city,

> ... a vast Lancia car has been parked on the front of the Palazzo Ducale. A giant Rolex watch has been draped over the Biblioteca Nazionale Marciana, also in St Mark's Square. And, by the Grand Canal the façade of the Ca'Rezzonico palazzo has been smothered with an advert for jeans.
>
> (Hooper 2008: 34)

The local administration in Venice has also allowed these advertisements to be lit at night which, according to the Chairman of the 'Venice in Peril' fund, takes away 'the wonderful darkness' of the city (Kington 2010: 11). The Italian government's heritage administrator in Venice, whose budget had been reduced by 25 per cent, responded to the inevitable criticism by saying: 'If the geniuses who criticize us give me the money for the restorations, I'll do away with [the giant ads] at once ... Otherwise, they should keep quiet. We don't have alternatives' (Hooper 2008: 34). However, this has not stopped some of the world's leading cultural experts from criticising these developments as violating Venice's UNESCO designation as a world heritage site by hiding many of the structures which are integral to the city's identity for tourists and residents alike (Kington 2010).

In contrast, in 2007, the city of Sao Paulo became the first city outside the communist world to implement a radical, near complete ban on outdoor advertising via its Clean City Law. Thus, billboards, outdoor video screens and adverts on buses were banned, and regulations introduced which drastically reduced the allowable size of storefront signage (Adbusters 2007). This has led to some unexpected – but ultimately rewarding – consequences, according to one Brazilian journalist:

It's weird, because you get lost, so you don't have any references any more … My reference was a big Panasonic billboard. But now my reference is an art deco building that was covered through this Panasonic. So you start getting new references in the city. The city's got now new language [*sic*], a new identity.

(Ibid.: 2–3)

This comment, relating to the means by which people orientate and navigate within urban environments recalls Lynch's (1960) well-established observations with regard to urban 'legibility' or 'imageability', which he considers an important function of well-designed cities. The legibility of the cityscape – defined by Lynch as 'the ease with which its parts can be recognized and can be organized into a coherent pattern' (ibid.: 2–3) – is a crucial aspect of urban design. By studying the ways in which people distinguish – and navigate through – urban landscapes, Lynch highlighted the importance of individual and collective cognition and perception of architectural patterns of a place. These investigations caused Lynch to conclude that cities are made from five, essentially architectural, constituents – paths, edges, districts, nodes and landmarks. Acknowledging that Lynch studied three American cities (Boston, Jersey City and Los Angeles) in the 1960s – at a time when billboards and mass advertisements were less prevalent – raises the provoking question as to the extent to which outdoor advertisements now constitute an additional element of contemporary urban legibility, and as such contribute to what Lynch considered to be good design.

Clearly, urban advertisement poses a new set of design questions for cities, which go beyond Lynch's concerns for spatial patterns and way-finding. For centuries, architects and planners followed design principles in which the façades of buildings determined not only the appearance of the building itself, but also contributed to a wider architectural ensemble and ultimately to an identity of place. This model required questions of architectural language or style, expressed by such design parameters as dimension, scale, openings, materiality and ornament, to be addressed by architects under the watchful eyes of planning officers and authorities. Yet today, all around the globe from Beijing to Prague to New York City, billboards and other forms of advertisement are being placed in front of existing façades, actively working against the intended design of carefully planned buildings. It would seem then, particularly in cases where advertisement boards have been installed *after* the building has been completed, the question here is not simply one of 'urban legibility'.

Guy Debord recognised modern society's increasing infatuation with signs and images, and the consequent formation of an urban spectacle in which 'the real world is transformed into mere images' and becomes a spatial commodity in a capitalist system of consumption (Debord 2002 [1967]: 8; see also Leach 1999; Kellner 2003). In his view, architecture and urban space have lost their role of contributing to good design or any function other than serving our need for entertainment, services and consumption. This, in turn, will lead to urban growth and ultimately to the 'explosion of cities into the countryside' (ibid.: 46). Despite such criticism, since advertising is often designed to appeal not to reason but to the emotions of the consumer, it could be argued that Sao Paolo's missing 'Panasonic billboard', mentioned earlier, also relates to a sense of place according to John Agnew's definition (Agnew 2002: 22; see also 1993), which emphasises the personal and emotional attachment people have to a place (see also Cresswell 2004; Tuan 1974).

In many cities today, outdoor advertising could be described as an after-thought in design terms. It is an aesthetic-economic trade-off, allowing local administrations to maximise a direct or indirect return (in monetary or in place marketing terms) that stems from advertising in urban landscapes. Yet, while such commercial interventions in public spaces may seem incompatible with principles of good design, it is an inescapable phenomenon which deserves further research. For instance, it raises the question of whether we should consider the placement of outdoor advertising as a design-related discipline, rather than seeing it a market-driven necessary evil and, in turn, whether we can design cities in such a way that advertising becomes part of a holistic urban design concept, rather than an afterthought? Conceptually, this might lead to a situation in which architecture in urban environments becomes a form of media itself, in which various ideological principles begin to overlap. Kenneth Frampton for instance, following the tradition of Gottfried Semper, notably saw the 'technological' and the 'scenographic' as two separate condi-tions in architectural practice – the latter representing 'abstract mystic or sym-bolic content as embodied in the surface' (Frampton 1995, 1983). Frampton gave this diagnosis in the 1980s and 1990s in the context of an emerging post-modernity in architecture. His response to the problem that 'the tactile opposes itself to the scenographic and the drawing of veils over the surface of reality' (Frampton 1983: 29) was to demand a tactile and tectonic response of architecture that would have the 'capacity to transcend the mere appearance of the technical in much the same way as the place-form has the potential to withstand the relentless onslaught of global modernization' (ibid.). It may be questioned whether this goal has been achieved in the last thirty years and, if not, whether the future integration of architectural design and outdoor adver-tisement might blur those well-established boundaries between the *technologi-cal* and the *scenographic*.

The above has drawn attention to contentious opinions with regard to the placement of advertisement in urban environments. What seems even more

Figure 7.2   Prague, Czech Republic. Large billboard mounted on top of building façade.

Figure 7.3   Liverpool. Large advertisement being mounted over entire façade.

controversial, however, is when our contemporary fixation on the *image* begins to challenge and contest the being, or in Heidegger's words, the *Dasein* of architecture. What happens when banners and signs in the city do not advertise products, films and services, but the city in which they are placed? What happens when architecture itself becomes a form of screen-based advertisement?

Chapter 8

Place Marketing: Urban Architecture as Image

Never have people been more the masters of their environment. Yet never has a people felt more deceived and disappointed. For never has a people expected so much more than the world can offer ... we have become so accustomed to our illusions that we mistake them for reality ... They are the world of our making: the world of the image.

(Boorstin 1992 [1962]: 4–6)

In the United Kingdom in 1998, Lord Rogers began to assemble a task force whose responsibility it was to identify the 'causes of urban decline' and to 'establish a vision for our cities, founded on the principles of design excellence, social wellbeing and environmental responsibility within appropriate delivery, fiscal and legal frameworks' (Rogers 2005: 2). A year later, the task force published the paper *Towards an Urban Renaissance*, which addressed the critical question of how to 'improve the quality of both our towns and countryside while at the same time providing homes for almost 4 million additional households in England over a 25 year period' (Urban Task Force and Rogers 1999: 7). The group identified five key areas, dealing with the sustainability/quality, management, land resources, financial investment and policy/political priority of urban environments (ibid.: 12–13), resulting in over one hundred recommendations for the UK government. In 2005, Rogers' short-term assessment concluded that 'English cities have established themselves as powerhouses in the UK economy and centres for cultural innovation' (Urban Task Force and Rogers 2005: 2). This raised the issue of the underlying importance of cities to the national economy. To ensure sustained economic benefits from cities, Rogers suggested that local councils should receive more rights to raise taxes and funds, and that Urban Regeneration Companies should be given the necessary powers to ensure that cities would continue to act as financial generators in the future (ibid.: 4).

Despite the ostensibly well-meaning aims of such initiatives, recent history has shown that this approach has led to an attitude in which cities in the United Kingdom are increasingly seen as a spatial commodity that needs to bring short-term return on investment. Many cities have chosen to focus their attention on cultural regeneration programmes, which, as Steven Miles notes, carries the danger of achieving the opposite effect, that is 'robbing them of their very identities and turn[ing] them into clones that tell us something profound about the nature of "consumerism as a way of life"' (Miles 2010: 2). City councils have sensed that their cities need to be advertised to national and international tourists and to capital investment markets. On the one hand, this puts cities in competition with each other, while on the other, the resulting investment attracts a generic consumer architecture – front façades that create a distinct indistinctness of urban centres. Regional centres, such as Liverpool, Birmingham or Bristol, suddenly see themselves not only in competition with each other, but also with international city destinations such as London, Paris and New York – places that have, for better or worse, already managed to form a strong city identity. As a result, cities are seen to be in need of *branding*, and branding is only effective in conjunction with marketing, particularly visual advertisement. Councils are spending considerable sums on logos and other graphics, posters and flyers, and even promotional films that showcase their cities as vibrant, dynamic, cultural and other 'buzz-wordy' centres. Since urban futures seem to depend on branding, it seems fruitful to make a brief excursion into the rich literature on marketing, advertisement and product placement.

Selling products in an increasingly advertisement-saturated and competitive environment is a complex and difficult task. Yet, regardless of how innovative, polished or expensive marketing strategies might appear, most of them rely on three basic principles to enhance the recognition of a product: *positioning*, *image creation* and *repetition* (Beasley and Danesi 2002: 49). Positioning deals with the market in which a product is advertised, image creation is important for later product recognition, and repetition aims to deepen this recognition and sustain the selling of a product.[1] I would argue that this three-part strategy is also employed in the advertisement of cities as places of investment and consumption, and that an interesting reading emerges if we apply these key principles to an architectural and urban context. Marketing specialists recognise with the term *positioning* 'the targeting of a product through appropriate advertisement for the right audience of consumers' (ibid.). This is familiar territory for regional development agencies, city councils and their respective place-marketing executives and managers. Urban regeneration programmes up and down the United Kingdom – and most likely also in other countries – promote cities to selected groups of people. City councils aim to attract external bodies, such as investors (e.g. for housing, corporations, national bodies) as well as tourists/visitors who choose places by the amount of spectacle they offer (e.g. cultural heritage, leisure, shopping). Judging by the amount of upmarket one-bedroom flats that are currently built in city centres (such as Liverpool, Manchester and other regional cities), a lot of marketing emphasis is also given to single occupants or couples: affluent recruits of a fresh urban knowledge economy. In other words, city marketing campaigns are geared towards shoppers of brand articles, customers of a rediscovered urban-cultural heritage, and speed-dating young professionals who enjoy taking part in a neourban tea/café culture.

The second principle, *image creation*, when seen in an urban context can have a double meaning. There is of course the important goal of creating an image to entice people to visit the city: the illusion of an overarching narrative. Examples include: Paris, the city of romance; Rome, the city of history; and New York, the city of crime. Certainly, the image of the city can be deeply rooted its cultural history and in this way be formed over a long period of time, but this does not mean that it is invariable or even fixed. James Donald notes, 'Unable to contain the unbound spread of London, Paris, Berlin, or New York in an all-encompassing image, we recall the city through metonymic images and fleeting events' (Donald 1997: 181). One can find, of course, evidence of unromantic spaces in and around Paris and ahistorical areas in Rome, but in terms of city branding the image of cities is often metonymic, exchangeable and reductionist. The image of a city can change quickly; we only have to think of the public perception of Berlin, which has undergone numerous transformations in the last eighty years. We can recall Berlin being variously a national socialist, divided, united, democratic and capital city. Such changes in the popular opinion of cities can happen rather suddenly, through for instance significant events that have a global relevance. Media plays an important role in the formation of a city image and creates regimes of representations, which Jonas and Wilson define as 'discourses of meaning that include whole sets of ideas, words, concepts, and practices' (Jonas and Wilson 1999: 38). Without intending to lessen the importance of other forms of media, it must be noted that film and television play a particularly important role in creating an image of the city. For example, the preconception by some that New York City is full of crime is both initiated and perpetuated by its sustained film presence as city in which crime takes place. The cinematic image then, has an influence on the perceived image of a city and can lead to situations whereby actual experiences on street level either confirm or contradict a previously held belief built up by film.

High-profile contemporary architectural projects – of the type encountered first in glossy magazine features, then in reality – can enjoy a status that is the secular equivalent to a site of pilgrimage, visited by devoted students, professionals and other admirers of good architecture and design. This magnetism has not gone unnoticed by city executives, whose ambition it is to bring media attention to their city and, in doing so, promote it as a place to visit. City councils and architectural professionals regularly refer today to the example of Bilbao, where a series of celebrated architectural interventions seemingly led to the capital city of the autonomous community of the Basque Country becoming a fixed point on the European cultural map. Using Bilbao as a case study, let us now turn to the third marketing principle, *repetition*. The so-called Bilbao effect, which is often wrongly attributed and reduced to the symbolic power Frank O. Gehry's Guggenheim Museum, was underpinned by a series of Strategic Plans for the Metropolitan Area of Bilbao (BM30), the first of which was approved in 1992.[2] The original plan focused at first on the hard city, that is on an architecturally-based regeneration, but following several reviews was eventually revised as a new, long-term plan that emphasised a qualitative approach towards urban regeneration. This revised plan recognised the need to invest in the softer aspects of urban revitalisation – such as the 'quality of life, universal education, access to information and knowledge, integration into global networks, the capacity to generate and attract new ideas and to innovate' – which would be necessary to promote Bilbao as a world-class city (BM30 2000: 6; see also 2001; González 2006: 847).[3] Unfortunately, Bilbao's success led to a series of copy-cat efforts in other European cities that aimed to replicate the positive effects by superficially imitating what could be 'seen' in northern Spain.

The visually appealing architecture of Gehry seems to have sparked an interest in the marketing revenue potential of landmark architecture designed by landmark architects. This short-term thinking relies on the belief that physical interventions in urban landscapes are, in economic terms, a universal remedy or (borrowing a term from David Harvey) a 'spatial fix' (Harvey 2001: 23–30). From Harvey's Marxist perspective, of course, 'the production, reproduction and reconfiguration of space have always been central to understanding the political economy of capitalism' and consequently the construction of landmark buildings amounts to little more than 'capitalism's insatiable drive to resolve its inner crisis tendencies by geographical expansion and geographical restructuring' (ibid.: 23–4). While Harvey's use of the term 'spatial fix' makes particular reference to an impulsive reaction, it also offers room for other interpretations. The Bilbao Guggenheim Museum demonstrates our *fixation* on the marketable and endlessly reproducible image quality of landmark architecture. The Guggenheim Museum has countless times been featured and replicated as the backdrop for product placements and advertisements in magazines and on television. With the Guggenheim, Gehry created more than a museum: he created a signature style – a titanium-clad and curvaceous brand product that can be bought on postcards in museum shops and which has been *repeated* in other places. Reincarnations appeared in the form of the Frederick R. Weisman Museum in Minneapolis and the Walt Disney Concert Hall in Los Angeles, demonstrating that Gehry's name as visionary architect and sculptor of places appeals to a wider group of people interested in 'selling the city'.[4]

It is evident, then, that Beasley and Danesi's three principles of product marketing (*positioning*, *image creation* and *repetition*) resonate strongly in the sphere of architecture and urbanity. In the light of city councils' mounting funding pressures and struggles for future survival, the increased commodification and spectacularisation of architecture and urban spaces – a concern first raised in debates of the 1960s and 1970s – seems today to be more acute and intensely discussed than ever (see, for example, Saunders and Frampton 2005; Landry 2006). Landry warns of the adverse effects of creating an artificial and economically-driven city image, specifically, the danger that people may not identify with it, which can cause the city and its citizens to drift further apart:

> Selling urban identity and the individuals within a city as a commodity is problematic given the differences between outsider and insider perceptions. When people do not participate in the story that is being sold about them, it creates resistance.
>
> (Landry 2006: 165)

While the above has begun to reflect on *image creation*, the following will examine this notion further in a simultaneously more literal and more radical way that finds concrete application in cities. Cities, after all, not only create images in our mind, as referred to with the examples of Paris, London and New York, but can themselves physically become three-dimensional image creations.

Architectural Iconography

It is an interesting phenomenon that until some years ago the term 'iconographic architecture' had a different meaning to how it is used today. The word 'iconic' seems to be used in rather inflationary terms in contemporary times. Before this is illustrated, however, it is worth bearing in mind that the term 'icon' (from Greek εἰκών *eikōn* translated as 'image') is historically rooted in the religious tradition of Byzantine art. Most of us are familiar with icons of the Christian Orthodox practice, with their gold-painted, stylised representations of religious figures. Slobodan Ćurčić recently curated an international exhibition of such art, entitled *Architecture as Icon: Perception and Representation of Architecture in Byzantine Art*, at the Princeton University Art Museum.[5] Ćurčić highlights in this exhibition that the representation of architecture and urban spaces played an important, yet 'completely ignored aspect of icons' in Byzantine art (Ćurčić 2010: 10; see also Ćurčić *et al.* 2010). Alongside the depiction of saints, Ćurčić argues, the representation of architecture and cities can have a central role in religious icons:

> Long dismissed as irrelevant background 'space fillers' for their idiosyncratic characteristics, representations of buildings and cities will be shown to be not the mindless 'decorative' insertions they were long considered but rather as playing active, substantive roles

that parallel and supplement the figures represented. Architecture, this exhibition sets out to demonstrate, *is also* the subject of icons in its own right.

(Ćurčić 2010: 10)

The term 'space fillers', in the context of iconography and architecture in Ćurčić's text, is an meaningful one to which I will return at the end of this section. But before that, I would like to ask what 'iconic architecture' means today. When using the term 'iconic' in the context of architecture, people normally refer to iconic buildings as structures that made a distinct or historical contribution to humanity, or at least the field of architecture. Leslie Sklair speaks of a relative consensus among experts as to what constitutes global architectural icons, citing examples such as the Egyptian Pyramids and the Sphinx in Giza, the Roman Pantheon and Coliseum, the Athenian Acropolis-Parthenon or the Taj Mahal (Sklair 2006: 42). For him, architectural 'icons' must have 'local, national or global significance and recognition or any mixture of these three' (ibid.: 37). In slightly more moderate terms, Pallasmaa sees 'iconic' realisations in architecture as 'buildings or projects which exemplify authoritatively and memorably a distinct formal approach' (Pallasmaa 2011: 83). Moving from the past to more recent times, there are plenty of architectural examples created throughout the twentieth century where, in the context of an emerging architectural modernity, the search for a new identity led to formally distinctive works. Examples include Gerrit Rietvelds's *Schröder House* (1924) in Utrecht, Le Corbusier's *Villa Savoye* (1928–29) in Poissy, Frank Lloyd Wright's *Fallingwater House* in Bear Run, Pennsylvania, and Mies van der Rohe's *Farnworth House* (1946–51) in Plano, Illinois. These examples, cited by Pallasmaa, could obviously be extended, yet it is significant that a good number of the same buildings are likely to be well-grounded in many western architects' minds due to their entrenched position in the academic canon of iconic twentieth century buildings.

At the beginning of the twenty-first century, it could be argued that the term 'iconic architecture' has suffered from some erosion. The time when the term was used in the context of landmark buildings produced exclusively by global architectural practices seems to have passed. Indeed, architectural offices led by Gehry, Foster, Libeskind, Alsop and others have in recent years come under increased scrutiny and received a fair share of criticism from the press. Commentators such as Giles Worsley wrote for *The Telegraph*:

Do we want icons? Or rather, do we want iconic architecture, big blowsy buildings that grab you by the throat and say 'look at me'? Buildings with curves, jagged edges, blobs, bulges, flashy materials and bright colours?

(Worsley 2004)

Yet it seems that in these fast-paced times, we have already passed this architectural moment. The 'iconic building' has become jargon that can refer to almost any type large-scale project, whose budget is large enough to require 'iconic' functions, whatever these are in a building. Every *regenerating* city today seems to demand an 'iconic' or at least a so-called 'gateway' building with 'iconic' functions. These subsequently tend to appear at random corners in the urban fabric, endowed with the purpose of polishing the image of a neighbourhood or city. It must be questioned whether such buildings fulfill the 'iconic' promise of making a lasting contribution to humanity. The reality is that big architectural projects are no longer designed under the authorship of a single architectural authority (the landmark architect of old), but by conglomerates of designers working for large developers. These pseudo-iconic structures often have a short life span, rendered ephemeral by their function as the image for a city or an institution, as such they tend to not fulfill Pallasmaa's definition of a building that exemplifies an authoritative and distinct formal approach.

The European bias of the examples cited above ought not to skew the picture. These examples and those that will be mentioned later in this chapter (some of which are found in the United Kingdom) draw attention to a phenomenon that is neither new nor exclusively European. There is of course no question that iconography is intrinsically linked to American architecture, in particular the debate on high-rise buildings. Due to the extensiveness of this topic, I would like to refer the reader to texts coming from a wide array of perspectives, such as Short's *The Urban Order* (1996), Neuman's *Architecture of the Night* (2002) or Langmead's *Icons of American Architecture* (2009). The following quote from Sinclair Lewis' novel *Babbitt* is also instructive, and could have been written equally as a commentary on European Capital of Culture activities today:

> Culture has become as necessary an adornment and advertisement for a city today as pavements or bank-clearances. It's Culture, in theatres and art galleries and so on, that brings thousands of visitors to New York every year and, to be frank, for all our splendid attainments we haven't yet got the Culture of a New York or Chicago or Boston – or at least we don't get the credit for it. The thing to do then, as a live bunch of go-getters, is to capitalize Culture; to go right out and grab it.[6]

> (Lewis 2002 [1922]: 261)

This quote ascertains that 'urban boosterism' (a term extensively used by Short and Sinclair) has a long tradition in the United States and has become part of the civic culture of capitalism today (Jonas and Wilson 1999: 37). According to Short, urban boosterism is deeply linked to the policies, economies and urban hierarchies found in the United States. It is attached to 'place-specific capital whose interests are bound up with the fortunes of a particular place' (Short 1996: 209–10; see also Short 1999). Emphasising the consumer-orientated and essentially capitalist function of iconic architecture, Sklair cites the concept of urban boosterism as 'the most common rationale for deliberately created iconic architecture' (Sklair 2006: 38). He also stresses a point similar to one examined earlier: 'Contemporary iconic architecture is now corporate to an extent that is historically unprecedented.' (ibid.: 42). Ironically, the corporate architectural 'icon' today has become Ćurčić's feared 'space filler' and regained the status of an irrelevant backdrop that has only recently been put aside in the study of Byzantine art.

Sign Structures

Each year since 1985, the European Union has selected a European city to carry the title European Capital of Culture, a programme intended to internationally recognise, promote and celebrate the culture of its award holder. Over the years, the programme has provided not only a platform for cultural events, but also a catalyst for financial investment in the nominated cities and, as a result, has come to be regarded as an opportunity to initiate a form of urban regeneration. The following will explore what I have termed *sign structures* in the specific context of Liverpool and its nomination as European Capital of Culture in 2008. Sign structures in this instance consisted of intensely coloured message-skins designed for Liverpool's 2008 celebrations. Prior to the events, Liverpool had been known for having a considerable number of vacant sites and empty buildings in the city centre, which arguably were not appealing to national and international visitors to the city. In response to this problem, the city council sponsored an initiative whereby buildings that were deemed undesirable by marketing strategists and the council would be entirely covered with a bright canvas on which cultural logos and other insignia were printed.[7] The surfaces of the screens were emblazoned with images of well-known architectural landmarks and notable cultural figures, such as (rather predictably) members of the Beatles. Paradoxically, these screens represent highly-visible signs of a meant-to-be invisible Liverpool, which seems to be based on a notion that is reductionist and contradictive.

The placement of large advertisement banners and protective screens on buildings in cities is common practice today – but the cited example is extraordinary in the sense that buildings were covered in their entirety and meant to function as images; a practice that is perhaps blazing a trail for other cities in a similar situations. Clearly, sign structures are not fit for human habitation, yet they have clear underlying design intentions and are meant to appeal to the aesthetic sense of the public. Sign structures started out as

Figure 8.1   Building on Liverpool's Strand before demolition (left). Concourse Tower, near Liverpool Lime Street Station, before demolition (right).

habitable buildings, yet somewhere in their evolution they have undergone a severe transformation in which the surface treatment of the building – its façade – superseded other aspects of the building in importance. This is not a new concept in architecture and we are reminded that during the Renaissance visionary architects and artists, such as Antonio Gambello and Mauro Codussi in Venice, or Leon Battista Alberti and Filippo Brunelleschi in Florence, equipped existing buildings with new façades for reasons that are not totally unrelated to the 'marketing of cities' that we discuss here. Notable in this regard are projects like the Roman basilica Santa Maria Maggiore, which saw extensions and rebuilds under the patronage of several popes and which, through its strategic location, was of particular importance in conveying a message of sovereignty (cf. Tafuri 1987: 67).[8] In our case, however, former buildings are transformed into something else, which raises profound questions as to what these large structures that occupy our shared public space actually are. Is it still a building, a piece of architecture, or simply a sign; and is it even appropriate in the twenty-first century that we draw a firm line between these norms?[9]

Ron Griffiths notes that 'place marketing works by creating a selective relationship between (projected) image and (real) identity' meaning that 'in the process of reimaging a city, some aspects of its identity are ignored, denied or marginalized' (Griffiths 1998: 53). Paul Jones and Stuart Wilks-Heeg conclude that the branding of cities goes hand-in-hand with an 'objectified, static, and necessarily narrow vision of a much wider, messier social reality' (Jones and Wilks-Heeg 2007: 204). Both observations find confirmation with these sign structures, where the reference to the city itself is highly selective and carefully crafted. This means also that sign structures are not architecture, but instead urban objects serving the place marketing of the city, relying on a mechanism that fosters 'a selective relationship between (projected) image and (real) identity'. In fact, the skin itself is designed to disguise and obscure the presence of a physical reality, thereby attempting to create a second-order simulation; a *simulacrum* that blurs the boundaries between reality and representation.[10]

Charles Burroughs remarks that the 'analogy of architecture and language is habitual', particularly in the context of late-medieval and Renaissance architecture (Burroughs 2002: 94). Thus, architecture, especially that of Brunelleschi, can be viewed as a materialisation of a system of communication that 'may resemble language' in terms of structure (i.e. grammar) or effect (i.e. rhetoric) (ibid.). Both the Renaissance city and the postmodern city, particularly with regard to the treatment of the façade, are places of *image production* whose differences lie in the mode of *delivery* and *consumption*. Whereas the Renaissance concepts of space are arguably based on a single-perspectival – a more static form of expression – the postmodern city operates on a layered, fragmented and palimpsestic mechanism. Hence, while the articulation of architecture and cities relied in the classical sense on permanent visible architectural signs that denoted private and public functions, such an acquired knowledge of place is compromised by impermanent sign structures, buildings and spaces that have lost their original function. Irrespective of any aesthetic judgment, the bright colouration of the banners can be seen as a rupture to the legibility of the urban fabric, directing attention to lines of sight that are not necessarily rooted in the *habitus* of a place. The new function is that of a sign that in semiotic terms (as in the example of Liverpool's Capital of Culture banner) is linked to what Roland Barthes called *myth*.

> [Myth] has turned reality inside out, it has emptied it of history and has filled it with nature, it has removed from things their human meaning so as to make them signify a human insignificance. The function of myth is to empty reality.
>
> (Barthes 1972: 142–3)

A myth 'essentially aims [at] causing an immediate impression' and is often made up of 'incomplete images, where the meaning is already relieved of its fat, and ready for a signification, such as caricatures, pastiches, symbols, etc.' (ibid.: 130; see also Warnaby and Medway 2010). As such, knowledge of place is no longer acquired through a series of visible buildings and spaces embedded in socio-spatial forms, functions and practices, but instead by image-generated myth that arguably can 'distort' an evolved urban legibility (ibid.). It seems fair to say that sign structures can take on a symbolic, if not iconic, role in the way they represent the city to the exterior world. Clearly, the aesthetic appearance of the structure is loaded with symbolic images of cultural icons, yet the structure itself does not seem to have the characteristics of an icon

Figure 8.2   Screenshot. *Brazil*. © Embassy International Pictures.

according to Sklair. He argues that iconic buildings 'tell us where we are, at a glance' (2006: 40). Indeed, while it is significant that the Liverpool structures qualify as being place-referential, their appearances being directly linked to a place – in this case a particular city – they do not take on the role of a global icon that is recognised beyond regional or even national boundaries.

If it becomes common practice in cities to cover up entire buildings, or what Frampton might call the 'drawing of veils over the surface of reality' (Frampton 1983: 29), cynical minds might want to ask whether this method of urban renewal is the new 'urban renaissance' and could be expanded to larger parts of the city – in other words, is there a limit to what the public would accept to be exposed to an artificial sense of reality. Such grotesque thoughts are in fact not entirely unexplored territory, at least in the context of film. Terry Gilliam reminds us in his film *Brazil* (1985) that the Ministry of Information, ruling a world increasingly dominated by bureaucracy, has the power to billboard entire streets, so covering up devastated postindustrial landscapes – necessary, apparently, to induce a sense of order in a world that has completely gone to pieces. One wonders if Gilliam dreamt of urban renewal programmes, such as those found in Liverpool and elsewhere, where the windows of entire streets of terraced houses earmarked for demolition are boarded up with signs and symbols of culture-led urban regeneration.

Street Canvases as Temporal Signs

We are all familiar with the sight of scaffolding on buildings and the large semitransparent nets or canvases that are sometimes attached to them. When we look back twenty or thirty years, most of these canvases simply served to check the fall of hazardous material and dust, in other words to protect the public while the building was under construction or repair. In recent years the sight of these canvases has notably changed; the materials used have become more sophisticated and the surface treatment has become more heterogeneous. Different categories and types of canvas-clad street scaffoldings have developed, and a once-inconspicuous element of urban reality – that had primarily utilitarian functions in the past – now fulfils multiple public duties.

The most common type of canvas-clad scaffolding has retained its function as a protective layer within the building industry. However, its appearance has considerably changed. Where in the past a builder might have used the canvas to display a company sign, we find today that companies entirely unrelated to the construction business print or attach large advertisements on to the screen. Most of us are familiar with such practices, which means that we can concentrate on another form of construction canvas. In historically- or commercially-sensitive environments, the canvases or nets rarely consist of monochromatic fabrics, but are often specially printed to precisely emulate the façade of the building they cover up. Examples of this practice can be found in the tourist-frequented pedestrian zones of almost every European city. The seemingly limitless scale and level of detail that can be achieved with these printed screens was demonstrated, for example, by the Munich *Residenzmuseum* at Max-Joseph-Platz, whose façade had been entirely covered up for the duration of its renovation. Pedestrians who passed by the historic building seem pleased with the fact that they had not to face the appearance of a building site. In fact, at historical buildings such as the *Residenzmuseum*, foreign tourists can be observed posing in front of the screen simulacra as if it were the original. What is interesting in this context is the sense of realism towards which these façades seem to strive. In Prague's Old Town Square, a building site was so realistically lit at night, with the shape of the windows cut out of the canvas so that the interior light could protrude the fake Baroque façade, that virtually no difference to the real building was detectable from a distance. It was only on closely approaching the building that a few wrinkles in the canvas disturbed the illusion of a solid façade – but even this went unnoticed by most visitors to this city square, who waded between the masses of other tourists and the semblance of an intact historic architectural ensemble.

What urban situations such as the ones described above have in common is that the images attached to the scaffolding are intended to give the impression of a completed building, thereby creating a three-dimensional illusion of a continuous space. By using software that can highlight even the smallest of details in materials and shadows, full-scale photorealistic images are produced, making it possible to create depth where there is none. The canvas in

Figure 8.3   Prague. Baroque façade covered up by canvas.

this instance fulfils multiple, temporary functions, such as: protecting the public from disturbing building works (falling materials and dust); providing visual continuity for the duration of the reconstruction; and presenting an 'image' of the future state of the building. While local residents might benefit from their presence indirectly, the investment in such screens is particularly meant to create an unspoiled experience for the economically important visitors to the city. While the above-cited projects are essentially temporary measures to preserve or reinstate an existing architectural condition, the following examples deal with buildings that are absent altogether.

Such variations of urban interventions by the means of scaffolding and screens can be found in Berlin, where dramatic political events – not just since the fall of the Berlin wall – left deep marks in the urban fabric of the city. A notable district in this regard is Berlin Mitte, situated between Unter den Linden and Leipziger Strasse. Here can be found, for example, the *Berliner Stadtschloss* (Berlin City Palace): Berlin's prestige project for which concrete yet controversial reconstruction plans exist. While some interest groups are keen to rebuild the palace (damaged by an Allied air raid in 1945 and later destroyed), other parties simply cannot imagine the reconstruction of this gigantic neoclassical complex. Not only is the site deeply imprinted with the recent memory of the *Palast der Republik* (Palace of the Republic), the seat of the East German government under Erich Honecker which was built after the Berlin City Palace was demolished, but also the fact that most Berliners simply have no recollection of the *Stadtschloss* as an intact building at this location. This lack of public imagination and visual reference is

Figure 8.4   Berlin. Bauakademie and Schleusenbrücke, *c.*1915 (left) and today (right). Photographs taken by Hermann Rückwardt (left) and Pazit Polalk (right).

addressed by a comparable scheme on a site nearby. The project in question is Karl Friedrich Schinkel's famous *Bauakademie*, the former technical and architectural school of Berlin built 1832–36, damaged during the Second World War and completely demolished by the East German government in 1961–62.

While the wisdom of the city of Berlin investing in the reconstruction of this historically-important building was still being discussed, a group of influential people took extraordinary steps to visualise the building on the site. In order to promote the reconstruction of the building, a small section of the brick façade was built at one corner of the site by students, while the rest was completed as full-size model made from scaffolding and PVC canvas to mark its volume and position.[11] The side of the simulated façade facing Schinkelplatz includes a projection screen that is used for the evening screening of films. The printed impression is so realistic that people passing by on Unter den Linden can hardly see that structure is an empty shell. The illusion is perfected by advertisement banners, such as those sponsored by Mercedes Benz, that are seemingly hanging from the features of the building's façade. Needless to say other advertisement campaigns have followed, using the popularity of the well-known project and, thereby, ideologically linking the campaigns with Berlin culture. The future of the *Bauakademie* is still uncertain at the time of writing this book. However, several offers by private investors and corporate housing associations to purchase the site from the city with the promise of reconstructing the building have given new impetus to the public discussion.

Another piece of urban plastic surgery lies at Leipziger Platz in close proximity to Postsdamer Platz. Leipziger Platz original served as Ceremonial Square for Friedrich Wilhelm I of Prussia. By the 1920s it had become an important focal point in the cultural and economic landscape of the city, featuring boulevards, parks, restaurants and department stores. Many buildings

Figure 8.5   Berlin. Leipziger Platz with Wertheim department store. Photograph taken by Waldemar Titzenthaler in the 1920s.

along the square were destroyed in the Second World War, while in the 1960s the division of the city at this point destroyed the last remnants of its former glory. After the unification of the city in 1989, Berlin put plans in place to develop the area around Potsdamer Platz and Leipziger Platz. In the case of the Potsdamer Platz, the masterplan was designed by Renzo Piano and the results of these undertakings are well established, although opinions regarding the success of their implementation remain divided. The situation around Leipziger Platz, being overshadowed by the Postdamer Platz development, does not enjoy the same prominence in the public realm, but it is a good site for the study of scaffolding architecture. After the fall of the Berlin wall, plans were drawn up for reconstruction of the square, retaining its octagonal shape and filling it with new buildings. When standing at the edge of Potsdamer Platz and looking east towards Leipziger Platz, we are presented with an extraordinary view.[12]

On the left side, facing Ebertsstrasse, a new building under construction is covered with printed PVC canvas of the type previously mentioned, making the building look complete and almost hyper-realistic. Towards the north-eastern corner of the square lies the last missing and very important piece in the jigsaw puzzle known as the Wertheim site. The building previously occupying this site was the famous Wertheim Kaufhaus; a department store that was once considered to be one of the most luxurious of its kind

Figure 8.6   Berlin. Leipziger Platz looking east.

in Berlin, whose name – if not the building itself – is remembered by many Berliners.[13]

So what do we see today if we look at this site? From a distance we see a multi-storey façade, giving the impression that a newly-developed building has completed the reconstruction of the square. The façade of the building looks picture perfect, blending in quite seamlessly with most of the other buildings around both squares. Only very observant pedestrians – mindful readers of this book perhaps – get a sense that something is not quite right with what we are presented. We might get a hint that its appearance is merely a cover-up for yet another building still under construction beneath. But nothing could be further from the truth. The full picture is only revealed when walking down Voßstraße, behind Leipziger Platz, which most people would not do. The entire structure, as well as another building on its left, is nothing more than a gigantic scaffolding, 105m wide by 38m high. The extensive scaffolding work has only one function: it serves as coat hanger for a printed image facing Leipziger Platz. The site – which has for years been the subject of legal disputes, financial crises and changing architectural proposals – will soon be occupied by a retail, hotel, entertainment, restaurant and residential complex. In the time leading up to this decision, the canvas served the Berlin authorities as a visual simulation of an architectural proposal by architects Kleihues + Kleihues and, in effect, showcased a completed geometry of the square. The printed screen functions to suggest a structure of volume and depth, where in actuality an empty landscape would apparently disrupt the visual perception of the site.

Figure 8.7   Berlin. View on to scaffolding from Voßstraße.

Figure 8.8   Behind the scenes of *Mon Oncle*. © Gaumont Distribution.

The *Bauakademie* and Wertheim examples, like some of the other cases mentioned earlier, illustrate that inner-city urban sites can have a quality that is not unlike that of a theatrical or filmic set design. In fact, the Leipziger Platz case recalls still photographs taken on the set of Jacques Tati's *Mon Oncle* (1958), where large-scale models of modern architectural office blocks are brought into play. In both cases, representations of architecture, which have no architectural functions in the traditional sense, are used to create a sense of place. It could be argued that the full-scale sets in Leipziger Platz are just as unreal or inauthentic as the architectural setting created in Tati's film. This notion of the city showing traces and trends of gaining a theatrical or even stage-like quality will be further explored in the next chapter, alongside the question of whether, perhaps, the spatial forms of media discussed here can lead us to think about the city in terms of a narrative and scopic regime that is multicentric; one that is not determined by a rationalised, utilised space within a fixed Cartesian system, but instead by a *transitory* and *immaterial* perception that is not unlike that of the dominant socio-cultural force in the twentieth century – film.

Marshall McLuhan (1964) coined the phrase 'the medium is the message' by which he means that 'the personal and social consequences of any medium – that is, of any extension of ourselves – result from the new scale that is introduced into our affairs by each extension of ourselves, or by any new technology' (McLuhan 2006 [1964]: 107). Translated into the sphere of iconic architecture, sign-structures or street canvases, this means that it is these new expressions of urban architectural form (spatial media) – the medium, and not necessarily their content (form, imagery, expressions) – that is 'the message'. Consequently, this *spatial media* is the driving force that 'shapes and controls the scale and form of human association and action' (ibid.: 108), which, in other words, can have a profound social effect or lead to a change in public attitudes. I would therefore argue it is important in the future that we are vigilant in recognising the importance of new forms of *spatial media* appearing in urban landscapes, as they can tell us much about the nature and attitude of our urban existence on a larger scale.

Chapter 9

Film Advertisement and Urban Spaces

Today the most real, mercantile gaze into the heart of things is the advertisement. It tears down the stage upon which contemplation moved, and all but hits us between the eyes with things as a car, growing to gigantic proportions, careens at us out of a film screen. And just as the film does not present furniture and façades in completed forms for critical inspection, their insistent, jerky nearness along with being sensational, the genuine advertisement hurls things at us with the tempo of a good film. Thereby 'matter-of-factness' is finally dispatched, and in the face of the huge images spread across the walls of houses, where toothpaste and cosmetics lie to hand for giants, sentimentality is restored to health and liberated in American style, just as people whom nothing moves or touches any longer are thought to cry again by films.

(Benjamin 2008 [1928]: 173)

In his 1928 essay *One-Way Street* (*Einbahnstraße*), Walter Benjamin compares the force with which gigantic advertisement boards hit the onlooker on the street of the modern city with the shock effects the film can have for the cinemagoer (Benjamin 1928).[1] The following will show that there are today again interesting correspondences to be observed between the visual culture of film and advertising – particularly with regard to spatial territories. At first glance, film space and urban space appear to be two distinct settings, each occupying its own separate dimension, one that is virtual and the other physical. However, on closer inspection there are signs that constituents from both spheres, normally anchored in one or other of the spatial dimensions, have crossed their boundaries. We are more familiar with movement in the direction from *solid to film*, in which real people, places and stories can of course dwell in film space. In the other direction, however, from *film to solid*, we are less consciously aware of such dimensional crossings. Film stars have for a long time appeared in urban space in the form of film posters or advertising banners. We take for granted sharing our urban environments with George Clooney, inviting us to drink more Nespresso coffee. And soon Angelina Jolie, who has just signed a contract with Louis Vuitton, will be showcasing fashion products in our streets. We notice the screen presence of these movie celebrities for what they are; not ordinary people, but actors whose personality is known to us only from our film and other moving image experiences. The image-based intervention of such stars in cityscapes, then, is linked to the roles they play and the filmic narratives that we know from the movies. While the advertisement-based presence of film stars in urban landscapes might be seen as a banal example of how film has infiltrated urban space, other, more recent phantasms are far more sophisticated.

A particularly fascinating phenomenon is the point of intersection between film and cities occupied by new film marketing campaigns. The costs of international film productions have steadily risen in recent years, with big-budget Hollywood productions reaching costs of $150 million or more. While the digital revolution has led to an exponential growth in small or micro budget films (cf. Finney 2010: 114) – technology that had allowed films to be made more quickly, more easily and thus more cheaply than even twenty years ago – the same cannot be said for the top end of the film market. In fact it seems that, at least when it comes to disaster movies in which cities and urban visualisations play an important role, the need for high-end digital animation work has added notably to the overall production bill. Such films include *212* (2005, $200 million), *King Kong* (2005, $207 million) and *Spiderman 3* (2007, $258 million). The bankruptcy of film giant Metro-Goldwyn-Mayer Inc. (MGM) in November 2010 is just one high-profile example of the tremendous pressure on studios to recover their production costs at the box office as quickly as possible. Rival production companies, particularly in the North American Theatre market, closely monitor and compete against the level of popular success achieved by each others' releases, that is, who is and who is not among the top-grossing pictures in the crucial first box office weekends.[2] This has led to a number of inventive ways in which production companies advertise their film productions and in which film and urbanity share a common space.

Cloverfield (2008)

One of the most impressive advertising campaigns for a film in recent years was for the Paramount production *Cloverfield*, directed by Matt Reeves and notably produced by Jacob J. Abrams – the creative mind behind *Mission Impossible III* (2006), *Star Trek* (2009), *Lost* (2004–10) and other film successes. The film, in which monsters threaten to destroy downtown New York, can be described as a documentary-horror movie, filmed using the first-person perspective of cinema-verité-style camera work. While neither the theme, setting nor plot of the film is entirely new, Paramount executives and producer Abrams decided to advertise the film through both traditional and innovative, non-traditional marketing strategies, for which they developed two distinct campaigns. The cost of the Hollywood production was relatively low at a reported $25–$30 million (Finney 2010: 138). Shooting began in relative secrecy in the spring of 2000, with the first teaser of the film being shown in cinemas a few months later. Unusually for such a trailer, no titles were given, no cast, no director; only the released date '1–18–08', which served at the same time as a synonym for a website (cf. Finney 2010: 136–7; Allen 2008: 93).

While a second, more revealing trailer, television advertisements, posters and other material appeared at a later stage,[3] from the beginning it is evident that Paramount harnessed the power of well-timed and diverse marketing strategies that would rely largely on online social networks and communities. Allen (2008: 93) quotes *Cloverfield* in his book on marketing strategies as an exemplary model in which a film was advertised substantially through so-called viral marketing techniques, whereby an awareness of and excitement for the film was created using social networks, websites, word-of-mouth and other self-replicating viral processes. Worth noting is the way in which Paramount created a sense of realism in the advertising campaign using, for instance, fake international news reports posted on YouTube.[4] This and other techniques clearly illustrate how *Cloverfield*'s advertising campaign aimed to blur the boundaries between fiction and reality, resulting in a promotional mode that coincides with the style of the movie itself.

It is of course not surprising that a production such as *Cloverfield* used web-based media to advertise the film, and other examples using a similar approach could be cited (e.g., *The Blair Witch Project*, 1999). But what is remarkable about these virtual/viral campaigns is how they penetrated and gained sub-stance in real architectural space. Numerous *Cloverfield* blogs appeared on sites such as Facebook, where users heatedly exchanged ideas as to what the film might be about.[5] Parallel to that, Paramount began to place billboards showing the film's title alongside a cleverly-composed image campaign for the film. The billboards made particular use of the spatial iconography of New York City, again a strategy that is not new and indeed shows considera-ble resemblance to the poster for *The Day After Tomorrow* (2004) showing a headless Statue of Liberty and the skyline of Manhattan (cf. North 2010: 85). These large-scale billboards and banners were placed at strategic locations on the East and West coasts of the United States, such as Times Square in New York City and at the corner of Cloverfield and Olympic in Santa Monica.

What happened next is remarkable. Online bloggers organised and embarked on billboard spotting tours with the objective of finding the *secret* locations of these advertisements, and dedicated web communities celebrated any finds of the film's giant signage with enthusiasm. What this shows is that, by animating people to look out for film imagery in cityscapes, a film such as *Cloverfield* has cleverly engaged with future box office customers of the film. As a further manifestation of the film in the landscape, a beheaded Statue of

Figure 9.1 *Cloverfield* billboard on Cloverfield Boulevard. © Dennis.

Figure 9.2 *Cloverfield* billboard wrapped around a storage facility in Los Angeles. © Dennis.

Liberty several metres-tall and known from the movie posters was placed was placed in front of Grauman's Chinese Theatre in Hollywood and Paramount Studios for the premiere of the film.

Importantly, the success of the campaign relied on active engagement, as highlighted by David Baronoff, new media executive at J. J. Abrams' Bad Robot Productions: 'We asked, how can we start telling the story of this movie right away and make the audience active and not passive?' (Brodesser-Akner 2008: 58). This led to the idea behind the film being circulated widely well before the film was released, a phenomenon that John Ellis calls the 'narrative image' of the film. 'The narrative image is

Figure 9.3 *Cloverfield* billboard on which passers-by have commented on the film (left). © Sean Ganann. Replica of Statue of Liberty at Paramount Studios (right). © Dennis.

decidedly less than the whole film: it is the promise, and the film is the performance and realisation of that promise' (Ellis 1992: 30; cf. North 2010: 78). It is arguably this *narrative image*, built up in our minds, and the corresponding mobilisation of people to actively seek out the film's enigmatic clues – which were partly *hidden* in the real city – that contributed to this redefinition of the boundary where a virtual campaign stopped and the physical space of the city began. On release, *Cloverfield* achieved one of the biggest January takings at the box office in film history, grossing *circa* $40 million in the first weeks (Finney 2010: 138) and by 2008 had topped $152 million worldwide (Brodesser-Akner 2008: 58).[6] The film is reported to have generated a gross income between $80–100 million (ibid.: 138; Allen 2008: 94). Not bad for a movie that, as mentioned in the beginning, cost a reported $25–$30 million.

District 9 (2009)

Cloverfield is not an isolated example of how film and cities share a common narrative space. The Sony science fiction thriller *District 9*, directed by Neill Blomkamp and produced by Peter Jackson and Carolynne Cunningham, employed another promotional campaign that is worth closer examination. The film was written by Blomkamp and Terri Tatchell and produced to a production budget of $30 million. The scenario begins with extraterrestrials having become stranded in a hovering spaceship over Johannesburg in South Africa, whereupon the government, which is keen to exploit their advances in technology, confines the aliens in non-human, slum-like refugee camps in a restricted area known as District 9. The title and plot make explicit reference to real historical events that took place in an area known as District

Six; a black residential neighbourhood in Cape Town, to which over 60,000 residents were forcefully relocated by the apartheid regime in the 1970s. Cinematographically, the film contains highly-realistic computer graphics that are paired with hand-held, news-style photography, aiming to create an eerie sense of realism. It was shot on location in Chiawelo, Soweto, an area that is best known for its real life battle with slum housing, unemployment and other serious problems. The film relies on the stereotypical portrayal of racial prejudice, which led, for instance, to the film being banned in Nigeria for the unjust portrayal of Nigerians as the ruling crime gang in District 9.

Critical press reports in South Africa and elsewhere shed light on the obvious danger of a large Hollywood production temporarily invading and profiting from Chiawelo as a setting, such as by the exploitative use of cheap extras (Smith 2009a, 2009b; *The Guardian* 2009). However, conversations with residents who lived in Johannesburg at the time when *District 9* was filmed paint a somewhat different picture. The choice of the location for the picture in and around Johannesburg was welcomed in particular by the younger population. Some locals felt a sense of pride that a Hollywood production gave Johannesburg its 'cinematic' seal of approval – irrespective of the fact that it was portrayed as the site of a neo-apartheid, anti-alien government. As in the case of Paramount's *Cloverfield*, Sony Pictures' *District 9* was launched with an extensive viral advertising campaign that took place partly in virtual space (e.g., websites, Facebook, Twitter) and partly in real space (e.g., New York). The film's main website not only shows the trailer of the movie,[7] but also functions as a knowledge centre of unprecedented depth, providing all sorts of information around the fictional scenario of aliens having populated planet earth; although, as the interactive map shows, they seem to be largely spotted in North America. The *District 9* web campaign includes elaborate maps, satellite imagery, training videos, safety downloads, employment opportunities, behaviour recommendations and more; it even streams a simulated live feed with 999 calls reporting non-human sightings in North America. But this is only part of the picture. Related sites, such as Multi-National United (MNU),[8] the 'global leader in technology and innovation' offer an online world of their own, in which the user and prospective *District 9* cinema-goer can dive into a strange near-future reality of a global corporate firm that has benefited from alien technology. As if this was not realistic enough, the *District 9* viral campaign acknowledges that any world – fictional or real – needs opposition. And so the online experience also offers a bi-lingual website (human/non-human) that is supposedly hosted by an antagonistic group calling for equal rights for non-humans.[9] Perhaps unsurprisingly, given the lurking legal ramifications of launching fake yet ultra-realistic doomsday scenarios, the terms of use issued by Sony Pictures for

Figure 9.4   *District 9* billboard at Times Square, NYC. © Rachel Berardinelli.

Figure 9.5   *District 9* advertisement on bench in Sherman Oaks, CA. © Alex Billington (left).
District 9 'Humans Only' warning sign (right).

these websites are almost as elaborate as the websites themselves. The character of this campaign brings to mind Orson Welles' radio adaptation of H. G. Wells' novel *The War of the Worlds* (Wells 1898), broadcasted in 1938 with preceding 'news bulletins' which gave the impression that an actual Martian invasion had taken place.

The second element of the campaign, as mentioned earlier, took place in real space and is of particular interest here. In Andrew Hampp's *Advertising Age* interview with Jeff Blake, chairman of Sony Pictures worldwide marketing, and Marc Weinstock, the studio's marketing president, both highlight the central importance of non-conventional marketing tools, some of which reach out into real space. The film's approach to marketing in cities provides a particularly rich case for the argument that *cinematic* narratives have impact on the quality of urban spaces. According to Weinstock, *District 9* 'was launched with a viral outdoor campaign on benches and kiosks featuring a silhouette of the film's signature prawn-like aliens and a 1–800 number' (Hampp 2010: 10). Weinstock's quote largely understates the actual dimension of *District 9*'s outdoor ventures. Sony launched a national and international advertising operation throughout dozens of large urban markets (cities) in the United States, Europe and elsewhere. Posters and other visual material, graphically designed like caution signs warning of aliens in public spaces, were not only placed on benches and kiosks, but also on buses, cars, underground trains, highways, indoor malls, telephone boxes and even public toilets. What this campaign demonstrates is the growing trend in film advertising towards the cinematisation of urban space and the corresponding amalgamation of virtual and real spaces. *District 9* achieves the latter by using the above-mentioned techniques of websites, Tweets, and YouTube films, as well as so-called QR-tags. These two-dimensional barcodes were printed on pavements, banners and posters, allowing the public to download movies and other server content directly to their smart phone displays.[10]

Did Sony's investment pay off in financial terms? The film opened simultaneously in over 3,000 theatres in the United States and Canada on 14 August 2009. It was produced for $30 million and, after an impressive weekend opening gross, generated a domestic income of $115 million (Hampp 2010: 10). The amount spent by Sony on the advertisement campaign has not been disclosed by official sources. The marketing of the film won numerous prizes for its viral outdoor campaign, including eight awards at *The Key Art Awards*, sponsored by *The Hollywood Reporter*, for outstanding achievements in the world of advertising. The invitation offered by one of the *District 9* associated websites to 'explore the District 9 Movie experience' reveals the nature of film marketing today. Movies are increasingly offering a cinematic experience that is infinitely more than a cinema or other screen-based experience; it is a multidimensional practice that can reach deep into public space (solid and virtual) and can modify the quality of what we perceive as real urban space.

Conclusion: The Near Future of Cinescapes

URBAN STAGE PHENOMENA

It is to be noted that a deserted street at four o'clock in the afternoon has as strong a significance as the swarming of a square at market or meeting times. In music, in poetry too, the silences have a meaning. Isn't Venice the example par excellence of this? Is this city not a theatrical city, not to say a theatre-city, where the audience [i.e. public] and the actors are the same, but in the multiplicity of their roles and their relations?

(Lefebvre 2004 [1992]: 96)

City as Theatre: The Staging of Architecture

As long as there have been cities, there has been a correlation between the concept of an open space and that of a theatre. Early notions of public places that also had representative and performance functions go back to the *Agora* of ancient Greece and the *Forum* of ancient Rome. The Athenian Agora, built around 600 BCE, had clearly-defined architectural boundaries (e.g. walls and colonnades), and fulfilled civic as well as commercial functions (Moffett *et al.* 2004: 60–1). When considering the range of different activities that took place in such an open square, it becomes clear that the Agora was, in ancient times, much more than merely a place for the exchange of commercial goods. The Greek term Agora (Greek: *Αγορά, Agorá*), commonly translated as 'place of assembly', denotes in ancient Athens a public square that played a central role in the educational, political, religious, philosophical, social and cultural life of the city. It is easy to see how the spatial setting for these functions can relate to that of a theatrical space, particularly because the nature of the aforementioned activities require a degree of 'performance', in the form of holding debates, the enactment of civic or religious rituals, or the promotion and selling of goods. Although only open to freeborn men of a higher social class and with considerable wealth, the Agora was a place of *assembly* and *exchange*. In fact, this double connotation is rooted in the etymology of the Greek term Agora, being from the Greek verb *αγείρω*, meaning 'to gather' or 'to bring together'. This stresses a historic civic, cultural and performative function, whilst, in a contemporary context, the word for marketplace (αγορά) and the verb 'to purchase' (αγοράζω) indicate that the Agora is a place of commercial exchange. It is interesting to see how this terminological shift in meaning is not only valid in an ancient Greek context, but also resonates with the reality of contemporary inner-city centres today, where public spaces have marginalised civic and emphasised retail functions. This is not to forget, of course, that there is a direct link between the Agora and the theatre, as its open spaces were also used for theatrical performances and dance (ibid.: 61).

Corrado Ricci observed that the 'first Greek stage was nothing but a platform more wide than deep and raised about two metres above the level occupied by the audience'. He further noted that the background of ancient theatre 'was nothing but a canvas coming forward at the sides and above, forming a kind of canopy' (Ricci 1928: 231). In contrast, the Italian theatres took significant steps towards a greater consciousness of performance space and resulted in more sophisticated design. In one of the most historically important writings on architecture, the *Ten Books on Architecture* or *De Architectura* (*On Architecture*), written around 15 BCE, Marcus Vitruvius Pollio (born *c.* 80–70 BCE, died *c.* 15 BCE) recognised the importance of the theatre. In the fifth book, he describes the architectural and spatial characteristics of the classical Augustan theatre, in terms of its layout, construction, acoustics and other properties, and compares it with those found in Greece. However, for many years the theatre played a subordinate role in public life, and it was only during the Renaissance period that many classical motives and values resurfaced, enabling the theatre to gain a renewed appreciation. This is evidenced in a number of texts, notably those by Leon Battista Alberti and the influential Italian writer and intellectual Pellegrino Prisciano (1435–1510). Both Alberti, in *De re aedificatoria* (*On the Art of Building*) published between 1443 and 1452, and Prisciano, in his unpublished *Spectaculum* of 1490, report on the vital role that theatre plays for the social and political welfare of citizens in society (Tylus 2000: 662). Prisciano mentions that

> ... those ancient and wisest of Greeks were the first, and after them the Italians, to institute theatres in their cities, to provide not only recreation and pleasure to their people, but a good deal of profit [*utilitate*] to their states.
>
> (Prisciano 1974 [1490]: 53; see Tylus 2000: 662)

The Renaissance period was marked by extraordinary artistic talent, technical achievement, power struggles and patronage, which brought forward remarkable examples of architecture, sculpture, painting and other arts. A characteristic of such works is not only its masterly execution at an artistic and technical level, but also its sophisticated narrative quality, which was particularly evident

Figure C.1   Fra' Carnevale, *Ideal City*, c. 1480–84.

in the drawings, paintings and frescos produced during this period. Piero della Francesca, Francesco di Giorgio Martini and Fra' Carnevale's works on ideal-ised cityscapes portray the city as both a rational and visionary construct in which stories are to be told.[1] The imagined urban situations, such as those presented in, for instance Fra' Carnevale's *Ideal City* (c. 1480–84), show the city as an empty stage on which observers can imagine themselves to be part of a narrative of an ideal, utopian urban life that is perhaps to come.[2] The theatrical stage-like paintings of Ambrogio Lorenzetti,[3] on the other hand, are often filled with people. Vladimir Mako notes on this: 'The city imaginary as scen-ery reveals in that way important aspects fundamentally linked to the story performed within it' (Mako 2008: 1). Mako sees, in literary visions and pain-terly representations of the city, sceneries that are more than just an aesthetic experience. They are metaphorical in nature and reveal the underlying narra-tive character of an urban space: '… the city imaginary as scenery is actually involved in the performance of a specific idea, as an important part of its essential character, rather than as pure decorum' (ibid.). This illustrates that imagery played an important role in public life during the Renaissance and imbued both architecture and art. Manfred Tafuri refers to this in his study of the Rome of Nicholas V to Giannozzo Manetti, by saying that the 'use of images and architecture as legitimation of the authority of the church of Rome in the eyes of the poor is a theme that emerges forcefully' and finds evidence in the use of 'allegorical images, rites and visual effects orchestrated in the heart of Rome' (Tafuri 1987: 63). In view of an apparent emphasis on a meta-phorical and allegorical visual and architectural culture, it is perhaps unsur-prising that Tafuri, who carefully studied the underlying civic, political and economic narratives of Renaissance Italy, asks the question: 'What else is architecture but a "theatre" of rationality?' (ibid.: 71).

The importance of the theatre in a western cultural context is further emphasised during the Baroque era, a period in which scenography advanced from a little-appreciated craftsmanship to a stagecraft of pan-European demand.

This shift can be attributed largely to three generations of artists in the northern Italian Galli da Bibiena family, who dominated European stagecraft throughout much of the seventeenth and eighteenth centuries.[4] Working for and in some of the most prestigious opera houses of the time – including those in Munich, Prague, Vienna, Bayreuth, Dresden and Berlin – Giuseppe, Carlo and other members of the Bibiena family developed elaborate stage backdrops that offered the audience a more realistic theatrical experience and placed stage design within the architectural dialectic of the theatre itself. This shows that the theatre was a potent space in the city, with influence that reached far beyond the boundaries of the stage. The theatrical developments during the era of the Bibiena family paved the way for significant changes to the relationship between the audience, the performance space and the stage, which transcended the nineteenth century and beyond. It was the work done by Giuseppe Galli Bibiena on the Margravial Opera House in 1744 which arguably drew Richard Wagner's attention to Bayreuth, and Reid Payne argues that, prior to Wagner and the Duke of Saxe-Meiningen (who had a particular passion for music and the theatre):

> … there is little evidence that anyone voiced the opinion that the [theatrical stage] set-ting did not really fit the tone of the play or opera or that they contributed in any real way to the totality of the production.
>
> (Payne 1993: 1)

All this changed with Wagner, who saw the relationship between his music, the stage and the performer not as superficial, but as intrinsically interconnected. Wagner, known as the great innovator of modern theatre, had an ambition to revive the unity of the arts of Greek tragedy, and developed the idea of the *Gesamtkunstwerk* (Kattenbelt 2006: 30), a concept that strove for realism through a perfect and immersive illusion. Consequently, Wagner intended to use his music as a means of reconnecting the head (through poetry) and the body (through dance) (ibid.: 30). This required profound changes to the way in which theatrical experience was staged for the audience, and in practical terms led to the notion that the orchestra, scenographer, director, costume designers and the remaining company should work together to deliver a single theatrical experience. In the case of the Bayreuth Festspielhaus, opened 1876, this meant that the orchestra pit was partially positioned under the stage and thus hidden from the view of the audience, who themselves were sitting in darkness (ibid.: 30). In fact, it could be argued that Wagner's theatrical concept in Bayreuth was proto-cinematic, whereby an aurally (music) and visually (stage design and action) modus operandi immersed the audience in the narrative world pre-sented on the stage. It also shows that Wagner realised that the immersive act of theatre (or, in this case, the film theatre) is neither solely acoustic nor visual, but one that is multisensory and connects the body and the mind.

In summary, the Renaissance was a time when the 'Italian city-states created the model of political organization that spread across Europe and found representation on the stage' (Kuritz 1988: 55). This interpretation can also be applied to the Baroque period, with Evers and Thoenes stating that Giuseppe Galli Bibiena, in *Architetture e Prospettive* (1740–44), elevated the 'synthesis of painting, architecture and scenography to a form of art in its own right, which had its greatest effect in the "staging" of architecture in the service of absolutist power.' (Evers and Thoenes 2003: 158). The same can be said about Richard Wagner, whose work was much admired by the leaders of the National Socialist regime, who had keen ambitions to translate the energy and dominance of Wagner's musical and theatrical work into a spatial manifestation of the Third Reich, both in terms of territorial expansion and the physical transformation of cities. In contrast to this, as will subsequently be explored, in the twentieth and twenty-first centuries it was no longer the theatre that played a heightened role in city life, but instead I argue that urban spaces and places have themselves begun to be viewed as theatrical spaces with their own narrative qualities.

City as Stage: The Theatre of Social Action

Erving Goffman, in *The Presentation of Self in Everyday Life* (1959), uses the metaphor of the stage as a way of showing how we all apply stage-management principles to our everyday lives. Although his text is not a study of urban life and its phenomena, it is tempting to relate his work to the environment in which most of us live: cities. Phil Hubbard applies these principles, and compares Goffman's 'stage' with the city. He summarises Goffman's position by stating that his work gives a 'detailed "theatrical" description and analysis of process and meaning in street interactions, suggesting we are on a "stage" when we are on the streets, constantly aware that we are presenting ourselves to an audience (of strangers)' (Hubbard 2006: 18). Both constituents of urban life, the stage (the city) and the stage action (our *being* in the city) are, of course, closely linked and can be traced back, according to Paul Makeham, to 'the historical traditions of classical architecture and civic participation' (Makeham 2005: 154). The Greek term *polis* makes reference to the ancient Greek 'city-state' being cognate with *polites*, or citizens, and, in this context, living in the city means more than simply being in or occupying a shared place. Instead, by participating with others in a complex social, cultural and political system that is integral to place (cf. ibid.: 154), we become citizens in a metropolis. Beginning with a quote from Lewis Mumford, I would like to draw attention to two areas: the theatrical and dramaturgical dimension of urban landscapes; and the role we play in them as everyday users.

> The city fosters art and is art; the city creates the theater and is the theatre. It is in the city, the city as theater, that man's more purposive activities are focused …
>
> (Mumford 2007 [1937]: 87)

In this text, Mumford explores the sociological nature of the modern city, describing it as a 'geographic plexus' that is a 'theatre of social action, and an aesthetic symbol of collective unity'. If we assume, as he asserts, that the modern city 'creates the theatre and is the theatre' (ibid.), then we can speculate that the manifestation of an urban place can be linked to some form of *narrative scenario*. Analogous with the theatre, the narrative quality of space may be defined by the social activities taking place (stage action) in a spatio-visual backdrop (stage set) that constitutes the formal qualities of the city. This is echoed by Jonathan Hale who notes that 'Countless times in the course of a normal day, similar "acts of theatre" take place, with architecture as an ever-present backdrop playing its part in the drama' (Hale 2000: 214). Some architects and planners might contest the notion that architecture is a mere backdrop to activity, as it implicitly questions the value and role of good design, but are architects responsible for the creation of narrative scenarios at a spatial level? While we might want to agree that it is the work of a designer to *set the stage* for social interactions, it would be fatal to suggest that architects should orchestrate the activities taking place in an urban realm.[5] Such an approach to urban planning failed spectacularly on many levels in the 1960s, not at least because an exclusive design process failed to identify with and give ownership to the local population. Architectural and urban design today and in the future will need to create flexible and adaptive spaces.

Why, then, is it important to consider the theatrical merits of a city and what sort of properties do both spaces have in common? Christine Boyer answers these questions by saying that: 'Both the theater and urban space are places of representation, assemblage, and exchange between actors and spectators, between the drama and the stage set' (Boyer 1994: 74). She argues further that 'theatrical and architectural space are both cultural prisms' through which we can experience 'social reality', and she sees the city and the theatre as 'viewing mechanisms that metaphorically spatialize reality' (ibid.). This is a useful point of departure as it illustrates that not only the theatre but also the city can be seen as a scopic regime through which we engage in social and spatial dimensions. The theatre-city is then an agent that enables us to have a collective narrative experience of either real or mediated everyday life situations. In this model of thought, the visible and physical form of cities – its architecture and infrastructure – can engage citizens in a sort of narrative act.[6] On this point, Mumford notes that:

> The physical organization of the city may deflate this drama or make it frustrate; or it may, through the deliberate efforts of art, politics, and education make the drama more richly significant, as a stage-set, well-designed, intensifies and underlines the gestures of the actors and the action of the play.
>
> (Mumford 2007 [1937]: 87)

Amongst other things, this quote highlights that Mumford believes the theatrical sensation of the city can cause people to have an active role in such space. Being active in a space changes the dynamic between that space and the people in it, and this argument aligns with that of Charles Landry, who refers to urban rituals (such as festivals which transform the city into a stage) as one of the methods of creating 'meaningful experiences' (Landry 2006: 180). Landry states that 'The urban theatre festival in Rome claims the territory of the city, transforming city spaces into stages. It invades random streets and surprises the public, not countenancing indifference' (ibid.: 181). Consequently, citizens become active agents that have an effect on the perceived form of the city. This means that if we look at the concept of the city as a stage, it is clear that the concept is meaningful only insofar as it denotes the idea of the city as a performative space; a space over which people take ownership. Such active engagement begins to contour urban space and thereby has palpable effects on the perceived reality of the city. This idea is succinctly expressed by Jonathan Raban:

> For at moments like this, the city goes soft; it awaits the imprint of an identity. For better or worse, it invites you to remake it, to consolidate it into a shape you can live in. You, too. Decide who you are, and the city will again assume a fixed form round you.
>
> (Raban 2008 [1974]: 2)

I would therefore argue, when engaging with the city in ways discussed in earlier chapters (such as in moments when we recall our own filmic experiences), Raban's words become a palpable reality. The city goes soft and begins to shape itself around our cinematic memory, or in other words, the city that exists in our minds begins to transform the city under our feet.

Writing in the late 1930s, Mumford asserted that the modern city can provide a stage for citizens and strengthen and emphasise their gestures like those of actors in a play. At this time, cinema had already made the reverse analogy with actors in a film behaving as if they were on stage, and thus providing the context for a reading of modern spaces. Man Ray's enigmatic film experiment, *Les Mystères du Château de Dé* (1928–29), shot in the *Villa de Noalilles* (1923–28) which was built by celebrated avant-garde architect Robert Mallet-Stevens in hills above Hyères in south-eastern France, exemplifies how acting out of, and a unique physical engagement with, this space animates a modernist building so that a new impression of it emerges. Man Ray's film features a series of surrealist figures in masks, who perform seemingly coincidental movements that recall ballet or sport both inside and outside the villa. The movement of these mysterious figures – which are reminiscent of the mannequins exhibited at the *Exposition Internationale du Surréalisme* at the Galerie Beaux-Arts in Paris in 1938 – begin to map the various spaces in the film, and thus give a multidimensional experience which brings to the foreground the sensual qualities of the architectural spaces in the villa which would otherwise be hidden behind the medium of film.[7] In one sense, the movement of these strange, faceless figures becomes an aesthetic symbol of Mumford's collective unity and translates the architectural spaces of the villa into macroscopic and indicative examples of fictional urban space. The context of the film's production is discussed in Helmut Weihsmann's detailed study, and he argues that there are 'two principal ways of perception of space in cinematography – the realist (pictorial) and the abstract (synthetic) approach' (Weihsmann 2010: 268). Similarly, by offering a unique visual intersection between L'Esprit Nouveau architecture and theatrical engagement with it, Man Ray's *Les Mystères du Château de Dé* provides the opportunity for an abstract reading of the represented profilmic space.

Consequently, the theatre and the city rely on a design that is thoughtful and supports wide-ranging narratives. Just as a theatre might have a repertoire of plays, a variety of seasons and themes, so a city has a repertoire of events and activities that occupy the foreground at various times. The theatre can raise serious questions for the audience, and engage theatre-goers in a critical discourse, whilst also being at times entertaining and fun, daring and imaginative. Arguably, cities and urban spaces should share these qualities, yet they are often underdeveloped or absent from the homogenised urban reality that dominates contemporary city centres. The stage is the focal point in theatrical productions, and a successful stage design draws people into the story. The same seems to be true for urban spaces. Urban narratives can hold spaces together, on a macro or a to micro level, and spatial situations, streets, districts and cities should be designed and planned in a way that allows such narratives to develop.[8] This may provide ways to shape cities and urban spaces which invite their inhabitants or visitors to actively engage with them. Spaces in which we are allowed *act* are likely to become places to which we attach stories; and it is these spaces that leave an impression on us, becoming memories to which we will eventually return.

City as *mise-en-urbanité*

If we consider the visual intensity that cities present today, through the presence of various forms of urban advertisement, and in particular through sign structures and street canvases, one wonders if these could be interpreted as mere requisites of a theatrical or cinematic play in which the city acts as a stage set for narratives that are directed by various interest groups. It seems possible to make a terminological analogy between such urban phenomena and film, but to do so we need to make a brief excursion into movie-making. While early film pioneers, such as the Lumière brothers, the Skladanowsky brothers or Thomas Edison, shot their films primarily *on location* in the streets of cities, George Méliès, coming from a theatrical background, became famous for shooting his films in a controlled studio environment with custom-made sets. Méliès' films were often comical filmic adaptations of popular and fantasy stories.[9] He understood stage design as a means of concealing his studio space and thus could create the illusion of a spatial atmosphere that complemented the narrative content of the scenes being shot.[10] In other words, Méliès showed a great consideration for the *mise-en-scène* – a term derived from theatrical practices and adopted by the film industry and relates to all the elements of production that are *put into a scene*. While architectural elements of the *mise-en-scène* might share a formal resemblance to those found in reality (such as a painting of a building or street), they do not normally fulfill the function they depict and are thus subservient to the spatio-temporal rationale of the plot. The same can be said for sign structures and street canvases, which means that these urban phenomena can be understood as parts of a full-scale set design. The primary function of these signs and urban infill – analogously *mise-en-urbanité* – is to support a narrative which rests on the imagination of urban marketing specialists and other interest groups.

Perhaps we can think about such phenomena in terms of Landry's idea of 'borrowing the landscape' (Landry 2006: 166). Thus, instead of tourists visiting cities in order to 'borrow someone else's landscape for their own personal pleasure and needs' (ibid.), the authorities behind the creation of the *mise-en-urbanité* can be seen as borrowing *our* landscape for the purpose of selling commodities that serve those needs. If we adopt this view, it seems plausible that recent years have seen a change in the way we judge the interplay between authentic and theatrical space. What does this mean? MacCannell discusses stage sets in the context of Disneyland and other entertainment parks, and notes that 'the only reason that need be given for visiting them is to see them – in this regard they are unique among social places; they are physically proximal to serious social activity, or serious activity is imitated in them' (MacCannell 1973: 597). This reveals an interesting postmodern, territorial shift. Inauthentic, set-like spaces are no longer confined to dedicated areas and are often located in a peripheral urban context, such as Annaheim or Orlando. They are spaces with a similar quality to those seen in inner cities today, with 'serious social activity' taking place within them, and becoming part of everyday life. Thus the danger lies in that we may confuse the much older notion of the *city as stage* with the much newer phenomenon of the *city becoming a stage set*. In the examples cited here (sign structures and street canvases), the city becomes a stage set which has to be viewed critically to avoid the obvious danger of getting the balance wrong (cf. Landry 2006: 167).

The concept of a *mise-en-urbanité* fits the picture we have about postmodern landscapes. David Harvey, for instance, sees in the ephemeral, eclectic and fragmentary nature of consumerist spaces the trademarks of a typical postmodern landscape:

> We can identify an albeit subterranean but nonetheless vital connection between post-Fordism and the postmodern penchant for the design of urban fragments rather than comprehensive planning, for ephemerality and eclecticism of fashion and style rather than the search for enduring values, for quotation and fiction rather than invention and function and, finally, for medium over message and image over substance.
>
> (Harvey 1989: 13)

From this we might conclude that the concept of cities having stage- and stage-set-like characteristics is pronounced in postmodern theory, and is confirmed through contemporary spatial reality by a manifestation of forms, functions and social interactions related to cities and architecture. While this might be the case, we should not forget that perspectives examined on the relationship between the city and theatre or urban and theatrical spaces were rooted in debates on modernity and affected by (as in the cases of Mumford and Ray) a critical engagement with architecture and urban spaces. Mumford's text and Man Ray's film seem to suggest that the *acting* of people in spaces, whether they are real or filmic, have an important bearing on the way we perceive or remember these spaces, and how they become real in our memory. Both men recognise the importance of the presence of the human body in the telling of stories and the development of narratives in a spatial context. This implies that the environment in which the majority of the population lives, in other words, cities – spaces that we either know reasonably well or that we inhabit and call our own – are deeply defined by a narrative relationship with space, and are therefore also defined by the way in which we engage with them bodily.

URBAN AUTHENTICITY

> A camera image defines space through objects, depth of field and interference of what is not in the frame, but is presumably part of the field of vision of the camera operator, and assumed to be understood by the audience.
>
> (Gaines 2006: 177)

Challenges Ahead

In the last 150 years, the industrial revolution brought a transformation from rural to urban environments and from small towns to cities across the western world. In 1900, London, Paris and New York were at the top of the leader board for being the largest city in the world. Believing that cities were places of opportunity and prosperity, more and more people decided to live in and adjust to the urban conditions presented in these cities. In the first decades of the twentieth century, cities in Europe, America and elsewhere suffered two world wars, financial crisis, overpopulation, environmental and man-made threats, unemployment, hunger and other ills, which exposed the vulnerable and malignant side of dense urban environments. Nevertheless, a century later, we seem to be more convinced than ever that living in cities offers indisputable benefits that outweigh such concerns. For the first time in history, more than half the world's population resides in cities and it is expected that this percentage will rise in the future. By 2030, the United Nations expects that over 8 billion people will occupy Earth, almost 5 billion will live in cities, with urban growth concentrated in Africa and Asia. Worryingly, according to the same source, 'most of the new growth will occur in smaller towns and cities, which have fewer resources to respond to the magnitude of the change'.[11]

While many of us are aware, through the media, of the rapid and precarious processes of the urbanisation of megacities on these continents, fewer people have a sense of the effects that such increases in population will have on cities worldwide, including those in the western world that are, as yet, less affected. This is unsurprising as, until about ten years ago, a good number of the 1980s and 1990s generations live in peace with relative material wealth across much of Europe, North America, Canada and elsewhere, and have experienced predominantly the benign condition of cities. This has engendered an image of the city that is characterised by economic, social and cultural rewards. Although there is reason to believe that this will change, with signs visible in the form of terror threats (New York, Madrid), street violence (Paris, Athens) and political upheaval and urban unrest at Europe's borders (Tunis, Cairo, Tripoli, Minsk), there appears to be little alternative to living in cities. However, we finally seem to have arrived at a point – many years after Georg Simmel warned of the dangers of the metropolis to our mental wellbeing (Simmel 2010 [1903]; original Simmel 1903) – where we have adapted to the complex challenges provided by dense urban environments.[12]

We inhabit city spaces that most believe to be a reflection of what might be called *urban reality* and trust that we know them fairly well. However, the physical nature of cities is, as Robert E. Park and other urban sociologists have demonstrated, more than a physical construct alone. As discussed in previous chapters, 'the city is [also] a state of mind' (Park 2005 [1925]: 25), and does not exist in a pure form (however this might be defined), but is increasingly filled with visual imagery, all of which has its own underlying agendas, and does not necessarily follow the logic of the urban fabric. The rise in population in urban environments today is perhaps a good reason to think again about the relationship between space, images and the body. A deeper understanding of film and moving images, whose influence on our life has grown at an equal pace to the size of cities, can arguably give us insights into the way we can engage with urban environments in the twenty-first century.

While the industrialisation of the twentieth century may be regarded as the industrial age of *collective* mass consumption – in terms of housing, consumer products and media – the twenty-first century is perhaps better understood as the age of *individual* mass consumption; the age of *pay as you go* and *on demand* television. While many enjoy being part of a society with shared values, we probably prefer to remain anonymous within the infinite matrix of space – virtual or otherwise – where we have a choice and can decide for ourselves what is right or wrong. This age of individualism stands in opposition to the spaces we inhabit; we live in increasingly denser places where we need to learn to share our presumed territory. Our urban future has already arrived in large parts of Asia, where space is regarded differently, having become an increasingly scarce resource as a consequence of a changing demography, a widening gap between rich and poor, a rising world population and more people wanting to live in cities. Powerful stakeholders demonstrate a willingness to reserve, imprint and further fragment the postmodern heterotopic city, through specialised zones for consumption, gated communities and advertising spaces. The challenge lying ahead is one of finding new ways to retain cities as meaningful places that both preserve old and create new quality spaces.

Pseudo Events and Staged Authenticity

If we begin to question the nature of postmodern cities, along the lines of an image-permeated phenomena or *mise-en-urbanité* as explored in Part III and as a spatial agent for which 'the medium is the message' (McLuhan 1964), a further question of the authenticity of our urban spaces and the things that surround us is also raised. This is engendered by the fact that urban culture is deeply entrenched in leisure, entertainment and consumption (activities that imply some sort of authorship), or an intellectual position in which the city is its own gigantic media apparatus. Walter Benjamin addressed this question in photographic- and film-theoretical terms with regard to the value of art in society in his seminal text *Age of Mechanical Reproduction* (Benjamin 1968 [1936]). He concludes that reproduced work is always of inferior quality because it lacks the 'aura' of the original; a position he also adopts in the context of film when landscapes are represented on the screen (ibid.: 221). The term *authenticity* also appears in an existentialist philosophical discourse led by Søren Kierkegaard, Jean-Paul Sartre and Martin Heidegger, but the emphasis here is predominantly inward through the recognition of our conscious self. Jean Baudrillard's landmark text *Simulacra and Simulation* (Baudrillard [2008] 1981) questions the authenticity of our perceived reality, arguing that we live in a society that is saturated with signs and symbols. According to Baudrillard, all images to which we are exposed in our everyday life can be categorised as a fourfold system that illustrates the transmutation from authenticity to simulacrum. Images either: (1) reflect a basic reality; (2) mask and pervert a basic reality; (3) mask the absence of a basic reality; or (4) bear no relation to a reality (Baudrillard 2008 [1981]: 4–5). He further states that 'When the real is no longer what it used to be, nostalgia assumes its full meaning. There is a proliferation of myths of origin and signs of reality; of second-hand truth, objectivity and authenticity' (ibid.: 4). While Baudrillard relates his study of simulacra and simulation to spatial phenomena, such as Disneyland and other pseudo-architectural environments, Kenneth Frampton asserts the importance of authenticity in the context of regular architectural practices. Relating to the existentialist position, he develops the concept of a 'critical regionalism' discussed previously, whereby architecture has a dialectical relationship to a place and its context (e.g. typography, climate, light and tectonic forms) (Frampton 1983). Similarly, Pallasmaa mentions in relation to the notion of authenticity that it is 'frequently identified with the ideas of artistic autonomy and originality' and he understands 'authenticity more as the quality of deep rootedness in the stratifications of culture' that allows us to 'dwell with dignity' (Pallasmaa 1994: 79). Pallasmaa believes that architecture faces new dangers in a consumer culture, and thus stipulates that 'The special mission of architecture today is to defend the feasibility of quality and authenticity, as well as the emancipation and autonomy of human experience' (Pallasmaa 2007: 42, cf. 2011: 23).

> The touristic experience that comes out of the tourist setting is based on inauthenticity, and as such it is superficial when compared with careful study; it is morally inferior to mere experience.
>
> (MacCannell 1973: 599).

With the rise of mass tourism in the 1980s and 1990s – fuelled in the United States by, for example, the opening of leisure resorts and theme parks in Florida, and new investment in gambling resorts like those at Atlantic City and Las Vegas – it is perhaps no coincidence that this correlates with emerging debates on the authenticity of space.[13] These discussions have, first and foremost, taken place in the widening field of human geography, especially in tourism studies' investigations into tourist experiences, as the MacCannell's quote illustrates. Rich texts discussing architectural space as a setting for an assumed cultural authenticity (or, rather, its absence in those mentioned above) were written by Relph (1981), Pearce and Moscardo (1986), Cohen (1988, 2007), Urry (1990), Harvey (1996), Wang (1999), Taylor (2001), Reisinger and Steiner (2006), Olsen, (2007), Pearce (2007), Ivanovic (2008), Vannini and Williams (2009) and Knudsen (2010). Although this incomplete list gives a sense of the enduring power and complex nature of this theme, it is also true that many of these debates have their ideological grounding in the concepts explored in texts by three key scholars in human geography dating from the late 1950s to the early 1970s: Erving Goffman's structural division of a 'front and back' (Goffman 1959); Daniel J. Boorstin's 'pseudo events' (Boorstin 1992 [1962]); and Dean MacCannell's 'staged authenticity' (MacCannell 1973).

> Firstly, there is the 'setting,' involving furniture, décor, physical layout, and other back-ground items which supply the scenery and stage props for the spate of human action played out before, within, or upon it.
>
> (Goffman 1959: 29)

Goffman argues in his seminal sociological text *The Presentation of Self in Everyday Life* (Goffman 1959) that our social life takes place in a spatial 'set-ting' that, not unlike in a theatre, contains scenery and stage props. He asserts that issues 'dealt with by stage craft and stage management are some-times trivial but they are quite general; they seem to occur everywhere in social life' (ibid.: 15). Goffmann relates our existence and participation in everyday-life activities to those found in a stage production, where certain actions are performed to an audience, whilst others are hidden from them behind the scenes (where there is, arguably, a higher degree of 'realness') (ibid.: 17). More than a decade later, this argument was readdressed by MacCannell, who alludes to the structural division of social establishments having a front, back and outside of stage – important in that it highlights a spatial division that explains the relationship between audience and stage (or, in this analogy, any architectural setting) (cf. MacCannell 1973: 590). Using a series of spatial and architectural metaphors, his essay *Staged Authenticity: Arrangements of Social Space in Tourist Settings* (ibid.) studies various types and degrees of staged experiences in social life, and he notes that 'a firm sense of social reality requires some mystification' (ibid.: 591). He describes 'almost authentic' experiences (ibid.: 596) such as guided tourist tours as being granted access to backstage where 'once a person, or an observer, moves off stage, or into the "setting," the real truth begins to reveal itself more or less automatically' (ibid.: 592). MacCannell's stage observations can be usefully employed in the context of urban experiences, where street frontages, signs or the design of façades often achieve an apparent mystification of a place. 'Mystification, then, can be the conscious product of an individual effort to manipulate a social appearance ...' (ibid.: 591). Boorstin's *The Image: A Guide to Pseudo-Events in America* (Boorstin 1992 [1962]) (one of a series of works by American sociologists which is further referred to by Debord in *Society of the Spectacle* (Debord 2002 [1967])) draws attention to so-called 'pseudo events'. His early 1960s social critique of contemporary American culture warns that America finds itself in an 'age of contrivance' and is increasingly faced by 'the menace of unreality' (Boorstin 1992: 240). While Boorstin argues that contemporary culture has a thirst for inauthenticity and the superficiality of modern life (see also Urry 1990: 9), Dean MacCannell disagrees, concluding that the 'rhetoric of tourism is full of manifestation of the importance of the authenticity of the relationship between tourists and what they see', in other words, tourists continually search for authentic experiences (MacCannell 1999 [1976]: 14).

Environmental Bubbles and Spatial Plagiarism

The arguments of Boorstin and MacCannell are made in the context of entertainment parks, such as Disneyland – so-called 'environmental bubbles' (Boorstin 1992 [1962]: 77) – and not cities *per se*. However, the 'almost authentic' and 'mystified' experiences described by MacCannell are not only found in popular tourist attractions (he cites Cape Kennedy), but also amidst our urban fabrics. Many of the aforementioned have followed this line and can therefore be seen in the context of Debord and the Situationist International. Unsurprisingly, Debord took a critical position towards the notion of commercial travel, with tourism for him being nothing more than 'human circulation packaged for consumption, a by-product of the circulation of commodities ... the opportunity to go and see what has been banalized' (Debord 2003: 67). He questions not only the notion that tourism is an act of consumption, but also the consequences it creates for the quality and authenticity of space. 'The economic organization of travel to different places already guarantees their *equivalence*. The modernization that has eliminated the time involved in travel has simultaneously eliminated any real space from it' (ibid.). What is relevant here is that Debord's notion of spatial equivalence is not confined to designated tourist settings (such as the amusement parks discussed above), but is directed and applicable to everyday scenarios found in inner-city centres across the western world. Paradoxically, we have come to accept the view that the majority of tourists (who leave their home to see and explore the unknown) apparently require a sense of familiarity for the perfect *away-from-home* experience, or

Figure C.2   Berlin. Kunsthaus Tacheles. © Mazbin.

rather expeditions in controlled environments. Consequently, from the perspective of tourist mass marketing, it is not necessarily problematic that the inner-city spaces of consumption found in London, Liverpool and Leicester barely differentiate themselves from those found in Lisbon, Vienna or Prague. The same is true for many cities on the North American continent, where the film industry has long taken advantage of this phenomenon, by allowing filming in cities that are not those that are being portrayed in the film. Instead, it is only important that our preconceived notion of a place is fulfilled, a challenge that can largely be achieved by the use of images and symbols in visual and architectural terms. Debord takes a clear ideological stance on the notion of *representation* which perhaps includes the representation of cities in film: 'In societies dominated by modern conditions of production, life is presented as an immense accumulation of *spectacles*. Everything that was directly lived has receded into a representation' (Debord 2003: 43). For him, urban life is both defined and exists through representation.

Today, a city that is full of representations, signs and symbols – not to mention 'staged authenticities' – is Berlin, the capital of Germany. One of many urban examples can be found at the Kunsthaus Tacheles in the Oranienburger Strasse, Berlin Mitte. The former meeting point of anarchist artists and squatters has, since the fall of the Berlin Wall, seen a remarkable transformation into a *touristified* version of itself. What continues to attract thousands of visitors to the dilapidated area – today framed by fashionable designer hotels and restaurants – is the fact that the Tacheles allows its visitors to go 'back stage' and enjoy cheap beverages or recreational drugs in 'architecturally untouched' or unrenovated indoor and outdoor environments.

Figure C.3 Dubai. Picture of the city with artificial archipelago, called *The World*, in background. The small islands are constructed in the shape of a world map (left). © Werner Paul. Picture taken from the Burj Khalifa, the tallest building in the world, showing The Dubai Mall (right). © Werner Paul.

Moving to the rear of the Tacheles is like crossing a threshold in time, although there is, of course, some doubt as to whether these ghostly spaces of the past are indeed more *authentic* examples of contemporary Berlin than the gentrified establishments nearby. However, this is not necessarily the concern of the numerous visitors who congregate to participate in the staged events of this area of Berlin. The popularity of places like the Tacheles, similar in effect to the themed hotels, restaurants, bars and other city venues, suggests that a high level of *realness* or *authenticity* of a place does not guarantee a high economic return for place marketing. In fact, quite the opposite can be the case. Significant numbers of people enjoy inauthentic places; places that are designed to be recreational and to tell their own story, providing a mediated reality or a perception of the world that is not dissimilar from our movie experiences. Consequently, millions of people each year enjoy visiting Las Vegas, perhaps the most artificial city in the world, and in the Middle East, major investment has transformed entire regions, on both land and water, into gigantic spatial simulacra. The secret of these places lies in their simple narrative quality, regardless of how obvious or dull the *spatial plagiarism* of, for example, a Venetian Canal rebuilt in the desert or on an island in the South China Sea, might be.[14] Rather, it is one that is not found in the fragmented, postmodern landscapes in which we live, but one that appeals to – or perhaps eases – the psychological disposition of poststructuralist, heterogeneous subjects.

So, does this mean that querying the authenticity of postmodern urban landscapes has lost its relevance and is a form of social critique that is now passé? Probably not, although we might have to come to terms with the fact that cities are increasingly viewed as *entertainment landscapes* by visitors, and places that allow for an engagement which enable people to – spatially or temporally – remove themselves from the actuality of everyday life.

Inauthentic spaces, such as those found in Las Vegas, Macau or Dubai, tend to have a style that reminds us of the mediated reality we recognise from watching *scenes* on a screen. In certain moments, when moving through the artificially-lit environments of casinos, it can feel like moving from one film set to another, again engaging with actual space in a way that seems like embodying a scene in film. In this sense there is a growing affiliation between cities and cinema, the latter being able to reflect upon a century of experience in the entertainment of people. Whilst the examples cited above are selected and isolated cases, urban regeneration strategists carefully monitor such apparently economically-successful examples. It is clear, echoing Landry's observations on the 'experience economy' (Landry 2006: 152), that it is only a matter of time and economic circumstance before urban spaces will begin to be seen, not only as a locale of social and economic exchange, but also as performative agents and places for entertainment. This invites us

Figure C.4   Macau. Picture taken outside and inside The Venetian Macau hotel and casino resort.

Figure C.5   Macau. Inside the MGM hotel and casino in Macau.

to further explore the duality of body and space in the context of the real city, and also how new screen technologies might change the way we perceive urban space.

URBAN SCREEN EVOLUTION: FROM 2D TO 4D

The electric light is pure information. It is a medium without a message, as it were, unless it is used to spell out some verbal ad or name. This fact, characteristic of all media, means that the "content" of any medium is always another medium. The content of writing is speech, just as the written word is the content of print, and print is the content of the telegraph. If it is asked, "What is the content of speech?," it is necessary to say, "It is an actual process of thought, which is in itself nonverbal."

(McLuhan 2006 [1964]: 107)

Iconic architecture, sign-structures, street canvases, film and other urban advertisement can be seen as symbols and cultural expressions that are essentially linked to an ideology of consumerism. Debord notes that 'today cities themselves are presented as lamentable spectacles, a supplement to the museums or tourists driven around in glassed-in buses' (quoted in Sadler 1999: 99). His remarks resonate with the urban-visual phenomena discussed above, as they are part of a marketing strategy that offers digestible imagery designed for the fleeting moments in which passers-by glance at eye-catching buildings and large-scale screens. However, in this argument it is easy to overlook the fact that whilst the appearance of the city might become more ephemeral through the use of screens with changing images, we face a more permanent change to the perception and consumption of imagery in urban environments. We are standing on the verge of a sizeable transformation in the relationship between screen-based media and urban landscapes which seemingly occurs unnoticed amongst the hype of image consumption, despite being right in front of our eyes. Some of the examples mentioned in this chapter have shown that visual urban phenomena typically associated with screens, such as advertisement and film, have begun to close the gap between two-dimensional representation and a three-, or four-dimensional experience.

The above quote from Marshall McLuhan's renowned and visionary text, *Understanding Media* (1964) highlights the somewhat self-referential nature of media, as each message it transmits refers both to its own medium and to other media (see also Nöth and Bishara 2007: 6). Regardless of the image content of urban sign-structures, street canvases or advertisements, the message would not exist without electric light (the medium), which in turn gives presence to these expressions of what Scott McQuire termed 'media city'.[15] Just as the electric light radically transformed the appearance of the modern city in the 1920s, so too do new technological innovations today promise a continuation of the impact

Figure C.6   Screenshots. *Blade Runner*. Nocturnal cityscape (left). © Warner Brothers. Hong Kong. LED advertisement (right).

that electric light has had on the city's appearance. Mitchell points out that advances in solid-state lighting technologies have dramatically advanced in recent years and it is now possible to assemble large light sources on any surface with highly-controlled and networked pixel information. He concludes that such advances led to the disappearance of traditional distinctions between architectural lighting and computer graphics, which has started, although not always convincingly, to transform the built environment (Mitchell 2005a: 88–9). Whilst it was Times Square in New York, Piccadilly Circus in London and the Shinjuku district in Tokyo that led the way in demonstrating the application of such light-emitting technologies in urban inner-city settings, many other cities now employ large screens for the dissemination of news and the display of advertisements which play an important role in the visual intensity of a place.

In fact, futuristic imagery of high-tech cityscapes, known from films such as *Blade Runner* (1982), in which flat media façades are mounted on building surfaces, are far from the cutting edge of today's technology and might soon be nostalgic visions of the past. Electric advertisements are transmitted in the form of pixels or beams, and started life simply as light bulbs before being replaced by cathode ray tubes (TV screens), semiconductors (LED displays), liquid crystals (LCDs) and now large-scale light projections, the last of which have finally begun to break away from the two-dimensional framework in which advertising operated for over a hundred years. This is perhaps the beginning of an era in which light-emitting screens are becoming more than just digital billboards, and are therefore no longer simply a replacement of static images by animated ones of which Mitchell disapproves (ibid.: 89). New technological innovations in the field of image visualisation has begun to do two things in relation to *space*; first, they have changed the measurable distance between the body and the screen (micro scale); and second, two-dimensional images have started to conquer three-dimensional space (macro scale).

On the micro scale, at the level of people's direct engagement with moving images, the distance between the human body and screens has systematically decreased over time and will, I predict, eventually shrink to nothing. In a conventional cinematic experience, the distance between the audience and the projection surface measured ten or more metres, depending on the size of the cinema and the seat position. Starting with the BBC's first transmission in 1936 and their proliferation during the 1950s, TV screens began to conquer our living rooms. This meant that the aforementioned distance was reduced to a few metres, enhanced further from the 1980s onwards as PC screens entered our workplaces and later our private homes. This further reduced the distance between us and the screens to under a metre, and today, as we carry handheld smartphones with us at almost all times, we have reduced the distance between our eyes and the screens to less than an arm's length. In recent years, several companies have offered wireless video glasses through which digital moving image content can be displayed right in front of our eyes. How much longer before a technological solution is found that will close the gap of the final centimetre that lies between us and the video screen? Back in 2001, I produced and directed the short film *Avenir*, which sketched a vision of a near future (2015) in which people would be wearing digital contact lenses capable of displaying e-mails, video conferences and live television directly on to our retina (the light-sensitive tissue lining the inside of the eye). Back then, I was surprised to learn from a representative of a large telecommunications company that their R&D department was considering the feasibility of just such a device. Only weeks before this book went into production, the *Journal of Micromechanics and Microengineering* published the results of a group of researchers from the University of Washington, Seattle, and Aalto University, Finland, which successfully tested a wirelessly-powered contact lens with an integrated micro-light emitting diode on live rabbits. The group's research is linked to that of Billinghurst and Starner (1999),[16] who emphasised in the late 1990s the advantages of wearable computers as a means of managing information. While, back then, the concept of cybernetics was science fiction, perhaps inspired by movies such as *The Terminator* (1984), it has today become a reality, and the direction that this research will take is clear. Augmented reality lenses will change the way we access information, as well as perceive and interact with the spatial environment we inhabit.

> Wearable computing will likely provide new ways to manage information and interact with the world. For example, personal see-through devices could overlay computer-generated visual information on the real world, providing immediate, handsfree access to information. … In the future, contact lens systems may receive data from external platforms (e.g. mobile phones) and provide real-time notification of important events.
>
> (Lingley *et al*. 2011: 1)

Figure C.7   Screenshots. Avenir wearing contact lenses with which she can receive video calls (left). POV of Avenir (right). © R. Koeck.

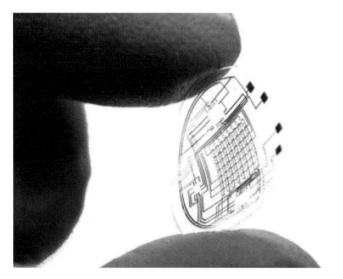

Figure C.8   Wireless LED contact lens. © University of Washington.

On the macro scale, at the level of architectural and urban spaces, so-called 3D projection mapping introduced a new way of projecting moving images on to buildings. This technique has its origins in an artistic context, where innovative groups and companies such as *Urbanscreen* in Bremen, Germany, or *NuFormer* in Zierikzee, The Netherlands, have begun to artistically engage with well-known pieces of architecture. The secret of such work lies not in the fact that moving image and light are projected on to an existing building, but that the 3D animations are precisely measured to fit an existing façade, thus creating the illusion of a building beginning to move, shift and reconfigure itself. In other words, a custom-made projection maps three-dimensional points on a two-dimensional surface, in this case, the façade of a building. Projects of note here are the screen installation *Kreisrot* (2009), which projected 3D graphics and images of people on to the façade of the Prellerhaus studio flats (1925–26) of the Bauhaus in Dessau designed by Walter Gropius,

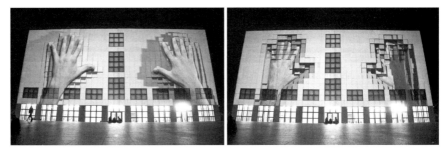

Figure C.9   Hamburg. Project 555 Kubik projected onto the Kunsthalle. © Urbanscreen.

or the award-winning *555 Kubik* (2009), which used the façade of the Hamburger Kunstalle (1993–27) designed by O. M. Ungers. The Hamburg audio-visual installation is an important example of how tailor-made digital content can be matched to an existing façade, to the extent that the side of the building seems to liberate itself from its static, two-dimensional existence and begins to venture into a third and even a fourth dimension.

Such innovative mapping of 3D projections quickly caught the attention of commercial industries, and these techniques have taken the world of advertisement by storm, culminating in extraordinary screening events in many European cities. Many examples could be cited here, and the following gives only a glimpse of some outstanding productions. In 2010, visitors were invited to see a 3D animation sponsored by Samsung which was mapped on to the Beurs van Berlage (1898–1903), and is noteworthy not only for the technical realisation of the animation, but also for its location. The Amsterdam Stock Exchange building, designed by Henrick Petrus Berlage, is a milestone in the history of twentieth century architecture, and was itself regarded as cutting-edge at the time of its construction. In the same year, BMW invited visitors and passers-by of the Suntec City Mall in Singapore to a show of similar techniques of 3D animation and motion graphics projected on to multiple buildings, the first of its kind in Asia. The screening experience was displayed under the motto *joy* and was intended to link BMW's automobile products with a positive emotional message. This was to be achieved by, among other illusions, digital animations that simulated the peeling off of the façade and the transformation of the buildings into animated 3D message boards. Although I have not spoken to people who attended the show, one can speculate that viewers were probably more interested in the entertainment aspect of the event, such as the spectacle of a building appearing to move, rather than to engage with an automobile product. Having this said, products sell through positive emotions.

Furthermore, in 2011 London became the setting for two extraordinary projection mappings in the centre of the city, designed and produced by the

Figure C.10   London. 3D mapping onto Millbank Tower, 2011. © James Perry.

London-based company Drive Productions. Finnish company Nokia invited guests to join them for a show on the occasion of the launch of their new Windows 7 Lumia 800 smartphone. The chosen location for this event was the Millbank Tower, a Grade II-listed skyscraper in Westminster on the banks of the River Thames, designed by Ronald Ward and Partners and built in 1963. The building is a well-known architectural landmark, but arguably what attracted thousands of people to the river bank was the announcement that Toronto-based world famous DJ and performance artist deadmau5 (aka Joel Zimmerman) would accompany the product launch with a remix of dance music. This clever marketing campaign, tailored to a particular generation of mobile phone users, also broke records technologically. The Millbank Tower event was the biggest projection mapping ever staged in London, and used an entire façade of the 118m tall building with massive loudspeakers mounted along the river. In order to achieve the desired visual effect for the night-time show, sixteen high-powered outdoor projectors, stationed 300 metres away on the other side of the Thames, beamed the light-animations on a façade with 800 windows, each of which had been covered with vinyl. Visitors who looked for an animation work that would intellectually engage with the characteristics of a listed landmark building were disappointed, but then they were probably in the minority. Instead, the event managed to deliver a stunning live audio-visual performance which maximised the potential of the tower as a giant vertical urban screen for entertainment and advertisement.

An equally stunning event produced by the same company was commissioned by the retail and fashion label Ralph Lauren in 2010, which saw giant 4D light shows in London and New York in what were called the 'ultimate fusion of art, fashion & technology – a visual feast for the 5 senses'.[17] Ralph Lauren's outdoor advertising event was intended to promote the launch of their new fashion collections and website, and incorporates a composite of

Figure C.11 London. Ralph Lauren 4D projection. © Charlie May.

live action film footage and digital animation work that was then projected directly on to the architectural façade of their flagship stores. The result was not only breathtaking, it raised profound questions about how we perceive the interplay between architecture, advertisement and art in an urban environment. In interview, David Lauren, Senior VP of Advertising, Marketing & Corporate Communications, pointed out that the show was linked to the company's new online presence and a marketing strategy they call 'merchantainment',[18] a phrase that blends merchandising and entertainment, and could have been coined by Debord. A quote by Charles Landry, made before such elaborate 3D projections, is visionary and fitting in this context:[19]

> ... the so-called 'experience economy' cannot be ignored – a rapprochement between everyday living, consumption and spectacle shaping what cities look and feel like ... This process is turning retailing into a part of the entertainment industry, often blurring the boundaries between shopping, learning and the experience of culture. In this process design, multimedia applications, theatrics and soundscapes move centre stage.
>
> (Quoted in Makeham 2005: 151)

The 3D projection mapping of architectural facades literally stitches moving images into an existing urban fabric, thus making a quite overt connection between filmic and architectural dimensions of space. It is therefore not surprising that film companies have begun to use the same three-dimensional projection technique to advertise their films. A trailer of Florian Henckel von Donnersmarck's *The Tourist* (2010), starring Angelina Jolie and Johnny Depp in lead roles, for instance, has been mapped into a 3D projection, 80 feet by 80 feet on the Praetorian Building at 1607 Main Street in Dallas, Texas. However, it is not only this new form of urban projection that has transformed the nature of advertisement, and, in so doing, challenges the known modes of perception of urban space. 3D technology has been present in film and television for some time, but the need to wear cumbersome glasses has prevented it from being as influential as it was perhaps expected to be. Today,

TV sets are currently available on the mass market that can show 3D images – Sky announced that 3D coverage would be available in the UK in March 2010 (although still with the need to wear special glasses). Recent developments in layered liquid crystal display (LCD) technology have dramatically changed the nature of the 3D screen technology market, and screen technology giants such as Samsung, Toshiba and Sony are investing heavily in the research and development of televisions capable of showing 3D images without glasses. In technologically-simplified terms, these screens use parallax barrier or lenticular lens technology, by which means very small lenses are integrated into the screen or monitor, shaped in such a way that different images can be displayed to each eye depending on the viewing angle. These TV sets can now produce moving images with a sense of depth that is similar to that of normal human experience. In January 2010 in Las Vegas, Samsung showed the first prototype of this autostereoscopic TV display at the International Consumer Electronics Show (CES), the world's largest consumer technology tradeshow; subsequently, Sony and Toshiba announced similar products and showed comparable TV sets at the 2011 CES.

One of the problems that prevent companies from developing larger TV screens is the offsetting of images that are displayed separately to the eyes when we move our head. This is an issue that all parallax barrier or lenticular lens screens have yet to overcome. However, this did not prevent the gaming industry implementing such technology in smaller, handheld devices, with Nintendo releasing their 3DS portable gaming console (equipped with an autostereoscopic display) in Japan in February 2011, and later across Europe, Australia and the United States. But do these screens really produce 3D images, or do they create a perception of three-dimensional depth for the viewer? Recently, Professor Laurence Nigay and Jérémie Francone from the Engineering Human Computer Interaction Research Group at the Laboratoire d'Informatique de Grenoble have found a method they call *Head-Coupled Perspective* (HCP), which simulates three-dimensional space and objects on ordinary iPhone or iPad screens. This software-based method creates interactive 3D scenes through head-tracking and uses the front-facing camera to recognise the angle at which the device is held.

The expectation is that it will take some time before any of the aforementioned technologies can be adapted for large-scale advertising billboards in cities, although it is worth noting that the industry has already started to find new technological solutions; some predict that holographic displays and volumetric displays (which do not have some of the shortcomings mentioned) will become the next phenomenon in digital screen technology. In the meantime, we can look to the near future by studying one of Samsung's TV commercials, produced by CHI & Partners, London, shot in Buenos

Aires and launched in April 2010 as part of an £8 million campaign to promote 3D TV sets. In this movie advertisement, we see gigantic screens built
from multiple TV sets mounted on buildings and laid out on the street. By
means of clever compositing and matching of screen content, and camera
movement on location, the viewer gets to see an optical illusion that gives a
sense of depth to the images on their TV screens. As a result, the viewer
gains an understanding of what it would be like if 3D television was installed
in a large city such as Buenos Aires, and how 3D images could become part
of our everyday environment. The advertisement shows how such televisions would not only revolutionise screen-based advertisements (eventually
replacing 2D images with digital 4D animations), but also gives us a glimpse
of a time when such technology will lead us into uncharted territory, in
terms of the appearance and perception of – as well as engagement with –
urban landscapes. We, the millions of viewers of these TV advertisements, are
invited to dream with Samsung about a future in which technology will
almost entirely abolish the boundary between the image and reality of urban
space.

Technological innovations in the field of image visualisation have not only
made us rethink our relationship with space, but also to *movement*. Whilst in
the history of film, it was images that began to move in front of our eyes,
facilitating a cultural revolution that was based on representation, in the
future it will be the movement of our body that will alter our relationship
with images in urban landscapes, and thus our understanding of the world.
On one hand, micro contact lenses will augment the spaces through which
we move, whilst other technologies might use our movement to change the
world we inhabit. Already we are all familiar with Internet search engines
providing customised advertising banners on our computer screens, and individualised relationships between people and product advertising is likely to
grow in the future. Mobile phone and Internet providers working together
are already capable of creating movement profiles of people through mobile
communication devices that enables our location to be made transparent to
whoever has access to such data. Future mobile phones might include radio-
frequency identification chips (RFID tags), which would enable the tracking
of a person's movement to an even higher degree, and it is only a matter of
time before interactive advertisement billboards (which we know from films
such as *Minority Report* (2002)) are able to recognise the identity of passers-by
and react to their movement. As it did with other areas of real-time visual
communication, it might be the computer gaming industry again that leads
the way in this field. Numerous gaming consoles, notably the Kinect for
Xbox 360, already show how responsive screen technology can be linked to
motion tracking of its users. UK marketing specialists Kinetic have recently

Figure C.12   Screenshot. *Minority Report*. © Twentieth Century Fox Film Cooperation.

conducted research on face-tracking technology in shopping malls with the Fraunhofer Institute, whereby cameras are placed on to digital screens that collect data on the people who pass by (Copley 2011). It only needs a little imagination to see how such technologies, when combined with and applied to advertising in urban environments, will open up enormous opportunities for change in our bodily existence and behaviour in urban space.

I have argued in this book that cities are increasingly defined through images, and that cinema and film contribute to new perspectives on how we view and engage with architectural spaces and urban environments. New digital technologies of visualisation and communication are increasingly infiltrating our most intimate spheres of personal space and, furthermore, through advertising and marketing, manifesting themselves in cities and their public spaces and places. The challenge for the future will be that we keep pace with these rapid developments and not get distracted by the content of the images. Instead, we must ask ourselves the larger question of how these new forms of media – and the *Cine-scapes* they create – can benefit both individuals and society at large.

Notes

Introduction

1 See also 'Liverpool in Film: J. A. L. Promio's Cinematic Urban Space' (Koeck 2009).

2 This is reference to Martin Scorsese's film *Taxi Driver* (1976). When Robert De Niro (aka Travis Bickle) is asked about the terms and conditions of his working as a New York City taxi driver, he answers 'I will work anytime, anywhere'.

3 *Modernity – an Incomplete Project* was the tile of Jürgen Habermas' lecture on the occasion of receiving the Theodor Adorno Prize in Frankfurt in 1980. Habermas saw postmodernism as a reaction to the failures of modernity so that it could be also be called 'Antimodernity'. It is worth noting that the Theodor Adorno Prize is not only given to sociologists, but also to filmmakers, including Jean-Luc Godard in 1995 and Alexander Kluge in 2009.

4 What is meant here is that cities changed in terms of their architecture, shape, density, infrastructure, pace, population and other key components.

5 See, for example, Christie (1994), Musser (1990), Toulmin (2006) and the edited volumes by Kessler *et al.* (1992–2006), Kessler and Verhoeff (2007), Elsaesser and Barker (1989).

6 To Moholy-Nagy's disappointment, only about nine seconds survived in the final cut of the film (Frayling 1995: 71–3). For further reading on the role of film in the representation and production of modern architecture, see Colomina 1994 and Albrecht 2000 [1986].

7 See also Bruno (2002: 67).

8 It is worth noting that founding member Andrea Branzi saw an affinity between their work and that of Ludwig Hilberseimer. Branzi admired the non-representative language of Hilberseimer's work. Aureli notes: 'For Branzi, such signs were the absolute minimum representations of a city liberated from its image, and thus from any recognizable values or civic iconography' (Aureli 2008: 75).

9 This does not apply to abstract film.

10 A similar point is raised by Steven Miles, but he emphasises that the city is, first and foremost, a product of the market system by which it is ruled (Miles 2010: 24).

11 Recent neurological research supports Simmel's remarks. A group of researchers around Professor Andreas Meyer-Lindenberg of the University of Heidelberg has recently stated that people living in cities show a 21 per cent increased risk of anxiety disorders and a 39 per cent increased risk of mood disorders. As such, for the first time in history, brain scanning technology (of the cingulate cortex and amygdala) has been used to evidence that the urban environment is linked to 'social stress processing', which suggests 'that brain regions differ in vulnerability to this risk factor across the lifespan' (Lederbogen *et al.* 2011: 498–501).

12 Fludernik (2009: 15) defines plot as being 'construed as the logical and chronological concatenation of these two or three events'.

13 Lowry and Buckland have summarised Souriau's definitions in short and precise terms and the following is, in part, indebted to their reading.

14 My discussion on Benjamin and Anderson is indebted to Douglas Smith and a conversation I had with him in Dublin in May 2011.

1 Tectonics of Film Space

1 Rothman argues that Alfred Hitchcock's film *Psycho* (1960) was a turning point for American filmmaking, marking the end of the 'classical era of American movies' (Rothman 2004: 281). He cites 1960 as the moment in the history of film when the New Wave 'broke on American shores' (ibid.), and alongside the earlier Film Noir movement, with films such as Jules Dassin's *The Naked City* (1948), made a distinct contribution to establishing the real city as a spatial setting for what would become a gigantic filmic industry.

2 This type of film practice refers to the work produced by film pioneers such as the Lumière brothers in cities like Liverpool (see Koeck 2009).

2 City in Our Mind

1 Andong Lu mentions 'episodic and situational narratives' in a different, architectural context. I have borrowed his terminology as it fits the case presented here (cf. Lu 2010: 237).

2 For New York and Washington DC, see On Location Tours, Inc., available on line at www.screentours.com (accessed June 2011). For Los Angeles, see All Los Angeles Tours, available online at www.alllosangelestours.com (accessed June 2011). For London, see Britmovietours, available online at britmovietours.com (accessed June 2011). For Paris, see Gridskipper, available online at gridskipper.com/archives/entries/061/61732.php (accessed June 2011). For Vienna, see Viennawalks, available online at http://www.viennawalks.com/?page=spezial (accessed June 2011). For Berlin, see Open Mind Event Management, available online at http://www.openmind-events.de/index.php?option=com_content&view=article&id=82&Itemid=97 (accessed June 2011).

3 One female visitor comments: 'We came here of course because it was the main set for the movie Amelie! Yes, it does look a little different than in the movie but essentially it is the same. I was sooooo excited to eat here!!! If you are a fan of the movie you have to go. The only thing was it was packed with people. I also wanted to take more photos but I didn't want to annoy people so the photos on the inside were limited. Outside though I took lots! The food was good too.' (www.virtualtourist.com/travel/Europe/France/Ile_de_France/Paris-99080/Restaurants-Paris-Cafe_des_Deux_Moulins-BR-1.html). Paris city guides, such as that by Fallon and Williams, mention the café specifically with reference to the film *Amélie*, advertised as 'walk up rue Lepic, which is lined with food shops, and halfway up on the left is the Café des Deux Moulins ..., where our heroine Amélie worked in the eponymous film' (Fallon and Williams 2008: 184).

4 My thanks to Dietrich Neumann who kindly provided an insight into this.

5 The ongoing presence of the film is also demonstrated in the blog of a young couple, who set up a website showing them standing in front of the fountain. Available online at dearoldhollywood.blogspot.com/2009/12/im-back-la-dolce-vita.html (accessed June 2011).

6 Milos Forman's famous film *Amadeus* (1984) features scenes set in Vienna that were not shot there. Forman felt that historical sites in Prague would be the better place to capture the atmosphere of this period film.

7 Executive producer Avril MacRory and director and writer Frederick Baker produced an informative BBC documentary *Shadowing The Third Man* (2004) which gives a good insight into the making of the film.

8 Some of Orson Welles' underground scenes were shot at Thames Water and not in the Viennese sewers. For information on guided tours, see www.drittemanntour.at/.

9 See Christie and Taylor (1994) for more information on Russian cinema, and pp. 69–73 and p. 93 for the *Kino-Eye* manifesto.

10 There are, of course, countless other cinematic spaces stitched into actual landscapes, not all of which are urban. The iconographic Villa Malaparte, for instance, built by Italian Rationalist architect Adalberto Libera in 1937, features prominently in Godard's landmark film Le Mépris (1963). I would argue that the building's spectacular cliff location on the Mediterranean Sea is interconnected with Godard's film and its narrative.

11 See *The Guardian*, online at www.guardian.co.uk/film/2010/jun/23/secret-cinema-review.

12 This term is borrowed from a BBC documentary *On the Brandwagon* (2008) presented by Jonathan Meades. This of course is not a North American phenomenon. As recently reported in *The Guardian* in the UK, the crisis-hit Greek government has unveiled plans to allow film companies to have access to its most precious cultural gems. Filming with the 5th century BCE Periclean masterpieces in the background are now being offered at a fee as low as 1600 Euros a day. 'Greece's ancient sites to play starring roe in recovery', available online at www.guardian.co.uk/business/2012/jan/20/greek-ancient-sites-for-rent (accessed January 2012).

13 On the topic of film-induced tourism as a destination motivator, see Urry 1990; Riley and van Doren 1992; Tooke and Baker 1996; Riley *et al.* 1998; Sharp 2000; Busby and Klug 2001; and Bolan and Davidson 2005.

14 On the topic of film-induced destination marketing, see Cohen 1986; Woodward 2000; Grihault 2003; Frost 2004; Beeton 2005; Connell 2005; Hudson and Ritchie 2006; and O'Connor *et al.* 2008.

15 'Tourism Marketing Campaign Promotes U.S. Destinations to Japanese Travelers'. Available online at trade.gov/press/publications/newsletters/ita_0706/tourism_0706.asp (accessed June 2011).

16 'U.S. Department of Commerce Unveils new Integrated Tourism Marketing Campaign for UK'. Available online at http://tinet.ita.doc.gov/about/us_promo_campaign/ukcampaign12142004.html (accessed June 2011). Additional information can be found in *The New York Times*, 15 December 2004, p. C2.

17 'Tourism Marketing Campaign Promotes U.S. Destinations to Japanese Travelers'. Available online at http://trade.gov/press/publications/newsletters/ita_0706/tourism_0706.asp (accessed June 2011).

18 Ibid.

19 Available online at http://www.empireonline.com/features/harry-potter-travel-guide/ (accessed June 2011).

20 Available online at www.movie-locations.com/ (accessed January 2012).

3 Existential and Experiential Notions of Space

1 Unlike during the Middle Ages, many large cities today grow rapidly and have no well-defined edges, with boundaries being determined by legislative, and not necessarily physical, terms.

2 De Certeau is discussed extensively in the next chapter; to avoid unnecessary repetition, his work is not examined here.

3 For an architectural reading of Heidgegger, see also Frampton (1996 [1974]).

4 The latter 'space' is meant here in a Euclidian sense.

5 Bullnow's original text reads: '… sondern daß der Mensch in seinem Dasein durch den Bezug zum Raum bestimmt ist' (1963: 500).

6 Bullnow's original text reads: '… sondern daß der Mensch nur in der Einheit mit einem konkreten Raum ein bestimmtes Wesen gewinnt; er hat es nich "an sich" und losgelöst vom jeweiligen Raum' (ibid.: 507).

7   Bullnow's original German text reads: '… sondern daß der Mensch in seinem Dasein durch den Bezug zum Raum bestimmt ist'.

8   This term is used in reference to René Descartes, who stated that, despite being essentially two separate entities, the mind interacts with the body, and therefore there is no such thing as a non-physical mind or a non-mental body. In a classical concept of dualism, mind and body occupy different entities.

9   I am aware that this hypothesis differs from the views of others, and it is certainly clear that the level of cinematic spatial memory varies depending upon the degree to which we engage with a film. I accept that a film studies student is likely to have a better awareness of film space than other groups of people.

4 Spatial Editing

1   An opposing strategy of this would be gated communities which, despite being problematic on many levels, have enjoyed an increasing popularity in recent years.

5 A Shared Space

1   This is changing today, and the newest digital projectors take film files from external storage devices, such as high-capacity hard drives and servers.

2   For the narrative quality and notion of journeys in Chinese gardens designs, see Lu (2011).

3   More recently, Tschumi has further developed his theories along the lines of the sequence of *Concept, Context, and Content* (Tschumi 2004) and *Concept and Form* (see Tschumi 2010).

4   The Brechtian theatre is also discussed by Roland Barthes, who provides a similar reading (see Barthes 1989 [1975]).

5   See *Anna Belle Serpentine Dance* (1895) shot by William Heise for the Thomas Edison Company.

6   The concept of an architectural path, Bruno notes, is further explored by Le Corbusier in the context of his design for the *Villa Savoye* in Poissy, and in relation to movement through Arabic architecture (Bruno 2002: 428, cf. Le Corbusier 1986: 24). Bruno also discusses the architectural promenade in her essay *Site-seeing* (Bruno 1997).

7   Of course, urban reality considerably limits the 'nearly unlimited' choice. Urban planning, the privatisation of space and other factors control and restrict the movement of people in cities. A notable exception is subversive urban tactics, such as Parkour.

8   The déjà-vu phenomenon explored previously is a good example of subversive tactics, but it is inward and not manifested through movement, which is central in de Certeau's argument.

9   Our binocular natural vision differs significantly from a 16:9 aspect ratio. The human eye has a fairly small focus area vision, whilst the rest is peripheral vision.

10   Some cubicles are populated with cardboard cutouts of people, which is almost unnoticeable because of Tati's skilled sound design that tends to override our flawed spatial perception.

11   In the case of recording on to film with a mechanical motion picture camera, the mechanics inside the camera, such as the gearing of the film transport mechanism and sprocket teeth, can lead to very small variations in the way that individual frames are exposed.

12   ASL is the length of a film divided by the number of shots in it, measured in seconds.

13 Martin Scorsese, for instance, used a handheld steadicam for the filming of *Raging Bull* (1980).

14 An example of such video art is *The Quintet of Remembrance*, which is one of four videos shot in extreme slow-motion created between 2000 and 2001.

15 Ben Highmore's book *Cityscapes* (2005), notably revisits Lefebvre's concept of rhythm analysis, and offers, through a study of movement and mobility, an excellent insight into the culture of cities.

16 The ease with which digital film can be used as an observational instrument in the urban realm has, in my view, revolutionised the possibilities of distilling urban rhythms that are normally hidden in spatial practices and the urban fabric of the everyday. Particularly worth mentioning here is a series of films that form a practice-led research project *In Time of Place*, produced by Dr Alan Marcus and filmed in Dachau, Venice, Prague and Boston (2006–10).

17 Friedrich Wilhelm Joseph von Schelling original text reads: 'Wenn die Architektur überhaupt die erstarrte Musik ist, ein Gedanke, der selbst den Dichtungen nicht fremd war …' (Schelling 1984 [1859]).

18 See also Robert Kronenburg's *Live Architecture: Venues, Stages and Arenas for Popular Music* (2012) which explores the physical form of popular music performance space from 1960 to the present day.

6 Architecture and Urban Form as Cinematic Apparatus

1 It has recently been reported in Germany that the number of deaths of people wearing headphones while walking or cycling through traffic has dramatically increased. New legislation prohibiting this practice is now being considered.

7 Urban Product and Advertisement

1 The quote is taken from an interview conducted on 14 February 2001. The original French text reads: 'Si on parle d'images, on parle surtout d'images figuratives, c'est à dire que tout est image … l'architecture en soi est image … on en prend connaissance par l'oeil et c'est avant tout une création d'ordre visuel.'

2 Parts of this section are much indebted to my colleague Gary Warnaby (Management School, University of Liverpool), with whom I am currently developing a research paper on outdoor advertisement.

8 Place Marketing: Urban Architecture as Image

1 Decisions as to how often an advertisement needs to be repeated in order for it to be effective in marketing terms depend on individual situations (cf. Vuokko 1997).

2 Other internationally renowned architects, such as Santiago Calatrava, Foster & Partners and Rafael Moneo, also made important contribution to the rebuilding of the port city.

3 Sara González gives good insight into Bilbao's entrepreneurial urban policy and investigates the concept of 'scalar narratives' – the cultural politics of scales as a form of study of urban policy.

4 This term is borrowed from Leeman and Modan (2010: 182–97) who explore the linguistic signs in an urban context.

5 This travelling loan exhibition was first shown in Princeton from 6 March to 6 June 2010. It was organised in collaboration with the Princeton University Art Museum.

6 My reference to Lewis's novel is indebted to the work of Short (1996: 210) and Jonas and Wilson (1999: 37). It seems so fitting to this section that I must use it again here.

7 In many cases these buildings have faced demolition at a later stage.
8 Some Renaissance artists and architects benefited from extraordinary patronage, and as such played a role with regard to civic, religious and political affairs. Alberti, for instance, stood in close relation to Pope Nicholas V, which is well illustrated by Tafuri (1987).
9 In another text I have framed this question around the classical Vitruvian definition of architecture – the trinity of *venustas*, *utilitas* and *firmitas*. See Koeck (2011: 73–93).
10 On Baudrillard's concept of a second-order simulation, see Baudrillard (2008 [1981]: 1, 21, 55 and 126–7). On the same subject and other perceptual dimensions, see also Carmona *et al.* (2003: 104).
11 The *Bauakademie* project is sponsored by the Association for the Promotion of the Academy of Architecture (*Förderverein Bauakademie*) headed first by architect Josef-Paul Kleihues and later Hans Kollhoff.
12 The picture was taken in October 2009.
13 Between 1896 and 1906, architect Alfred Messel planned and built the department store in several phases along Leipziger Strasse and Voßstraße. Because of its enormous success and popularity as one of Berlin's premier shopping locations, the store was expanded in 1911–12 by Heinrich Schweitzer and in 1926–27 by Eugen Schmohl and Paul Kolb.

9 Film Advertisement and Urban Spaces

1 See Janet Ward's book *Weimar Surfaces* (2001: 134–40) for more information on the notion of this shock technique in the context of film and advertisement culture.
2 A good online source of information for box office revenue is Box Office Mojo, produced by IMDb. It is available at http://boxofficemojo.com (accessed July 2011).
3 One blogger reports that *Cloverfield* cups and postcards were handed out at the Rose Bowl Parade at Times Square.
4 Available at www.youtube.com/watch?v=v5Lvl7FORI8; www.youtube.com/watch?v=mTXQVOs3Kxs (accessed July 2011).
5 For more information about the online discussions see Facebook Group 'Cloverfield/1-18-08', available at www.facebook.com/group.php?gid=5445894786 (accessed July 2011). Also Cloverfield Blog, 'Cloverfiled Clues', available at cloverfieldclues.blogspot.com (accessed July 2011).
6 Box office takings dropped significantly thereafter (Finney 2010: 138).
7 Website produced by Sony Pictures Digital (2009). Available at www.d-9.com (accessed July 2011).
8 Website produced by Sony Pictures Digital (2009). Available at multinationalunited.com (acccssed July 2011).
9 Website produced by Sony Pictures Digital (2009). Available at mnuspreadslies.com (accessed July 2011). There are further websites linked to the *District 9* campaign, such as Humanbeingsaregreat.com, available at www.humanbeingsaregreat.com (accessed July 2011).
10 QR-tags were placed, for instance, in Lower Manhattan New York, between 4th and 10th Street.

Conclusion: The Near Future of Cinescapes

1 Examples include Francesco di Giorgio Martini's *The Ideal City* (1480–90) and his *Trattato di Architettura* (1530s).
2 Please see a text in a wonderful exhibition catalogue by Ruth Eaton (2000: 119–31), *Utopia: The Search for the Ideal Society in the Western World*, in which she explores 'the city as an intellectual exercise' and draws upon examples of Renaissance art and architecture.

3 For example, the fresco entitled *Effects of Good Government on City Life* (c. 1338–40) at the Palazzo Pubblico, Siena.

4 Influential scenographers of this family included Giovanni Maria Galli da Bibiena (1618/19–65), Francesco Galli da Bibiena (1659–1739), Ferdinando Galli Bibiena (1657–1743), Alessandro Bibiena (1686–1748), Antonio Galli da Bibiena (1700–74), Giuseppe Galli Bibiena (1696–1757) and Carlo Galli da Bibiena (1728–87).

5 The terminology of 'setting the stage' can mean, in this context, creating adaptable buildings and spaces that can accommodate changing user groups or activities which, next to environmental concerns, is arguably one of the biggest challenges in architectural design today.

6 This notion of a collective narrative act also chimes with Baudrillard, who says of Los Angeles' freeways that they are a 'Gigantic, spontaneous spectacle of automotive traffic. A total collective act, staged by the entire population, twenty-four hours a day' (Baudrillard 1988 [1986]).

7 The *Exposition Internationale du Surréalisme* was organised by writer André Breton (1896–1966) and poet Paul Éluard (1895–1952) and included artists such as Salvador Dalí, Marcel Duchamp, Joan Miró, and, important here, Man Ray.

8 This is not to be confused with a sense that cities need to have a narrative structure implemented from the top down, although there are cases where this might be necessary.

9 Many of George Méliès' films were based on the novels of Jules Verne.

10 Méliès' studio comprised a converted glasshouse.

11 See United Nations (2004) and United Nations Population Fund, www.unfpa.org/pds/urbanization.htm.

12 Recent medical research suggests that there is an area in our brain that is particularly active in people living in cities. The study also shows that city dwellers are more likely to suffer from mood and anxiety disorders (Lederbogen *et.al.* 2011).

13 In Florida, the Walt Disney World Resort opened in 1971, followed by Magic Kingdom (1982), Epcot Center (1982), Hollywood Studios (1989), and Disney Animal Kingdom (1998). Gambling in Atlantic City began in the late 1970s, and added to the economic pressure that Las Vegas experienced in the 1980s. In Las Vegas, this ultimately led to new investment and increased building activity along the Strip, such as the opening of *The Mirage* (1989), *Treasure Island* (1989), *The Excalibur* (1990), *The Forum Shops at Caesars Palace* (1992), *The Luxor* (1993), and *MGM Grand* (1993) to name a few. See Moehring and Green (2005: 206–7).

14 This refers to *The Venetian*, a casino resort in Las Vegas, Nevada, USA and the newly opened casino resort, *The Venetian Macao*, in Macau, China.

15 On the notion of *Electropolis* and McLuhan's *Understanding Media*, see also *The Media City* (McQuire 2008: 113–29).

16 In their article, Billinghurst and Starner discuss the idea of an unobtrusive interface in the shape of a micro-optical head-mounted display and cloth keyboard, as developed at the MIT Media Lab (Billinghurst and Starner 1999: 57–8).

17 Website produced by Ralph Lauren Media LLC. Available at 4d.ralphlauren.com/?ab=int_120110_FRONTDOOR_LIGHTSHOW_LEARNMORE (accessed July 2011).

18 The interview was conducted by F. Tape in 2010 and is available at vimeo.com/16727532?ab (accessed July 2011).

19 Charles Landry's talk, *Tapping the Potential of Neighbourhoods: The Power of Culture and Creativity*, was given at the International Conference on Revitalizing urban Neighbourhoods, Copenhagen, 5–7 September 2001. See Makeham (2005: 151, 159).

Bibliography

Abbott, H. P. (2008) *The Cambridge Introduction to Narrative*. Cambridge: Cambridge University Press.

Adbusters (2007) 'São Paulo: A City Without Ads'. Available online at adbusters.org/print/magazine/73/Sao_Paulo_A_City_Without_Ads.html (accessed May 2010).

Agnew, J. A. (1993) 'Representing Space: Space, Scale and Culture in Social Science', in J. Duncan and D. Ley (eds) *Place/Culture/Representation*. London: Routledge.

Agnew, J. A. (2002) *Place and Politics in Modern Italy*. Chicago, IL: University of Chicago Press.

Agrest, D. and Gandelsonas, M. (1995) *Agrest and Gandelsonas: Works*. New York, NY: Princeton Architectural Press.

Aitken, S. C. and Zonn, L. (1994) *Place, Power, Situation, and Spectacle: A Geography of Film*. Lanham, MD: Rowman & Littlefield.

Alberti, L. B. (1988 [1452]) *On the Art of Building in Ten Books (De Re Aedificatoria)*. Cambridge, MA: MIT Press.

Albrecht, D. (2000 [1986]) *Designing Dreams: Modern Architecture in the Movies*. Santa Monica, CA: Hennessey + Ingalls.

Alexander, C. (1977) *A Pattern Language: Towns, Buildings, Construction*. Oxford: Oxford University Press.

Allen, K. (2008) *Viral Marketing: 100 Success Secrets*. Newstead: Emereo Publishing.

Allen, S. and Agrest, D. (2000) *Practice: Architecture, Technique, and Representation*. Australia: G+B Arts International.

AlSayyad, N. (2006) *Cinematic Urbanism: A History of the Modern from Reel to Real*. New York, NY: Routledge.

Altman, C. F. (1977) 'Psychoanalysis and Cinema: The Imaginary Discourse', *Quarterly Review of Film Studies*, 2(3): 157–272.

Altman, R. (1992) *Sound Theory, Sound Practice*. New York, NY: Routledge.

Altman, R. (2008) *A Theory of Narrative*. New York, NY: Columbia University Press.

Andrew, D. (2000) 'The "Three Ages" of Cinema Studies and the Age to Come', *Modern Language Association*, 115(3): 341–51.

Arnheim, R. (1954) *Art and Visual Perception: A Psychology of the Creative Eye*. Berkeley, CA: University of California Press.

Arnheim, R. (1957) *Film as Art*. Berkeley, CA: University of California Press.

Astruc, A. (1968 [1948]) 'The Birth of a New Avant-Gard: La Camera Stylo (Du Stylo à la Caméra et de la Caméra au Stylo)', in P. J. Graham (ed.) *The New Wave: Critical Landmarks*. London: Secker & Warburg, pp. 17–23.

Augé, M. (1995) *Non-Places: Introduction to an Anthropology of Supermodernity*. London: Verso.

Augoyard, J.-F. (2007 [1979]) *Step by Step: Everyday Walks in a French Urban Housing Project*. Minneapolis, MN: University of Minnesota Press.

Augoyard, J.-F. and Torgue, H. (eds) (2005 [1995]) *Sonic Experience: A Guide to Everyday Sounds*. Toronto: McGill University Press.

Aumont, J., Bergala, A., Marie, M. and Venet, M. (2004 [1983]) *Aesthetics of Film*. Austin, TX: University of Texas Press.

Aureli, P. V. (2008) *The Project of Autonomy: Politics and Architecture Within and Against Capitalism*. New York, NY: Temple Hoyne Buell Center for the Study of American Architecture, Princeton Architectural Press.

Barber, S. (2002) *Projected Cities: Cinema and Urban Space*. London: Reaktion Books.

Barthes, R. (1972) *Mythologies*, trans. A. Lavers. London: Vintage.

Barthes, R. (1989 [1975]) 'Brecht and Discourse: A Contribution to the Study of Discursivity', in S. Mews (ed.) *Critical Essays on Berthold Brecht*. Boston, MA: G. K. Hall & Co.

Barthes, R. (1997 [1967]) 'Semiology and the Urban', in N. Leach (ed.) *Rethinking Architecture: A Reader in Cultural Theory*. New York, NY: Routledge, pp. 156–72.

Barthes, R. and Heath, S. (1977) *Image, Music, Text*. New York, NY: Hill & Wang.

Baudrillard, J. (1988 [1986]) *America*. London: Verso.

Baudrillard, J. (2008 [1981]) *Simulacra and Simulation*, trans. S. F. Glaser. Ann Arbor, MI: The University of Michigan Press.

Bazin, A. (2005 [1967]) *What is Cinema? Volume I*. Los Angeles, CA: University of California Press.

Bazin, A. (2005 [1971]) *What is Cinema? Volume II*. Los Angeles, CA: University of California Press.

Bazin, A. and Truffaut, F. (1974) *Jean Renoir*. New York, NY: W.H. Allen.

Beasley, R. and Danesi, M. (2002) *Persuasive Signs: The Semiotics of Advertising*. Berlin: Mouton de Gruyter.

Beeton, S. (2005) *Film-induced Tourism*. Clevedon: Channel View Publications.

Beller, J. (2006) *The Cinematic Mode of Production: Attention Economy and the Society of the Spectacle*. Hanover, NH: Dartmouth College Press.

Benjamin, W. (1928) *Einbahnstraße*. Berlin: Rowohlt Verlag.

Benjamin, W. (1968 [1936]) 'The Work of Art in the Age of Mechanical Reproduction', in H. Arendt (ed.) *Illuminations*, first published in *Zeitschrift für Sozialforschung*, 5(1), pp. 40–68. New York, NY: Schocken Books, pp. 217–51.

Benjamin, W. (1974–89) 'Das Passagen-Werk', in R. Tiedemann and H. Schweppenhäuser (eds) *Gesammelte Schriften*, vol. 5. Frankfurt am Main: Suhrkamp Verlag.

Benjamin, W. (2008 [1928]) 'These Surfaces for Rent', in W. Benjamin (ed.) *The Work of Art in the Age of Its Technological Reproducibility, and Other Writings on Media*. Cambridge, MA: Belknap Press of Harvard University Press, pp. 173–5.

Billinghurst, M. and Starner, T. (1999) 'Wearable Devices: New Ways to Manage Information', *Computer*, 32(1): 57–64.

Blandford, S., Grant, B. K. and Hillier, J. (2001) *The Film Studies Dictionary*. Oxford: Oxford University Press.

BM30 (2000) *Bilbao 2010: Reflections on Strategy*. Available online at www.bm30.es/plan/Bilbao2010-StrategicReflection.pdf (accessed March 2011).

BM30 (2001) *Bilbao 2010: The Strategy*. Available online at www.bm30.es/plan/Bilbao2010-TheStrategy.pdf (accessed March 2011).

Bois, Y.-A. (1989) 'Introduction: Montage and Architecture', *Assemblage*, 10 (December): 110–15.

Bolan, P. and Davidson, K. (2005) 'Film Induced Tourism in Ireland: Exploring the Potential', in S. Boyd (ed.) *Tourism and Hospitality Research in Ireland: Exploring the Issues*. Proceedings of University of Ulster Conference, Portrush, pp. 1–19.

Boorstin, D. J. (1992 [1962]) *The Image: A Guide to Pseudo-Events in America*. New York, NY: Vintage Books.

Borden, I. (2011) 'The Limehouse Link: The Architectural and Cultural History of a Monumental Road Tunnel in London's Docklands', *The Journal of Architecture*, 16(5): 589–611.

Borden, I., Kerr, J., Pivaro, A. and Rendell, J. (eds) (1996) *Strangely Familiar: Narratives of Architecture in the City*. London: Routledge.

Bordwell, D. (1981) *The Films of Carl-Theodor Dreyer*. Berkeley, CA: University of California Press.

Bordwell, D. (1985) *Narration in the Fiction Film*. Madison, WI: University of Wisconsin Press.

Bordwell, D. (2006) *The Way Hollywood Tells It: Story and Style in Modern Movies*. Berkeley, CA: University of California Press.

Bordwell, D., Staiger, J. and Thompson, K. (1985) *The Classical Hollywood Cinema: Film Style & Mode of Production to 1960*. New York, NY: Columbia University Press.

Boyer, M. C. (1994) *The City of Collective Memory: Its Historical Imagery and Architectural Entertainments*. Cambridge, MA: MIT Press.

Boyer, M. C. (1996) 'Twice-told Stories: The Double Erasure of Times Square', in I. Borden, J. Kerr, A. Pivaro and J. Rendell (eds) *Strangely Familiar: Narratives of Architecture in the City*. London: Routledge, pp. 70–6.

Branigan, E. (1992) *Narrative Comprehension and Film*. London: Routledge.

Bright, M. (1984. *Cities Built to Music: Aesthetic Theories of the Victorian Gothic Revival*. Columbus, OH: Ohio State University Press.

Brodesser-Akner, C. (2008) 'Cloverfield', *DIGITAL ISSUE: THE A-LIST*, 79(11): 58.

Bruno, G. (1997) 'Site-seeing: Architecture and the Moving Image', *Wide Angle*, 19(4): 8–24.

Bruno, G. (2002) *Atlas of Emotions: Journeys in Art, Architecture, and Film*. New York, NY: Verso.

Brunsdon, C. (2007) *London in Cinema: The Cinematic City Since 1945*. London: British Film Institute.

Buckland, W. (2000) *The Cognitive Semiotics of Film*. Cambridge: Cambridge University Press.

Budzynski, S. (2011) 'Continous Space: Object and Imagination in Superarchitettura', *Palinsesti*, 1(1): 1–19.

Bullnow, O. F. (1963) 'Der Mensch und der Raum', *Universitas*, 18: 499–515.

Burch, N. (1973) *Theory of Film Practice*. London: Secker & Warburg.

Burroughs, C. (2002) *The Italian Renaissance Palace Façade: Structures of Authority, Surfaces of Sense*. Cambridge: Cambridge University Press.

Busby, G. and Klug, J. (2001) 'Movie-induced Tourism: The Challenge of Measurement and Other Issues', *Journal of Vacation Marketing*, 7(4): 316–32.

Calvino, I. (2009 [1972]) *Invisible Cities*, trans. W. Weaver. London: Vintage Books.

Canudo, R. (1988a [1911]) 'Birth of a Sixth Art', in R. Abel (ed.) *French Film Theory and Criticism*. Princeton, NJ: Princeton University Press.

Canudo, R. (1988b [1923]) 'Reflections on the Seventh Art', in R. Abel (ed.) *French Film Theory and Criticism*. Princeton, NJ: Princeton University Press.

Carmona, M., Heath, T., Oc, T. and Tiesdell, S. (2003) *Public Places, Urban Spaces*. Oxford: Architectural Press.

Carney, S. (2005) *Brecht and Critical Theory: Dialectics and Contemporary Aesthetics*. London: Routledge.

Chatman, S. B. (1978) *Story and Discourse: Narrative Structure in Fiction and Film*. Ithaca, NY: Cornell University Press.

Chion, M., Gorbman, C. and Murch, W. (1994) *Audio-vision: Sound on Screen*. New York, NY: Columbia University Press.

Choisy, A. (1899) *Histoire de l'Architecture*. Paris: Gauthier-Villars.

Christie, I. (1994) *The Last Machine: Early Cinema and the Birth of the Modern World*. London: BBC and British Film Institute.

Christie, I. and Taylor, R. (1993) *Eisenstein Rediscovered*. London; New York, NY: Routledge.

Christie, I. and Taylor, R. (1994) *Inside the Film Factory: New Approaches to Russian and Soviet Cinema*. London; Routledge.

Clarke, D. B. (1997) *The Cinematic City*. London: Routledge.

Cohen, E. (1988) 'Authenticity and Commoditization in Tourism', *Annals of Tourism Research*, 15(3): 371–86.

Cohen, E. (2007) '"Authenticity" in Tourism Studies: Après la Lutte', *Tourism Recreation Research*, 32(2): 75–82.

Cohen, J. (1986) 'Promotion of Overseas Tourism Through Media Fiction', in J. W. Bendy (ed.) *Tourism Services Marketing: Advances in Theory and Practice*. Proceedings of the Special Conference on Tourism Services Marketing. Cleveland, OH: TTRA, pp. 229–37.

Colomina, B. (1992) 'The Split Wall: Domestic Voyeurism', in B. Colomina and J. Bloomer (eds) *Sexuality & Space*. New York, NY: Princeton Architectural Press.

Colomina, B. (1994) *Privacy and Publicity: Modern Architecture as Mass Media*. Cambridge MA: MIT Press.

Connell, J. (2005) 'What's the Story in Balamory?: The Impacts of a Children's TV Programme on Small Tourism Enterprises on the Isle of Mull, Scotland', *Journal of Sustainable Tourism*, 13(3): 228–55.

Cook, P. (1999) *The Cinema Book*. London: BFI Publishing.

Cooper, M. G. (2002) 'Narrative Space', *Screen*, 43(2): 139–57.

Copley, J. (2011) 'Case Study: Face Tracking the Mall Consumer', On the Threshold of Change: The Future of Out of Home Media in the UK. The Industry, Consumers and Technology to 2020, July: 1–68.

Coste, D. (1989) *Narrative as Communication*. Minneapolis, MN: University of Minnesota Press.

Coyne, R. (2010) *The Tuning of Place: Sociable Spaces and Pervasive Digital Media*. Cambridge, MA: MIT Press.

Cresswell, T. (2004) *Place: A Short Introduction*. Malden, MA: Blackwell Publishing.

Cullen, G. (2005 [1961]) *The Concise Townscape*. Oxford: Architectural Press.

Culler, J. D. (1981) *The Pursuit of Signs: Semiotics, Literature, Deconstruction*. Ithaca, NY: Cornell University Press.

Ćurčić, S. (2010) 'Architecture as Icon: Genesis of an Idea', *30th Anniversary Yale, Wintermagazine*: 10–11.

Ćurčić, S., Chatzētryphōnos, E., McVey, K. E. and Saradi, H. (2010) *Architecture as Icon: Perception and Representation of Architecture in Byzantine Art.* Princeton, NJ: Princeton University Art Museum; distributed by Yale University.

De Certeau, M. (1988 [1980]) *The Practice of Everyday Life.* Berkeley, CA: University of California Press.

Debord, G. (2002 [1967]) *Society of the Spectacle,* trans. K. Knabb. London: Rebel Press.

Debord, G. (2003) *Complete Cinematic Works: Scripts, Stills, Documents.* Oakland, CA: AK Press.

deNora, T. (2000) *Music in Everyday Life.* Cambridge; New York, NY: Cambridge University Press.

Deriu, D. (2007) 'Montage and Modern Architecture: Giedion's Implicit Manifesto', *Architectural Theory Review,* 12(1): 36–59.

Derrida, J. (1979) 'Living On', in H. Bloom (ed.) *Deconstruction and Criticism.* New York, NY: Seabury Press.

Derrida, J. (1997 [1986]) 'Point de Folie-Maintenant l'Architecture', in N. Leach (ed.) *Rethinking Architecture: A Reader in Cultural Theory.* New York, NY: Routledge, pp. 324–36.

Dimendberg, E. (2004) *Film Noir and the Spaces of Modernity.* Cambridge, MA: Harvard University Press.

DiNapoli, T. P. and Bleiwas, K. P. (2010) *The Film and Television Production Industry in New York State.* New York, NY: Office of the State Comptroller, New York City Public Information Office, pp. 1–2.

Donald, J. (1992) 'Metropolis: the City as Text', in R. Bocock and K. Thompson (eds) *Social and Cultural Forms of Modernity.* Oxford: Polity Press in association with the Open University, pp. 417–70.

Donald, J. (1997) 'This, Here, Now: Imagining the Modern City', in S. Westwood and J. Williams (eds) *Imagining Cities: Scripts, Signs, Memory.* London: Routledge, pp. 181–201.

Donald, J. (1999) *Imagining the Modern City.* Minneapolis, MN: University of Minnesota Press.

Dovey, K. (2002 [1999]) *Framing Places: Mediating Power in Built Form.* London: Routledge.

Dudley, A. (1984) *Concepts of Film Theory.* Oxford: Oxford University Press.

Eaton, R. (2000) *Ideal Cities: Utopianism and the (Un)built Environment.* New York, NY: Thames & Hudson.

Eisenstein, S. (1974) 'Montage of Attractions: For "Enough Stupidity in Every Wiseman"', *The Drama Review: TDR,* 18 (1, March, Popular Entertainments): 77–85.

Eisenstein, S. (1989 [*c.* 1938]) 'Montage and Architecture', *Assemblage* 10 (December): 110–31.

Ellis, J. (1992) *Visible Fictions: Cinema, Television, Video*. London: Routledge.

Elsaesser, T. and Barker, A. (eds) (1989) *Early Cinema: Space, Frame, Narrative*. London: British Film Institute.

Elsaesser, T. and Hagener, M. (2010) *Film Theory: An Introduction Through the Senses*. New York, NY: Routledge.

Evers, B. and Thoenes, C. (2003) *Architectural Theory: From the Renaissance to the Present*. Köln: Taschen.

Fallon, S. and Williams, N. (2008) *Paris: City Guide*. Hawthorn; Oakland, CA: Lonely Planet Publications.

Finney, A. (2010) *The International Film Business: A Market Guide Beyond Hollywood*. New York, NY: Routledge.

Fludernik, M. (2009) *An Introduction to Narratology*. London: Routledge.

Frampton, K. (1983) 'Towards a Critical Regionalism: Six Points for an Architecture of Resistance', in H. Foster (ed.) *The Anti-aesthetic: Essays on Postmodern Culture*. Seattle, WA: Bay Press.

Frampton, K. (1995) *Studies in Tectonic Culture: The Poetics of Construction in Nineteenth and Twentieth Century Architecture*, Cava, J. (ed.). Cambridge, MA: MIT Press.

Frampton, K. (1996 [1974]) 'On Reading Heidegger', in Nesbitt, K. (ed) *Theorizing a New Agenda for Architecture: An Anthology of Architectural Theory, 1965–1995*. New York, NY: Princeton Architectural Press, pp. 440–6.

Frayling, C. (1995) *Things to Come*. London: British Film Institute.

Freud, S. (1901) *Zur Psychopathologie des Alltagslebens: Vergessen, Versprechen, Vergreifen: Nebst Bemerkungen über eine Wurzel des Aberglaubens (Psychopathology of Everyday Life)*. Berlin: S. Karger.

Frost, W. (2004) 'Braveheart-ed Ned Kelly: Historic Films, Heritage Tourism and Destination Image', *Tourism Management*, 27: 247–57.

Gaines, E. (2006) 'Communication and the Semiotics of Space', *Journal of Creative Communications*, 1(2): 173–81.

Gandelsonas, M. (1979) 'From Structure to Subject: The Formation of an Architectural Language', *Oppositions*, 17 (Summer): 7–29.

Gandelsonas, M. (1998) 'From Structure to Subject: The Formation of an Architectural Language', in K. M. Hays (ed.) *Oppositions Reader: Selected Readings from a Journal for Ideas and Criticism in Architecture, 1973–1984*. New York, NY: Princeton Architectural Press, pp. 200–24.

Genette, G. (1966) 'Frontières du Récit', in *Communications*, (8): 152–63. Reprinted in *Figures II*.

Genette, G. (1972) *Figures III*. Paris: Seuil.

Genette, G. (1982 [1966]) 'Frontiers of Narrative', in *Figures of Literary Discourse*. New York, NY: Columbia University Press, pp. 126–44.

Giedion, S. (1995 [1928]) *Building in France, Building in Iron, Building in Ferro-Concrete*. Los Angeles, CA: Getty Research Institute.

Gillespie, D. (2000) *Early Soviet Cinema: Innovation, Ideology and Propaganda*. London: Wallflower Press.

Goffman, E. (1959) *The Presentation of Self in Everyday Life*. Garden City, NY: Doubleday.

González, S. (2006) 'Scalar Narratives in Bilbao: A Cultural Politics of Scales Approach to the Study of Urban Policy', *International Journal of Urban and Regional Research*, 30(4): 836–57.

Graham, P. J. (1968) *The New Wave*. London: Secker & Warburg.

Greimas, A. J. (1966) *Sémantique Structurale, Recherche de Méthode*. Paris: Larousse.

Griffiths, G. and Chudoba, M. (eds) (2007) *City + Cinema: Essays on the Specificity of Location in Film*. Tampere: Department of Architecture, Tampere University.

Griffiths, R. (1998) 'Making Sameness: Place Marketing and the New Urban Entrepreneurialism', in N. Oatley (ed.) *Cities, Economic Competition, and Urban Policy*. London: Paul Chapman Publishing, pp. 41–57.

Grihault, N. (2003) 'Film Tourism: The Global Picture', *Travel & Tourism Analyst*, 5: 1–22.

Gunning, T. (1991) *D. W. Griffith and the Origins of American Narrative Film: The Early Years at Biograph*. Urbana, IL: University of Illinois Press.

Hale, J. A. (2000) *Building Ideas: An Introduction to Architectural Theory*. Chichester: John Wiley.

Hampp, A. (2010) 'In a Banner Year for Film, One Studio Stands Tall', *Advertising Age*, 81(21): 10–1.

Haralovich, M. B. (1990) 'All that Haven Allows: Color, Narrative Space, and Melodrama', in P. Lehman (ed.) *Close Viewings: An Anthology of New Film Criticism*. Tallahassee, Gainesville, FL: Florida State University Press, pp. 57–72.

Harvey, D. (1989) *The Condition of Postmodernity: An Enquiry into the Origins of Cultural Change*. Oxford: Blackwell.

Harvey, D. (1996) *Justice, Nature, and the Geography of Difference*. Cambridge, MA: Blackwell Publishers.

Harvey, D. (2001) 'Globalization and the "Spatial Fix"', *Geographische Revue*, 2: 23–30.

Heath, S. (1976) 'Narrative Space', *Screen*, 3, Autumn (17): 68–112.

Heath, S. (1981) *Questions of Cinema*. Bloomington, IN: Indiana University Press.

Heidegger, M. (1971 [1951]) *Poetry, Language, Thought*. New York, NY: Harper & Row.

Heidegger, M. (2005 [1962]) *Being and Time*. Malden, MA: Blackwell Publishing.

Highmore, B. (2005) *Cityscapes*. New York, NY: Palgrave.

Hill, J. (2006) *Immaterial Architecture*. New York, NY: Routledge.

Hooper, J. (2008) 'Outrage in Venice as giant ads smother cultural jewels', in *The Guardian*. Online, 22 November 2008. Available at www.guardian.co.uk/world/2008/nov/22/venice-advertisments-restoration-funding-berlusconi (accessed June 2010).

Hubbard, P. (2006) *City*. New York, NY: Routledge.

Hudson, S. and Ritchie, Brent J. R. (2006) 'Film Tourism and Destination Marketing: The Case of Captain Corelli's Mandolin', *Journal of Vacation Marketing*, 12(3): 256–68.

Ivanovic, M. (2008) *Cultural Tourism*. Cape Town: Juta.

Jacobs, J. (1961) *The Death and Life of Great American Cities*. New York, NY: Random House.

Jameson, F. (1981) *The Political Unconscious: Narrative as a Socially Symbolic Act*. Ithaca, NY: Cornell University Press.

Jonas, A. E. G. and Wilson, D. (eds) (1999) *The Urban Growth Machine: Critical Perspectives Two Decades Later*. Albany, NY: State University of New York Press.

Jones, P. and Wilks-Heeg, S. (2007) 'Packaging Culture, Regulating Cultures: The Re-branded City', in C. Grunenberg and R. Knifton (eds) *Centre of the Creative Universe: Liverpool & the Avant-garde*. Liverpool: Liverpool University Press in association with Tate Liverpool; distributed by University of Chicago Press.

Jousse, T. and Paquot, T. (eds) (2005) *La Ville au Cinéma*. Paris: Cahiers du Cinéma.

Kafka, F. (1991 [1923]) *The Great Wall of China and Other Short Works*, trans. M. Pasley. London: Penguin Books, p. 185 *et seq*.

Kattenbelt, C. (2006) 'Theatre as the Art of the Performer and the Stage of Intermediality', in F. Chapple and C. Kattenbelt (eds) *Intermediality in Theatre and Performance*. Amsterdam: Rodopi, pp. 29–40.

Kaye, N. (2000) *Site-specific Art: Performance, Place, and Documentation*. London: Routledge.

Kellner, D. (2003) *Media Spectacle*. London: Routledge.

Kessler, F. (2007) 'Comment Cadrer la Rue?', in E. Biasin, G. Bursi and L. Quaresima (eds) *Lo Stile Cinematografico (Film Style)*. Udine: Forum, pp. 95–101.

Kessler, F. and Verhoeff, N. (eds) (2007) *Networks of Entertainment: Early Film Distribution 1895–1915*. Eastleigh: John Libbey & Co.

Kessler, F., Lenk, S. and Loiperdinger, M. (eds) (1992–2006) *KINtop*. Frankfurt: Stromfeld.

Kington, T. (2010) 'Norman Foster joins world culture leaders' protest at adverts "ruining" Venice's beauty', *The Observer*, 3 October: 11.

Knabb, K. (2006) *Situationist International Anthology*. Berkeley, CA: Bureau of Public Secrets.

Knudsen, B. T. (2010) 'The Past as Staged-real Environment: Communism Revisited in the Crazy Guides Communism Tours, Krakow, Poland', *Journal of Tourism and Cultural Change*, 8(3): 139–53.

Koeck, R. (2008) 'Cine-tecture: A Filmic Reading and Critique of Architecture in Cities', in J. Hallam, R. Koeck, R. Kronenburg and L. Roberts (eds) *Cities in Film: Architecture, Urban Space and the Moving Image*. Liverpool: Liverpool School of Architecture.

Koeck, R. (2009) 'Liverpool in Film: J. A. L. Promio's Cinematic Urban Space', *Journal of Early Popular and Visual Culture*, 7(1): 63–81.

Koeck, R. (2011) 'Urban Regeneration in Liverpool: Sign-structures of the Visible and the Invisible', in J. Harris and R. Williams (eds) *Regenerating Culture and Society: Architecture, Art and the Global-politics of City Branding*. Liverpool: Liverpool University Press/TATE, pp. 73–93.

Koeck, R. and Roberts, L. (eds) (2010) *The City and the Moving Image: Urban Projections*. London: Palgrave.

Koeck, R. and Warnaby, G. (2012) 'Outdoor Advertising and the Urban Built Environment: Economy, Legibility and Aesthetics', unpublished paper.

Konstantarakos, M. (2000) *Spaces in European Cinema*. Exeter: Intellect.

Koolhaas, R. (1978) *Delirious New York: A Retroactive Manifesto for Manhattan*. New York, NY: Oxford University Press.

Koolhaas, R., Mau, B., Sigler, J., Werlemann, H. and Office for Metropolitan Architecture (1995) *S, M, L, XL: Office for Metropolitan Architecture, Rem Koolhaas, and Bruce Mau*. New York, NY: Monacelli Press.

Kronenburg, R. (2012) *Live Architecture: Venues, Stages and Arenas for Popular Music*. London: Routledge.

Kruger, L. (2004) *Post-imperial Brecht: Politics and Performance, East and South*. Cambridge: Cambridge University Press.

Kuritz, P. (1988) *The Making of Theatre History*. Englewood Cliffs, NJ: Prentice Hall.

Lamster, M. (2000) *Architecture and Film*. New York, NY: Princeton Architectural Press.

Landry, C. (2006) *The Art of City-making*. Sterling, VA: Earthscan.

Langmead, D. (2009) *Icons of American Architecture: From the Alamo to the World Trade Center*. Westport, CO: Greenwood Press.

Le Corbusier (1927 [1923]) *Towards a New Architecture (Vers une Architecture)*. New York, NY: Payson & Clarke.

Le Corbusier (1986) *Oevre Complète*. London: Ellipsis.

Leach, N. (1999) *The Anaesthetics of Architecture*. Cambridge, MA: MIT Press.

Lederbogen, F., Kirsch, P., Haddad, L., Streit, F., Trost, H., Schuck, P., Wüst, S., Pruessner, J. C., Rietschel, M., Deuschle, M. and Meyer-Lindenberg, A. (2011) 'City Living and Urban Upbringing Affect Neural Social Stress Processing in Humans', *Nature*, 474 (23 June 2011): 498–501.

Leeman, J. and Modan, G. (2010) 'Selling the City: Language, Ethnicity and Commodified Space', in E. Shohamy, E. Ben-Rafael and M. Barni (eds) *Linguistic Landscape in the City*. Clevedon: Multilingual Matters, pp. 182–97.

Lefebvre, H. (1991 [1974]) *The Production of Space (La production de l'espace)*. Oxford: Blackwell Publishing.

Lefebvre, H. (2003 [1970]) *The Urban Revolution*. Minneapolis, MN: University of Minnesota Press.

Lefebvre, H. (2004 [1992]) *Rhythmanalysis: Space, Time, and Everyday Life*. London: Continuum.

Lewis, S. (2002) 1922]) *Babbitt*. New York, NY: The Modern Library.

Lingley, A. R., Ali, M., Mirjalili, R., Klonner, M., Sopanen, M., Suihonen, S., Otis, B. P., Lipsanen, H. and Parviz, B. A. (2011) 'A Single-pixel Wireless Contact Lens Display', *Journal of Micromechanics and Microengineering*, 21(125014): 1–8.

Loos, A. (2000 [1908]) *Ornament und Verbrechen*. Wien: Prachner.

Lowry, E. (1985) *The Filmology Movement and Film Study in France*. Ann Arbor, MI: UMI Research Press.

Lu, A. (2010) 'The Telling of a Spatial Allegory: The Danteum as Narrative Labyrinth', *Architectural Research Quarterly*, 14(3): 237–46.

Lu, A. (2011) 'Deciphering the Reclusive Landscape: A Study of Wen Zheng-Ming's 1533 Album of the Garden of the Unsuccessful Politician', *Studies in the History of Gardens & Designed Landscapes*, 31(1): 40–59.

Lynch, K. (1960) *The Image of the City*. Cambridge, MA: MIT Press.

Lyotard, J.-F. (1984) *The Postmodern Condition: A Report on Knowledge*. Minneapolis, MN: University of Minncsota Prcss.

MacCannell, D. (1973) 'Staged Authenticity: Arrangements of Social Space in Tourist Settings', *The American Journal of Sociology*, 79(3): 589–603.

MacCannell, D. (1999 [1976]) *The Tourist: A New Theory of the Leisure Class*: Berkeley, CA: University of California Press.

MacGilvray, D. F. (1992) 'The Proper Education of Musicians and Architects', *Journal of Architectural Education*, 46(2): 87–94.

McLuhan, M. (1964) *Understanding Media: The Extensions of Man*. London: Routledge & Kegan Paul.

McLuhan, M. (2006 [1964]) 'The Medium is the Message', in M. G. Durham and D. Kellner (eds) *Media and Cultural Studies: Keyworks*. Oxford: Blackwell Publishers, pp. 107–16.

McQuire, S. (2008) *The Media City: Media, Architecture and Urban Space*. Los Angeles, CA: Sage Publications.

Madanipour, A. (2003) *Public and Private Spaces of the City*. London: Routledge.

Makeham, P. (2005) 'Performing the City', *Theatre Research International*, 30(2): 150–60.

Mako, V. (2008) 'Imagining the City Scenery: Categories of Renaissance Aesthetics and Architectural and Urban Metaphors', *Design Discourse*, 3(4): 1–9.

Mallet-Stevens, R. (1925) 'Le Cinéma et les Arts, l'Architecture', *Les Cahiers du Mois*, (16–17): 96.

Mallgrave, H. F. (2011) *The Architect's Brain: Neuroscience, Creativity and Architecture.* Chichester: Wiley-Blackwell.

Malpas, J. (2006) *Heidegger's Topology: Being, Place, World*. Cambridge, MA: MIT Press.

Marcus, A. and Neumann, D. (eds) (2007) *Visualizing the City*. London: Routledge.

Matthews, E. (2006) *Merleau-Ponty: A Guide for the Perplexed*. London: Continuum.

Meecham, P. and Sheldon, J. (2005) *Modern Art: A Critical Introduction*. London: Routledge.

Mennel, B. (2008) *Cities and Cinema*. London: Routledge.

Merleau-Ponty, M. (1962 [1945]) *Phenomenology of Perception*. New York, NY: Routledge.

Merleau-Ponty, M. (1963 [1942]) *The Structure of Behavior*. Boston, MA: Beacon Press.

Merleau-Ponty, M. (1964) *Sense and Non-sense*. Evanston, IL: Northwestern University Press.

Metz, C. (1974) *Film Language: A Semiotics of the Cinema*. New York, NY: Oxford University Press.

Miles, S. (2010) *Spaces for Consumption*. Thousand Oaks, CA: Sage Publications.

Mitchell, W. J. (2005a) *Placing Words: Symbols, Space, and the City*. Cambridge, MA: MIT Press.

Mitchell, W. J. (2005b) 'There are No Visual Media', *Journal of Visual Culture*, 4(2): 257–66.

Moehring, E. P. and Green, M. S. (2005) *Las Vegas: A Centennial History*. Reno, NV: University of Nevada Press.

Moffett, M., Fazio, M. W. and Wodehouse, L. (2004) *A World History of Architecture*. Boston, MA: McGraw-Hill.

Monaco, J. (2002) *The New Wave: Truffaut Godard Chabrol Rohmer Rivette*. New York, NY: Harbor Electronic Pub.

Muecke, M. W. and Zach, M. S. (2007) *Essays on the Intersection of Music and Architecture*. Ames, IA: Culicidae Architectural Press.

Mumford, L. (1938) *The Culture of Cities.* London: Secker & Warburg.

Mumford, L. (2007 [1937]) 'What is a City?', in R. T. LeGates and F. Stout (eds) *The City Reader.* New York, NY: Routledge, pp. 85–9.

Musser, C. (1990) *The Emergence of Cinema: The American Screen to 1907.* New York, NY: Charles Scribner.

Neumann, D. (ed.) (1999) *Film Architecture: Set Design from Metropolis to Blade Runner.* Munich: Prestel.

Neumann, D. (2002) *Architecture of the Night: The Illuminated Building.* Munich: Prestel.

Neupert, R. J. (2007) *A History of the French New Wave Cinema.* Madison, WI: University of Wisconsin Press.

Norberg-Schulz, C. (1971) *Existence, Space & Architecture.* New York, NY: Praeger.

Norberg-Schulz, C. (1979 [1963]) *Intentions in Architecture.* Cambridge, MA: MIT Press.

Norberg-Schulz, C. (1980) *Genius Loci: Towards a Phenomenology of Architecture.* New York, NY: Rizzoli.

Norberg-Schulz, C. (1988) *Architecture: Meaning and Place.* New York, NY: Electa/Rizzoli.

Norberg-Schulz, C. (2000) *Architecture: Presence, Language, Place.* Milan: Skira.

North, D. (2010) 'Evidence of Things Not Quite Seen: *Cloverfield's* Obstructed Spectacle', *Film & History*, 40(1): 75–92.

Nöth, W. and Bishara, N. (2007) *Self-reference in the Media.* Berlin: Mouton de Gruyter.

Nouvel, J. (2001) 'Everything is Image'. Online Interview, 14 February 2001. Available at www.jeannouvel.com (accessed June 2011).

O'Connor, N., Flanagan, S. and Gilbert, D. (2008) 'The Integration of Film-induced Tourism and Destination Branding in Yorkshire, UK', *International Journal of Tourism Research*, 10: 423–37.

Olsen, K. (2007) 'Staged Authenticity: A Grande Idée', *Trousim Recreation Research*, 32(2): 83–5.

Onega, S. and Landa, J. Á. G. (eds) (1996) *Narratology: An Introduction.* London: Longman.

Pallasmaa, J. (1994) 'Six Themes for the Next Millennium', *Architectural Review*, 196(1169): 74–9.

Pallasmaa, J. (2001) *The Architecture of Image: Existential Space in Cinema.* Helsinki: Rakennustieto.

Pallasmaa, J. (2005) *The Eyes of the Skin: Architecture and the Senses.* Chichester, NJ: Wiley-Academy; John Wiley & Sons.

Pallasmaa, J. (2006) 'Hapticity Vision', *A.D., Architectural Design*, 75(4): 137–8.

Pallasmaa, J. (2007) 'An Archipelago of Authenticity: The Task of Architecture in Consumer Culture', in G. Caicco (ed.) *Architecture, Ethics, and the Personhood of Place*. Hanover: University Press of New England, pp. 41–9.

Pallasmaa, J. (2009) *The Thinking Hand: Existential and Embodied Wisdom in Architecture*. Chichester, NJ; John Wiley & Sons.

Pallasmaa, J. (2011) *The Embodied Image: Imagination and Imagery in Architecture*. Chichester, NJ: John Wiley & Sons.

Paalman, F. (2011) *Cinematic Rotterdam: The Times and Tides of a Modern City*. Rotterdam: 010 Publishers.

Park, E. R. (2005 [1925]) 'The City: Suggestions for the Investigation of Human Behavior in the Urban Environment', in K. Gelder (ed.) *The Subcultures Reader*. London: Routledge, pp. 25–34.

Payne, D. R. (1993) *Scenographic Imagination*. Carbondale, IL: Southern Illinois University Press.

Pearce, P. L. (2007) 'Persisting With Authenticity', *Tourism Recreation Research*, 32(2): 86–90.

Pearce, P. L. and Moscardo, G. (1986) 'The Concept of Authenticity in Tourist Experiences', *Australian and New Zealand Journal of Sociology*, 22: 121–32.

Peirce, C. S. (1960–66 [1903–4]) *Collected Papers of Charles Sanders Peirce,* Vols 1–6, edited by C. Hartshorne and P. Weiss; Vols 7–8, edited by A. W. Burks. Cambridge, MA: Harvard University.

Piaget, J. (1955) *The Child's Construction of Reality*. London: Routledge and Kegan Paul.

Poe, E. A. (1842) *Masque of the Red Death*. Available online at books.eserver. org/fiction/poe/masque_of_the_red_death.html (accessed April 2012).

Pramaggiore, M. and Wallis, T. (2011) *Film: A Critical Introduction*. Boston, MA: Pearson Allyn & Bacon.

Priest, S. (1998) *Merleau-Ponty*. London: Routledge.

Prince, G. (1982) *Narratology: The Form and Functioning of Narrative*. Berlin: Mouton.

Prisciano, P. (1974 [1490]) 'Spectacula', in F. Marotti (ed.) *Lo Spettacolo dall'Umanesimo al Manierismo*. Milan: Feltrinelli.

Raban, J. (2008 [1974]) *Soft City*. London: Picador.

Rasmussen, S. E. (1959) *Experiencing Architecture*, trans. E. Wendt. Cambridge, MA: Technology Press of Massachusetts Institute of Technology.

Rattenbury, K. (1994) 'Echo and Narcissus', *A.D., Architectural Design*, 64(12): 35–7.

Reeves, T. (1999) *Worldwide Guide to Movie Locations*. Chicago, IL: Titan Publishing Group.

Reeves, T. (2008) *Movie London: Exploring the City Film-by-Film*. London: Titan Books.

Reisinger, Y. and Steiner, C. (2006) 'Reconceptualising Object Authenticity', *Annals of Tourism Research*, 33(1): 65–86.

Relph, E. C. (1976) *Place and Placelessness*. London: Pion.

Relph, E. C. (1981) *Rational Landscapes and Humanistic Geography*. London; Totowa, NJ: Croom Helm; Barnes & Noble Books.

Relph, E. C. (1987) *The Modern Urban Landscape*. Baltimore, MD: Johns Hopkins University Press.

Ricci, C. (1928) 'The Art of Scenography', *The Art Bulletin*, 10(3): 231–57.

Riley, R. W. (1994) 'Movie Induced Tourism', in A. V. Seaton (ed) *Tourism: The State of the Art*. Chichester: John Wiley & Sons, pp. 453–8.

Riley, R. W. and Van Doren, C. S. (1992) 'Movies as Tourism Promotion: A "Pull" Factor in a "Push" Location', *Tourism Management*, 13: 267–74.

Riley, R. W., Baker, D. and Van Doren, C. S. (1998) 'Movie Induced Tourism', *Annals of Tourism Research*, 25: 919–35.

Ripley, C., Polo, M., Wrigglesworth, A. and Ryerson University (2007) *In the Place of Sound: Architecture, Music, Acoustics*. Newcastle: Cambridge Scholars Publishing.

Rogers, R. (2005) 'The Urban Renaissance Six Years On', in Urban Task Force (ed.) *Towards a Strong Urban Renaissance*. London: Urban Task Force, 2.3.

Rothman, W. (2004) *The 'I' of the Camera: Essays in Film Criticism, History, and Aesthetics*. Cambridge: Cambridge University Press.

Rowe, C. and Koetter, F. (1984 [1978]) *Collage City*. Cambridge, MA: MIT Press.

Rudrum, D. (2005) 'From Narrative Representation to Narrative Use: Towards the Limits of Definition', *Narrative*, 13(2): 105–24

Sadler, S. (1998) *The Situationist City*. Cambridge, MA: MIT Press.

Sadler, S. (1999) *The Situationist City*. Cambridge, MA: MIT Press.

Salt, B. (2009 [1983]) *Film Style and Technology: History and Analysis*. London: Starword.

Sanders, J. (2001) *Celluloid Skyline: New York and the Movies*. New York, NY: Knopf.

Saunders, W. and Frampton, K. (eds) (2005) *Commodification and Spectacle in Architecture: A Harvard Design Magazine Reader*. Minneapolis, MN: University of Minnesota Press.

Schafer, R. M. (1969) *The New Soundscape: A Handbook for the Modern Music Teacher*. Don Mills: BMI Canada.

Schafer, R. M. (1970) *The Book of Noise*. Vancouver: Privately printed by Price Print.

Schafer, R. M. (1977) *The Tuning of the World*. New York, NY: A. A. Knopf.

Schelling, F. W. J. v. (1984 [1859]) *Schelling's Werke: Zur Philosophie der Kunst: 1803–1817*. München: Beck.

Schelling, F. W. J. v. and Stott, D. W. (1989 [1859]) *The Philosophy of Art*. Minneapolis, MN: University of Minnesota Press.

Scholes, R. and Kellogg, R. L. (1966) *The Nature of Narrative*. New York, NY: Oxford University Press.

Seattle Mayor's Office (2003) *The Economic Impact of Film and Video Productions on Seattle. A Report for the Seattle Mayor's Office of Film and Music*. Portland, OR: The Firm.

Secret Cinema. Facebook site. Available online at www.facebook.com/pages/Secret-Cinema/46896241052?sk=info (accessed January 2011).

Sharp, J. (2000) 'Towards Critical Analysis of Fictive Geographies', *Area*, 32(3): 327–34.

Sharr, A. (2007) *Heidegger for Architects*. London: Routledge.

Shiel, M. and Fitzmaurice, T. (2001) *Cinema and the City: Film and Urban Societies in a Global Context*. Oxford: Blackwell.

Shohat, E. and Stam, R. (1994) *Unthinking Eurocentrism: Multiculturalism and the Media*. London: Routledge.

Short, J. R. (1996) *The Urban Order: An Introduction to Cities, Culture, and Power*. Cambridge, MA: Blackwell Publishers.

Short, J. R. (1999) 'Urban Imagineers: Boosterism and the Representation of Cities', in A. Jonas and D. Wilson (eds) *The Urban Growth Machine: Critical Perspectives Two Decades Later*. Albany, NY: State University of New York Press.

Simmel, G. (1903) 'Die Grosstädte und das Geistesleben', in T. Petermann (ed.) *Jahrbuch der Gehe-Stiftung*. Dresden, pp. 185–206.

Simmel, G. (2010 [1903]) 'The Metropolis and Mental Life', in G. Bridge and S. Watson (eds) *The Blackwell City Reader*. Oxford: Wiley-Blackwell, pp. 103–10.

Sinclair, I. (1997) *Lights Out for the Territory: 9 Excursions in the Secret History of London*. London: Granta Books.

Sipière, D. (2008) 'Souriau Revisited by the Matrix: A few Questions About the Status of the Real in Film Fiction', *Cercles*, 18: 11–19.

Sklair, L. (2006) 'Iconic Architecture and Capitalist Globalization', *City*, 10(1): 21–47.

Smith, D. (2009a) 'Soweto residents report mixed feelings as *District 9* grosses $90m at box office', in *The Guardian*. Online, 2 September 2009. Available at www.guardian.co.uk/world/2009/sep/02/district-9-soweto-residents-exploitation (accessed July 2011).

Smith, D. (2009b) 'The real District 9', in *Mail & Guardian Online*. Online, 5 September 2009. Available at www.mg.co.za/article/2009-09-05-the-real-district-9 (accessed July 2011)

Soja, E. W. (1989) *Postmodern Geographies: The Reassertion of Space in Critical Social Theory*. London: Verso.

Souriau, É. (1951) 'La structure de l'Univers Filmique et le Vocabulaire de la Filmologie', *Revue Internationale de Filmologie*, 2(7–8): 231–40.

Stam, R., Burgoyne, R. and Flitterman-Lewis, S. (1992) *New Vocabularies in Film Semiotics: Structuralism, Post-structuralism, and Beyond*. London: Routledge.

Stevenson, D. (2003) *Cities and Urban Cultures*. Maidenhead: Open University Press.

Stewart, M. (1997) 'The Impact of Films in the Stirling Area – A Report', *Scottish Tourist Board Research Newsletter*, 12: 60–1.

Sullivan, G. H. (2006) *Not Built in a Day: Exploring the Architecture of Rome*. New York, NY: Carroll & Graf.

Sultanik, A. (1995) *Camera-cut-composition: A Learning Model*. New York, NY: Cornwall Books.

Tafuri, M. (1987) '*Civies esse non licere:* The Rome of Nicholas V and Leon Battista Alberti: Elements Towards a Historical Revision', *Harvard Architectural Review*, 6: 61–75.

Taylor, J. (2001) 'Authenticity and Sincerity in Tourism', *Annals of Tourism Research*, 28(1): 7–26.

The Guardian (2009) 'Soweto: District 9 residents forced to leave', 2 September. Available online at www.guardian.co.uk/world/gallery/2009/sep/02/southafrica (accessed July 2011).

Thomas, M. (2003) 'Beyond Digitality: Cinema, Console Games and Screen Language – The Spatial Organisation of Narrative', in M. Thomas and F. Penz (eds) *Architectures of Illusions: From Motion Pictures to Navigable Interactive Environments*. Bristol: Intellect Books, pp. 51–134.

Thomas, M. and Penz, F. (eds) (1997) *Cinema and Architecture: Méliès, Mallet-Stevens, Multimedia*. London: British Film Institute.

Todorov, T. (1969) *Grammaire du* Décaméron. The Hague: Mouton.

Tooke, N. and Baker, M. (1996) 'Seeing is Believing: The Effect of Film on Visitor Numbers to Screened Locations', *Tourism Management*, 17(2): 87–94.

Toulmin, V. (2006) *Electric Edwardians: The Story of the Mitchell & Kenyon Collection*. London: BFI Publishing.

Toy, M. (1994) 'Editorial', in *A.D. Special Issue Architecture and Film, Architectural Design*, (112).

Tschumi, B. (1976–81) *The Manhattan Transcripts*. London: Academy Editions.

Tschumi, B. (1977) *The Screenplays*. Unpublished. Extracts reproduced in B. Tschumi (1996) *Architecture and Disjunction*. Cambridge, MA: MIT Press.

Tschumi, B. (1994) *Event-cities: Praxis*. Cambridge, MA: MIT Press.

Tschumi, B. (1996) *Architecture and Disjunction*. Cambridge, MA: MIT Press.

Tschumi, B. (2000) 'Six Concepts', in A. Read (ed.) *Architecturally Speaking: Practices of Art, Architecture and the Everyday.* London: Routledge, pp. 155–76.

Tschumi, B. (2004) *Event-cities 3: Concept, Context, and Content.* Cambridge, MA: MIT Press.

Tschumi, B. (2010) *Event-cities 4: Concept and Form.* Cambridge, MA: MIT Press.

Tuan, Y.-F. (1974) *Topophilia: A Study of Environmental Perception, Attitudes and Values.* New York, NY: Colombia University Press.

Turok, I . (2009) 'The Distinctive City: Pitfalls in the Pursuit of Differential Advantage', *Environment and Planning* A, 41(1): 13–30.

Tylus, J. (2000) 'Theater and Its Social Uses: Machiavelli's *Mandragola* and the Spectacle of Infamy', *Renaissance Quarterly*, 53(3): 656–86.

Tzonis, A. and Lefaivre, L. (1986) *Classical Architecture: The Poetics of Order.* Cambridge, MA: MIT Press.

United Nations (2004) 'World Population to 2300', *Department of Economic and Social Affairs* (ST/ESA/SER.A/236), 1–240.

Urban Task Force and Rogers, R. (1999) *Towards an Urban Renaissance.* London: Spon Press.

Urban Task Force and Rogers R. (2005) *Towards a Strong Urban Renaissance.* London: Urban Task Force.

Urry, J. (1990) *The Tourist Gaze: Leisure and Travel in Contemporary Societies.* London: Sage.

Vannini, P. and Williams, J. P. (2009) *Authenticity in Culture, Self, and Society.* Farnham: Ashgate Publishing.

Venturi, R., Scott Brown, D. and Izenhour, S. (1977) *Learning from Las Vegas: The Forgotten Symbolism of Architectural Form.* Cambridge, MA: MIT Press.

Vertov, D. and Michelson, A. (1984) *Kino-eye: The Writings of Dziga Vertov.* Berkeley, CA: University of California Press.

Vidler, A. (1995) 'Refiguring the Place of Architecture', in D. Agrest and M. Gandelsonas (eds) *Agrest and Gandelsonas: Works.* New York, NY: Princeton Architetural Press, pp. 7–17.

Vidler, A. (1996) 'The Explosion of Space: Architecture and the Filmic Imaginary', in D. Neumann (ed.) *Film Architecture: Set Design from Metropolis to Blade Runner.* Munich: Prestel.

Vidler, A. (2002) *Warped Space: Art, Architecture, and Anxiety in Modern Culture.* Cambridge, MA: MIT Press.

Virilio, P. (1994) *The Vision Machine.* Bloomington, IN: Indiana University Press.

Vogt, G. (2001) *Die Stadt im Kino: Deutsche Spielfilme 1900–2000.* Marburg: Schüren.

Vuokko, P. (1997) 'The Determinants of Advertising Repetition Effects', in W. D. Wells (ed.) *Measuring Advertising Effectiveness.* London: Psychology Press, pp. 239–60.

Walters, D. and Brown, L. (2004) *Design First: Design-based Planning for Communities*. Oxford: Architectural Press.

Wang, N. (1999) 'Rethinking Authenticity in Tourism Experience', *Annals of Tourism Research*, 26: 66–74.

Ward, J. (2001) *Weimar Surfaces: Urban Visual Culture in 1920s Germany*. Berkeley, CA: University of California Press.

Warnaby, G. and Medway, D. (2010) 'Semiotics and Place Branding: The Influence of the Built and Natural Environment in City Logos', in G. Ashworth and M. Kavaratzis (eds) *Brand Management for Cities: The Theory and Practice of Effective Place Branding*. Cheltenham: Edward Elgar, pp. 205–21.

Webber, A. and Wilson, E. (eds) (2008) *Cities in Transition: The Moving Image and the Modern Metropolis*. London: Wallflower.

Weihsmann, H. (1988) *Gebaute Illusionen: Architektur im Film*. Vienna: Promedia.

Weihsmann, H. (1995) *Cinetecture*. Vienna: PVS Verleger.

Weihsmann, H. (1997) 'The City in Twilight: Charting the Genre of the "City Film", 1900–1930', in M. Thomas and F. Penz (eds) *Cinema and Architecture: Méliès, Mallet-Stevens, Multimedia*. London: British Film Institute, pp. 8–27.

Weihsmann, H. (2010) 'Let Architecture "Play Itself": A Case Study', in R. Koeck and L. Roberts (eds) *The City and the Moving Image: Urban Projections*. London: Palgrave, pp. 253–70.

Wells, H. G. (1898) *The War of the Worlds*. London: Heinemann.

Westwood, S. and Williams, J. (1997) *Imaging Cities: Scripts, Signs, Memory*. London: Routledge, p. 12.

Wollen, P. (2002) *Paris Hollywood: Writings on Film*. London: Verso.

Woodward, I. (2000) 'Why Should the UK's Tourism Industry be Interested in Bollywood Films?', *Insight* 12: 23–6.

Worsley, G. (2004) 'Review 2004: Architecture', *The Telegraph*, 18 December: n.p.

Wunderlich, F. (2008) 'Walking and Rhythmicity: Sensing Urban Space', *Journal of Urban Design*, 13(1): 125–39.

Filmography

2001: A Space Odyssey (1968, Kubrick, S.)

212 (2005, Ng, A.)

À bout de soufflé (1960, Godoard, J.)

A Clockwork Orange (1971, Kubrick, S.)

A Nous la Liberté (1931, Clair, R.)

Amadeus (1984, Forman, M.)

Amélie (2001, Jeunet, J.)

Anna Belle Serpentine Dance (1895, Heise, W.)

Avenir (2001, Koeck, R.)

Bad Timing (1980, Roeg, N.)

Before Sunrise (1995, Linklater, R.)

Beverly Hills Cop II (1987, Scott, T.)

Blade Runner (1982, Scott, R.)

Brazil (1985, Gilliam, T)

Chicago (2002, Marshall, R.)

Citizen Kane (1941, Welles, O.)

Cloverfield (2008, Reeves, M.)

Dark City (1998, Proyas, A.)

Der Golem, wie er in die Welt kam (1920, Boese, C. and Wegener, P.)

District 9 (2009, Blomkamp, N.)

Forrest Gump (1994, Zemeckis, R.)

Hiroshima Mon Amour (1959, Resnais, A.)

I, Robot (2004, Proyas A.)

In Time of Place (2006–10, Marcus, A.)

James Bond: The Living Daylights (1987, Glen, J.)

King Kong (2005, Jackson, P.)

Kino Eye (1924, Vertov, D.)

La Dolce Vita (1960, Fellini, F.)

Ladri di Biciclette (1948, De Sica, V.)

L'Agent (1928, L'Herbier, M.)

L'Architecture d'Aujourd'hui (1931, Le Corbusier and Chenal, P.)

L.A. Story (1991, Jackson, M.)

L'Avventura (1960, Antonioni, M.)

Le Diable au Coeur (1928, L'Herbier, M.)

Le Mépris (1963, Godard, J.)

Le Nouveau Messieurs (1928, Feyder, J.)

Le P'tit Parigot (1926, Le Somptier, R.)

Le Vertige (1926, L'Herbier, M.)

Les Mystères du Château de Dé (1928/29, Ray, M.)

Let Los Angeles Play Itself (2003, Anderson, T.)

Lime Street (1897, Promio, A.)

L'Inhumaine (1924, L'Herbier, M.)

Lost (2004–2010, Abrams, J. J., Lieber, J. and Lindelof, D.)

Maid in Manhattan (2002, Wang, W.)

Matrix (1999, Wachowski, A. and Wachowski, L.)

Minority Report (2002, Spielberg, S.)

Mission Impossible III (2006, Abrams, J. J.)

Mission Impossible IV (2011, Bird, B.)

Mon Oncle (1958, Tati, J.)

Panorama pris du chemin de fer électrique I–IV (1897, Promio, A.)

Pink Floyd: The Wall (1982, Parker, A.)

Playtime (1967, Tati, J.)

Psycho (1960, Hitchcock, A.)

Raging Bull (1980, Scorsese, M.).

Roma Città Aperta (1945, Rossellini, R.)

Ronin (1998, Frankenheimer J.)

Run Lola Run (1998, Tykwer, T.)

Shadowing The Third Man (2004, Baker, F.)

Spiderman 3 (2007, Raimi, S.)

Star Trek (2009, Abrams, J. J.)

Streets of Fire (1984, Hill, W.)

Taxi Driver (1976, Scorsese, M.)

The Avenging Conscience (1914, Griffith, D. W.)

The Birth of a Nation (1915, Griffith, D. W.)

The Blair Witch Project (1999, Myrick, D. and Sánchez, E.)

The Day After Tomorrow (2004, Emmerich, R.)

The Italian Job (1969, Collinson, P.)

The Man with a Movie Camera (1929, Vertov, D.)

The Naked City (1948, Dassin, J.)

The Quintet of Remembrance (2000 and 2001)

The Terminator (1984, Cameron, J.)

The Third Man (1949, Reed, C.)

Things to Come (1936, Korda, A.)

Tron (1982, Lisberger, S.)

Une Femme est une Femme (1961, Godard, J.)

Virgin Spring (1960, Bergman, I.)

Viva Las Vegas (1964, Sidney, G.)

Index